Praise

THE MIRACLE CHILD

"Michael and Kelly Lang's memoir, *The Miracle Child: Traumatic Brain Injury and Me*, is a brutally honest and compelling accounting of a tragic car accident that left Olivia, their three-year-old daughter, in a coma with a traumatic brain injury. Readers will be inspired by the Lang's overriding commitment to family during countless medical challenges that ultimately earned Olivia the nickname 'the Miracle Child.'"

—Lee Woodruff
New York Times Best-Selling author of *In an Instant*

"*The Miracle Child* is a testament to parental love and the power of family. In the wake of a terrible tragedy, Kelly and Mike harnessed their faith and became the fiercest of advocates for their daughter Olivia. Their story teaches us that brain injury not only affects individuals, it transforms families. Told with honesty and determination, their journey is one of profound love—the love of two parents fighting for their child's future."

—Abby Maslin
Author of *Love You Hard*

"It's been a long, long time since I've read a book in one day. Through your journey I felt close to Olivia and your family and felt the emotions through every twist and turn. It's true—tell your loved ones many times a day how much you love them, many times. Well done!"

—Marie Scott
Coaching Widows and Widowers to Live Well, Laugh More, and Love Again!

"Brain injury advocate Kelly Lang epitomizes the struggle and promise of our generation—resilience in the face of tragedy and hope in a time of despair. With this book, she and her husband generously offer solace to fellow parents struggling to nurture a family in the aftermath of a life-changing accident."

—Ada Calhoun
Author of *Why We Can't Sleep*

"What happened to your family was horrific, but you and Mike tell your story with great humanity and compassion, and with honesty about how you felt and what devastation the accident caused to your family. The details you put in about the hospitals and various treatments that Olivia had in the first few weeks made for compelling reading."

—Laurence French
Beta Reader

The Miracle Child:

Traumatic Brain Injury and Me

By Kelly and Michael Lang

ISBN 978-1-64663-730-0

Published by

köehlerbooks™

3705 Shore Drive
Virginia Beach, VA 23455
800—435—4811
www.koehlerbooks.com

THE

MIRACLE CHILD

TRAUMATIC BRAIN INJURY AND ME

KELLY AND MICHAEL LANG

VIRGINIA BEACH
CAPE CHARLES

TABLE OF CONTENTS

AUTHORS' NOTE

In many cases, names have been changed to protect people's privacy. Much of this story comes from journals we kept during Olivia's hospitalizations as well as afterward. The information contained is our perception of the events. The timeline in our book starts in detail at the beginning. Of course, documenting certain significant events would make this book a bit . . . challenging, so we decided to create a general timeframe after 2001.

This book has been a labor of love. We feel strongly this story needs to be told so others can find hope and inspiration even in the worst hours of their lives. We have been blessed with three daughters, but this book focuses on our story along with Olivia's.

For more information, please visit The Miracle Child at www. themiraclechild.org.

PART 1
FAR FROM HOME

DAY ZERO

"Mike, this is Kristin. Kelly and the girls were in a car accident," the recording from my answering machine says in the stillness of my home. I hold my breath and wait for the next line, telling me, "But everyone is all right." It never comes . . .

—Tuesday, November 27, 2001

A Normal Day
Kelly, Morning/Afternoon

It is a day like any other . . . arranging an afternoon playdate for Hannah, our kindergartener, squeezing in some holiday shopping between delivering and picking up Olivia, our preschooler, and getting in a few minutes on the treadmill.

Hannah auditioned for a role in *The Nutcracker* production her ballet studio presents each holiday season. She is so excited to have gotten the role of the Hot Chocolate Gift Bearer. The costume is perfect for her—bright red with black trim.

Tonight's rehearsal is throwing off our routine a bit, and I don't expect Mike home from his consulting job until tomorrow, so dinner will be a quick pasta dish—with the option of a cookie if the girls eat their dinner—before getting Hannah to the first night of rehearsals for *The Nutcracker*.

The Arrival Home
Mike, Late Evening

I have been in New Hampshire for a few days, working a short-term consulting job I landed right after Thanksgiving. My project ended a day earlier than expected, so I'm scrambling to make an earlier flight back to Washington Dulles. I'm so pressed for time trying to catch my flight that I do not get a chance to call Kelly.

I make it to our house in Leesburg, Virginia, between 8:30 and 9 p.m., turning the lights on in our strangely dark and empty kitchen as I enter. Our five-year-old, Hannah, had a *Nutcracker* ballet rehearsal tonight, but I expected Kelly, Hannah, and three-year-old Olivia would be home by now. Of course, it's probably just another drawn-out practice stretching much longer than everyone initially expected. Not too unusual. But it's crazy to keep the little ones out so late . . . and the overtaxed parents!

I walk past the answering machine with the blinking light to unload a couple of my bags, then return to my car, which is still running in the driveway, and park it in the garage. When I walk back to the kitchen, I listen to the messages.

The message starts. "Mike, this is Kristin. Kelly and the girls were in a car accident," the recording from my answering machine says in the stillness of my home. I hold my breath and wait for the next line, telling me, "But everyone is all right." It never comes . . .

Five Miles from Home
Kelly, Early Evening

I quickly try to clean up the kitchen and send the girls to get ready before we leave.

The girls gather activities to keep them busy during the numerous unstructured gaps of time at rehearsal. We say goodbye to our cat, Liberty, and dog, Gallagher, and head into the garage. As we pull out of the driveway—it is around 5:45 p.m.—Olivia asks to listen to a *Blue's Clues* CD, and the girls immediately start singing along. We begin our drive to the studio.

Five miles from home, I slow to a stop as a yellow light turns red, the girls still singing along to the CD . . . and then it all goes dark.

Lost in the Fog and Anger
Mike, Late Evening

The next message is another from Kristin. She says something about bringing a change of clothes because Olivia is being transferred to Inova Fairfax to stay overnight. I'm paralyzed; I want to leave immediately, but I'm confused about the message, which continues, saying that Olivia is unconscious. My mind races as I battle a numbness in my body. Did I hear those words correctly? My heart pounds against my rib cage and finally breaks through the shock. I shift into autopilot, fixated on getting to that hospital. There are no competing factors at that moment . . . nothing else matters, only the hospital.

I run to my car but stop short. Our good friend Mary is pulling up in her car. She calmly tries to tell me what happened, but the words coming out of her mouth are not sticking—I just want to leave! Then Hannah steps out of the car. I rush over and pick her up, asking how she is. She says she's fine, and I see that she only has a slight bruise over the bridge of her nose. She gives me a big hug and seems to be in good spirits. Finally able to focus for just a moment on what Mary is saying, I learn she's going to keep Hannah for a sleepover tonight so Kelly and I can spend time with Olivia.

I drive down Belmont Ridge, a dark road with many curves, to get onto the toll road that will get me to the other hospital quicker— but I am not thinking of the best way to get to the hospital; I just know that I must drive, and that I was not there in that time of need. The thought circles over and over: *I was not there. I was not there. I should have been there.*

In the heavy mist and fog, apparitions of other vehicles and trees seem to float by. A slow-moving car blocks me from quickly getting to my destination. I am livid, but I know that the dark, rural road needs to be taken with caution. I must not become another injured Lang.

Another strong realization grows in me: I need to be a rock throughout whatever situation awaits me at the hospital.

Tell Me This Is a Dream
Kelly, Early Evening

"Mommy, Mommy! Wake up!"

My head is groggy. It feels like I'm waking up from a nap as Hannah calls me. Another voice comes from my left side: Is anyone sitting in the third row of my minivan? Their tone comes with heavy concern and urgency. I respond with a no.

An instinct tells me something is wrong with Olivia. She is sitting directly behind me in a five-point harness car seat. More people ask questions. They want to know how old she is. I start yelling. They must save her!

Still struggling through the haze filling my head, I hear someone talking to Hannah, calming her down while another someone takes Olivia and her car seat out of the minivan. Sirens and flashing lights surround us, the sound a painful groan in my ears. Someone in an emergency uniform tells me we are being taken to Loudoun Hospital Center. They put me in one ambulance, Hannah in another, and Olivia in a third.

When we get there, Hannah is examined and appears to be fine. The doctors quickly decide that they are not equipped to treat Olivia in her condition. She must be transferred to a pediatric trauma center immediately.

When I finally break free from the fog, the nurse shows me the information I gave her. I gave her Kristin's phone number, and she headed to the hospital as soon as they called. But the nurse continues to ask me how to reach Mike. The question confuses me. Why can't she reach him? In my discombobulated state, I mistakenly gave her all of Mike's former work information. I also asked her to call the church I have been attending the past three years.

Hannah's little voice comes from the corner of the room, reminding me that Mike is returning from a business trip. I had not seen her until this moment.

Kristin arrives and seems very relieved to see Hannah. The hospital told her that Hannah and I were injured, but they never mentioned Olivia, so she assumed Olivia was not in the car with us. When the nurse explains the situation more clearly, Kristin fervently agrees to accompany Olivia to Fairfax Hospital Center, the closest trauma center.

Hannah is discharged with the advice that she should be given Tylenol if she has any soreness or pain during the night. Mary comes to pick her up so she can go to school tomorrow. She is excited as I tell her goodbye, happy to have a school-night sleepover with her friend Katherine.

After Hannah is gone, they escort Kristin to Olivia. The ER nurse explains I will have to undergo some tests before discharge. As I'm wheeled to radiology, a nurse asks if I would like to see Olivia before she is transferred. They wheel me to her. She is on a backboard and has a cervical spine collar on. She looks like a little angel sleeping on the gurney. I try to sit up but cannot. Only now do I realize that I am strapped down as well. The emergency technicians lift my backboard so I can see and touch Olivia.

Looking at my little girl, I am in complete shock. Life is so incredibly fragile. I touch her cheeks and tell her I love her, then ask Kristin and the technicians to take good care of her.

Tests, Bare Feet, and Fear
Kelly, Evening

Olivia is transported while I have a CT scan and X-rays. I complain of leg, ear, and nose pain, but the doctors tell me the tests do not show anything broken. Somewhere in the middle of testing, Susan, Kristin's sister-in-law, arrives. She tells me Kristin called her and asked her to drive me to the trauma center where they have taken Olivia.

When I'm discharged, the nurses give me scrubs to wear; my pants were cut by the EMTs when they took me out of the car. My shoes were left at the accident scene, so I'm left to walk barefoot.

As Susan and I walk toward the exit, a woman escorts a man out. I realize he's the same man I saw being treated in the ER across from me. In fact, he was questioned by the same police officer I was. Can that be the man who hit us? No, surely not. If he were, wouldn't he say he is sorry or ask how my daughters are?

On the car ride to Fairfax, I am frustrated and dazed. I still don't remember the accident. All I can say is "I can't believe this is happening." It seems surreal. Susan talks with me, and her words calm me down. Her voice is soothing. She went through her own tragedy many years before I met her. She knows how things can change in the blink of an eye.

Kristin calls and gives updates as they drive her and Olivia to the hospital. The EMTs have allowed her to ride in the back with Olivia during transport. Olivia is not responding to anything they try. The

EMT tells Kristin that Olivia is lucky she is a big kid because that must be what saved her.

When Kristin and Olivia arrive at the trauma center, a team awaits their arrival. Olivia is whisked into a treatment room for examination. I worry the hospital will not allow me to enter without shoes, but we walk right in and head straight for the Pediatric Intensive Care Unit.

That's My Little Girl
Mike, Late Evening

I finally make it to the trauma center and rush to the ER. It takes the security guard a while to find out where Olivia is. My anxiety reaches a boiling point. I cannot stand the delays every step of the way, everything repeatedly grinding to a complete stop!

Finally, I am given the room number. As I approach, a social worker tries to talk to me, stopping me again. She is so calm and smiling, which only heightens my anger. I want to shove her aside and shout, "Get out of my way so I can see my little girl!" but instead I mumble a thank-you and walk past her. Then I see Kristin, Susan, and Kelly. Kelly has a black eye from the car crash and seems so fragile. She does not say anything. We both just want to get to our Olivia.

I turn, and my eyes drop to the hospital bed where my three-year-old daughter lies, the center of attention for the doctors and nurses tending to her. She has a little blood on her nose, and her mouth is twisted to accommodate the surgical tape and various tubes. She wears a surgical collar. Hooked up to a ventilator, she also has what seems like yards and yards of IVs and other tubes uncoiling from her limbs. The only thing covering her is a diaper. Although she is breathing and her chest is moving up and down in a slow, consistent pattern, I must remind myself that the ventilator—not Olivia—is doing the work. So strange. She seems to be resting peacefully.

I've only received bits of information about the incident since

I arrived at the hospital. A reckless driver hit several other cars, went through a red light, and rear-ended our van . . . Something about hitting a guardrail. The details don't matter at the moment. What sticks with me most is the thought that Olivia would have been medevacked and treated more quickly had the weather not been so awful. I wonder, *Would that have made a difference for her? Would she be awake right now?*

Kelly keeps saying that we did everything parents are supposed to do; we had a highly regarded minivan, a 2000 Toyota Sienna. We had the kids in child car seats, and they were buckled in properly. So how could this be happening?

After trying and failing to find words to explain and rationalize for the both of us, I finally settle on saying the whys are not important, especially now.

We both stay the night in the hospital. My suitcase is still packed from my trip, and Kristin has given Kelly clothes and toiletries she thought to bring from our home. I come so close to breaking down. I start to cry on several occasions, but somehow, I can't let it all out. I'm not sure why. My beautiful little girl might die. I don't even know if she can hear me say that I love her.

But the doctors say it might be helpful to talk to her and touch her. Kelly leaves the room to find some things to bring back, so I pick up one of Olivia's favorite books, *The Little Mermaid*, and try to read it aloud. I choke up on the first few words and can't finish. It takes some effort, but I'm somewhat composed by the time Kelly returns. I'll try reading to Olivia again later.

Nothing to Do but Wait
Kelly, Late Evening

After we arrive at Olivia's room, the doctor explains that she has a traumatic brain injury, and they don't know when or if she will wake up. I can't believe what I'm hearing. They say she has a few brain bleeds, but they want to wait to do more tests. They also tell us that her Glasgow Coma Scale (GSC) was a six at the time of admission—a severe injury. They continue, saying the GCS is a neurological scale that aims to give a reliable, objective way of recording the conscious state of a person for initial as well as subsequent assessment.[1]

We're told to sit and talk to her quietly. They suggest reading a book or magazine she enjoys to stimulate brain activity. Once again, Kristin comes to our rescue. She pulls some *Ranger Rick* magazines out of her bag. Her husband, David, has come to the hospital along with their three-week-old baby, Camryn. Father John, the Episcopalian priest from the church I have been attending, is here as well.

With nothing else to do but wait, we tell Kristin, Susan, David, and everyone else that we're all right and they can go home. We thank them over and over. Had they not answered our pleas for help, we shudder to think where we would be right now.

The neurosurgeon on duty recommends surgery to alleviate the pressure of the bleeding and swelling in Olivia's brain. It's a terrifying thought! We have no idea what all this means. I have never heard of a swollen brain. When chief of neurosurgery Dr. Lee reviews Olivia's condition in a consultation via a phone call from his home, he vetoes this decision and instead orders an intracranial pressure monitor (ICP) be placed in her skull. They will drill the ICP into the left side of Olivia's skull, and then a machine will constantly record the pressure in her brain, with hopes that the swelling will go down on its own. If the monitor reaches a high point, then surgery will be necessary.

We are asked to leave the room while the monitor is inserted. Mike and I sit on a bench outside of the Pediatric Intensive Care

---

1   A patient is assessed against the criteria of the scale, and the resulting points give a patient a score between 3 (indicating deep unconsciousness) and either 14 (original scale) or 15 (the more widely used modified or revised scale). Generally, brain injury is classified as
•   Severe, with GCS ≤ 8
•   Moderate, GCS 9–12
•   Minor, GCS ≥ 13

Unit (PICU). All I can think is *If Olivia dies, I don't know how I will go on*. I think about Hannah and what this will do to her, and all I feel is utter despair. My heart is being crushed under the weight of everything happening.

As we wait, I find a restroom and notice my reflection in the mirror. I feel as though I am floating in the atmosphere, looking down on myself. I gently touch the area underneath my left eye and realize it's tender. I'm testing to make sure this is me I'm seeing and not someone else. I have not one but two black eyes, along with blood all over my nose and upper lip. I quickly grab a paper towel and wet it with water. I try to clean the blood gently, but the paper towel is rough on my skin. I immediately remember Hannah saw me like this. She witnessed so much more than any five-year-old should. I am incredulous that no one mentioned these injuries to me or gave me a way to clean myself up.

Once the ICP is in place, the doctors tell us not to touch her or stimulate her as that will increase the pressure on her brain. They are closely monitoring the pressure, and if it escalates too high, she will require surgery. I never imagined a day when I would be told to refrain from touching, holding, or soothing my own child. If I don't obey, my child may need brain surgery.

We're told to get some rest. What exactly are they expecting? How do you rest when your "baby" is breathing through a ventilator and has a monitor in her skull, and you are unable to hold or console her? Getting some rest is a near impossible task.

WEEK ONE, DAY ONE

The walls are so thin I can hear the screams of others in the middle of the night, leaving me to wonder whether the child in the next room made it.

—Wednesday, November 28, 2001

Hopeless and Helpless

Mike, Early Morning

Kelly and I feel even more helpless today. Olivia has another CT scan scheduled incredibly early this morning to determine whether the swelling or bleeding in her brain increased or decreased overnight. Since she is hooked up to so many machines, it takes a team of more than five nurses and assistants to move her down to radiology. I can't get my mind around what I'm seeing. So many people, so many machines and tubes, my daughter helpless and limp in their arms.

While she has her CT scan, the chief of neurosurgery meets with us and tells us the back of Olivia's skull was fractured in the incident and it will take six months to heal. He also explains why he didn't want surgery conducted last night—to avoid risking complications unless there are no other options.

We're told that all we can do at this time is wait and see how Olivia progresses. He reiterates, more than once, that it is imperative Olivia not be touched or spoken to because these "stressors" can raise the pressure in her brain and bring on further complications. Kelly and I look at each other. Did he just tell us, her parents, not to talk to our child? Not to touch or try to let her know that we are here with her?

We will do anything for her. If it means that type of separation, well, we will do just that. Even though it runs contrary to every fiber in our bodies and souls.

With the probe tracking her brain activity, we see by way of the monitors when extra pressure is being exerted. As parents, we feel useless—as if we are giving up our innate duty to comfort our child. I feel like I'm letting Olivia down . . .

Unpredictable Waiting
Kelly, Early Morning

Morning takes forever to arrive. Sitting in a hospital, I'm not a part of the world outside. Time stands still. There are windows, but they only allow filtered light, so it always feels gray and cloudy. The smell of antiseptic permeates every cell of my body. The air is so dry that my throat and skin feel like I haven't had anything to drink for months.

We ask Dr. Lee what to expect, and he can't tell us. He explains all brain injuries are unique and do not follow a predictable timeline. We return to Olivia's room, and I sit in the dark, cool room and pray for my baby.

As the day goes on, we receive a lot of visitors. Kristin comes by with toiletries and food and to check on Olivia. She approaches

Olivia and gives her a careful kiss. The EMTs who transported Olivia come by to check on her while they're at the hospital on another call. I see the concern on their faces and am so touched they've taken the time to check on her. It makes me wonder how many times they take care of someone and never find out how they are or whether they recover. I wonder whether they ever get any closure.

The Incident . . . Not an Accident
Mike, Late Morning

I pace the hallway outside the waiting room—back and forth as far as I can go. I must have covered a couple miles by now, replaying the story of the "incident" in my mind. I can't call this event an "accident." To me, an accident means that no one is at fault or that it happened without intention. Someone has to be accountable as my three-year-old fights to stay alive . . .

What happened just a fleeting time ago gets a bit clearer as more information is relayed to me. Early yesterday evening, Kelly was driving the kids to the ballet rehearsal. They were only a few miles from our house when Kelly felt a crushing impact from the back of the van. A man driving a white Toyota 4-Runner had hit five vehicles on the main route into and out of Leesburg, then went through a red light, hitting our van while Kelly was stopped at a light.

The 4-Runner somehow locked its bumper with the van, and the powerful impact pushed our vehicle from the right lane across the other lanes, smashing the van into a guardrail. The force of the crash was so powerful that the van ended up perpendicular to the ground. The emergency responders immediately asked if anyone was in the third row of the van because the rear was so compressed that it didn't exist anymore.

Briefly, I think, *Why? How could this be happening to us?* Our entire world is crumbling before me. With all that has happened this year—me losing my job right after moving into our new home with a new mortgage, Kelly suffering a miscarriage—watching my motionless daughter in a coma and not being able to even hold her hand and tell her that I love her is too cruel for anyone to confront. I wonder whether God is putting us through some type of test. But why, and what could my family or I have possibly done to deserve this?

Then my mind goes to the tragedies in New York City, DC, Pennsylvania, and the events of September 11 a few months before. The whole nation is experiencing a time like no other. I join thousands of others in asking these questions. There is no sense and no explanation to be found.

Right then, I decide to concentrate on my family. I choose to never think back to those probing questions. I will get my family whole and together again, even if I don't know what that will look like or what it means.

Not long after I return to Olivia's room, Father John enters. He is a kind, young priest. I've met him a couple times before and am always struck by just how down-to-earth he is. He asks if Kelly and I will join him in a prayer for Olivia. Strange that a moment later I am standing and holding Kelly's hand as Father John gives his prayer. My Judaism is important to me, but if anyone wants to say a prayer for Olivia, it doesn't matter what their religion is. I know what they feel in their hearts, and the more support expressed for Olivia, well, it can't hurt.

New Tortures
Kelly, Midmorning

Father John tells us that God is crying along with us. I keep asking how God could let this happen, and he tells me that God does not cause these things, nor can he stop them from happening. He explains God gave us free will and cannot alter what happens. God could not stop the driver from hitting us, and He is praying for Olivia's survival as much as we are. This gives me so much comfort.

By midmorning, her temperature has risen, and she starts vomiting. There are also problems with her breathing, so a respiratory therapist is called. She is examined by more doctors, and they conclude she is developing pneumonia due to aspiration in her lungs. Another thing added to the list of worries.

Her lungs are suctioned on a regular basis, and the sound the machine makes is frightening. Her temperature keeps rising, so they remove all her clothes except for a diaper. Her sheets are removed from the bed, and the temperature in her room is lowered to keep her as cool as possible.

The social worker comes into the room repeatedly. She takes all our insurance information and assures us she will handle everything with the insurance company. We opted to take COBRA health insurance when Mike was laid off weeks ago, which has allowed us to keep the insurance we had without any lapse of coverage. I can't imagine what would have happened if we hadn't done this.

We are encouraged to get snacks and drinks in the PICU kitchen; we aren't allowed to eat in the hospital room. We decide to sneak in food as much as possible so we don't have to leave her bedside. How can they expect us to leave our child alone in the PICU so we can eat? It's hard enough for me to leave the room to use the restroom; each time I do, I hurry, just in case something happens while I'm gone.

In the PICU, each room faces the nurses' station through a glass wall so when the doctors make rounds or want to discuss cases with the residents, they can peer at each child. The walls are so thin I can hear the screams in the middle of the night, leaving me to wonder whether the child in the next room has made it. Yet I'm not allowed to hear the doctors discussing my own child's case because I'm not privy to the information. Monitors and alarms go off, and nurses can't always respond quickly.

The glass denies us any semblance of privacy. But we don't care. We anticipate her waking up and are anxious. Will she know us? My thoughts constantly pore over the questions she may have and the ones running through my mind: What will she be like? How will she act toward us?

Wrestling with Control
Mike, Afternoon

I call home to tell my parents what has occurred. My mom answers, and though it doesn't take long to get to the point, I only manage a few shaky words. I say that there was a crash and Olivia is hurt. I choke up. Kristin takes the phone and updates my mother.

I regain my composure and want to wrestle the phone back from Kristin. I need to do this my way, but I'm not sure what that even means. It is abundantly clear that I can't control various situations; as a planner, I find this exceedingly frustrating. I'm not sure how I'm supposed to feel beyond the deep sadness and helplessness that has taken over.

After I get back on the phone and manage to talk a bit with my mother, I gather my thoughts, starting the task of going down the list of calls that I need to make.

The Calls Begin
Kelly, Afternoon

Mike makes a lot of other phone calls that need to be made, as I am incapable of doing these. Mike is a type A person and can't sit still, so he keeps himself busy. He calls Olivia's preschool and informs them of the accident and then notifies friends who we planned to meet up with during the week. He checks on Hannah, notifies other family members, and finds someone to take care of our pets. He also calls the insurance company regarding our totaled van, the rescue squad that responded to our accident to get more information, and the towing company. It is a never-ending list.

Another Day Ending
Kelly, Evening

Tonight, I lie down on one of the chair cots, an exact duplicate of the cots in every patient room, and try to get as comfortable as possible. I recline in the semi-dark, wondering how this story will end. Will there be a positive outcome? I drift in and out of sleep all night long. Monitors constantly go off in rooms all over the PICU, including Olivia's. Are other parents receiving tragic news? Are any children dying in this place? Nurses and respiratory therapists come in during the night to check Olivia's status, fluids, and other vitals. Their presence is another alarm, waking me each time they step in the room.

WEEK ONE, DAY TWO

Now and then we say a quick hello in the hallway—but that is the extent of the conversation. Maybe it's that we're all too scared to ask why the other child is here . . . not wanting to hear a story worse than our own.

—Thursday, November 29, 2001

Deafening Codes
Kelly, Morning

I am awake to see the sun rise. Though the night was fitful, I'm happy we made it through another one.

My neck feels stiff. I fold the blanket, put the pillow aside, and then try to move my head from side to side. At first, I think this is just the result of sleeping on the cot for the past two nights, but even after a very quick shower, I still can't move it much.

When Mike arrives, he encourages me to go downstairs and have someone in the emergency room look at my neck and determine how serious it is. I reluctantly agree but worry something will happen while I'm away from Olivia.

I don't know if the worry I'm consumed by is because I feel guilty for not being able to protect her in the accident or something else, but I'm very reluctant to leave. This hospital is quite large, and I'm not familiar with it. I ask a nurse for directions, but the hallways seem to turn into mazes as I head to the ER.

I ride the elevator down to the main level. Looking at the others, I can't help wondering what their stories are. Are they visiting friends or family during a joyous time such as the birth of a baby? Are they coming to say goodbye to a loved one at the end stage of life? I hope it's for joyful reasons . . . not reasons like mine.

The emergency room is a busy place for a Thursday morning. I fill out paperwork and wait for someone to call my name. When I'm finally called into the triage room, the nurse asks a lot of questions. I explain that my three-year-old daughter is in a coma upstairs and I would like to get back as quickly as possible. I'm hoping this will expedite my exam and any tests they feel are needed. But deep down, I doubt anything will make the process quicker.

The doctor orders an X-ray, since a CAT scan was completed two nights ago. My time waiting in the exam room feels like an eternity. Codes like the ones in the PICU echo through the entire hospital. They never seem to stop, even for a moment. They are deafening, and I can't drown out or ignore all the sounds.

Knowing Olivia is in the hospital just upstairs, it is difficult, even painful, to hear "Code blue in the ER," "Code yellow, sixth floor west wing," etc. I keep waiting to hear something concerning Olivia. I want to be there when Olivia wakes up; I don't want her to think I've abandoned her.

Never Fast Enough
Kelly, Early Afternoon

I can't wait any longer. The doctor tells me I'm probably suffering from whiplash and will need physical therapy. He instructs me to take ibuprofen for the discomfort. All that time away from Olivia, and I'm simply told to take something for the pain.

I want to run through the hospital to reach her room, but I can't. I hurry back to make sure she's all right. I know Mike is with her and that he's doing everything in his power to help her, but I want to be there too.

When I enter, Mike's parents have arrived. Both wearing looks of concern and shock, they keep remarking how small Olivia looks lying on the bed, hooked up to so many machines. They stay with us for a little while before they head out to pick up Hannah and take her home. They tell us they will stay at our house and take care of Hannah for as long as we need.

So Much Food, but No Appetite
Mike, Afternoon

Family and friends start calling. Others send more food than we can eat. Friends, neighbors, and acquaintances stop by. We can't help but feel overwhelmed by the thoughtfulness of so many.

As they come, they express words of sympathy: "I'm so sorry," "Please let me know what I can do," "I can't believe this," "You're in our prayers," etc. Some show up so distraught that they don't say anything. They just reach out to us and give us a hug. It's ironic that I feel sorry for them—people who genuinely want to help but don't know what to do, how to act, or what to say. For us, it really doesn't matter what the gesture is; what's most significant is that they are thinking of us. As people come and go, I wonder how some of them heard of the incident. I'm seeing in real time how fast news travels, and it is amazing to witness.

Many of the conversations happen in a blur. Moments after the words come out of my mouth, I don't remember what I've said. Simply saying "Thank you" isn't nearly enough to show our appreciation toward so many thoughtful and understanding people. I know they aren't necessarily seeking a response from Kelly and me. They just want to give a bit of themselves and let us know that they support us.

It doesn't take long for Olivia's room to grow crowded with all the food. It doesn't help that we've been warned not to eat in her room since there is an insect problem in the hospital. *No need to worry about breaking that rule*, I think; Kelly and I find it difficult to eat much at all. I'm worried about the toll this is taking on my wife. She seems fragile and a bit withdrawn, understandably. I want to provide some type of comfort. I feel her isolating herself under all the strain and worry.

Oblivious and Self-Absorbed

Kelly, Afternoon

The phone in the hospital room is our main mode of communication. We have cell phones, but we can't use them as our primary numbers while we're in the hospital. Cell signals interfere with the medical equipment. Anyone trying to reach us has to call the hospital.

Mike leaves the room for a bit of air, and as I'm sitting by Olivia's bed, my mother calls the hospital room. She is returning Mike's call. As many children do, I have a tumultuous relationship with my parents but especially my mother. The last time I spoke with her was prior to Thanksgiving. She and my dad told me they weren't coming for Christmas this year because they were worried about getting the flu.

As I answer the phone, rather than asking me how Olivia is, my mother tells me she doesn't know where my father is. That he keeps leaving the house for hours. She then asks me what she should do. I don't have a whole lot of advice for her. She goes on to tell me she hopes I never have to deal with the kind of crisis she is in. At this point, anger is seething out of me—like the pictures of monsters with steam coming out of their heads. I tell her I can't speak about this right now; she becomes very agitated with me. I explain that my three-year-old is lying in a hospital bed on life support and I need to focus on her healing and well-being. She never once asks how I or Hannah are doing. The conversation finally ends when I hang up in frustration and anger.

This phone call is particularly hard to bear. A familiar rage comes over me; over the past few years, these conversations have been difficult and fraught with so much emotion. I decide my focus needs to be on my daughter and try to block my mother out of mind for the time being.

Feeling the Frustration
Kelly, Evening

Mike is going home for the evening so he can spend time with Hannah and hopefully get a good night's sleep.

Susan comes to visit and brings me a home-cooked meal. It's times like this that the true nature of friendship and community shine through. Especially in these little gestures. Our former neighbors come by, too, with a huge bag full of snacks for Mike and me and cards for Olivia and Hannah made by all their children. Their thoughts and gestures are so incredibly special.

The next time I see the nurse, I ask if we can give Olivia a bath. She has vomited a few times, and though her diaper has been changed, giving her a sponge bath may help clean her up more. I would feel like I'm helping, too. I'm told a sponge bath isn't allowed while she's hooked up to so many machines. I really want to take care of my little girl, and since I can't hold her, lie down with her, or feed her, I want to be able to do something.

Life in the PICU feels like it's becoming our normal. I've started to recognize the faces of fellow parents and the nursing staff. The parents never speak much. Now and then we say a quick hello in the hallway—but that is the extent of the conversation. Maybe it's that we're all too scared to ask why the other children are here . . . not wanting to hear a story worse than our own.

The nurse stationed outside of Olivia's room tonight is one of those I could do without. All she does is complain about her job and how the day shift left all the paperwork for her to complete and how busy she is looking for a new job. Doesn't she already have an important job? Isn't it her job to make sure my daughter and the other children in this hospital receive the best care?

Each time Olivia's machines beep, it seems to take forever for this nurse to come in and check to make sure everything is all right. I don't expect to get much sleep tonight. I'll be trying even harder to catch the attention of the nurse, on top of trying to cope with the overwhelming worry I feel.

WEEK ONE, DAY THREE

She asks how Olivia is and if she likes the pictures she drew. Hannah has always liked receiving praise, especially for her drawings. I don't know how to respond . . .

    —Friday, November 30, 2001

I Gasped
Mike, Morning

Before heading to the hospital this morning, I stop by the wrecking yard to get our personal items out of the Toyota Sienna minivan. It's hard to describe the dread and the tightness in my stomach as I drive. I don't know what to expect or what condition the van will be in.

I stop one of the guys who works there and follow him to the vehicle. It is an astonishing sight—this van that housed my family in the tragic event. A gasp escapes me, and I take a deep breath. My knees buckle a bit. After a moment, I snap some photos with my camera because, well, I feel like I should. I methodically take photos from several angles, trying to be somewhat of a historian rather than someone who feels the air getting thicker, making it difficult to breathe. I tell myself to treat this moment objectively and capture the evidence.

The rear of the burgundy Sienna is . . . gone. The impact compressed the rear end all the way to the middle row where Olivia and Hannah sat.

The front of the van is compressed, too, but not to the extent of the rear. The van's cabin is remarkably intact. I look inside and find one of the girls' pink umbrellas. The other one is stuck in the rear, lodged between the collapsed seats and metal. I can't pull it out.

Driving Through the Fear

Kelly, Early Afternoon

Father John comes to visit, bringing me a latte from the coffee stand in the lobby. I am touched by the gesture. He talks with us and then asks to say a prayer over Olivia. Of course, we say yes. He again speaks about this event not being Jesus's doing, reminding us that Jesus is crying and praying alongside us. Father John prays for strength and knowledge for the nurses and doctors treating Olivia. It's hard to believe the sense of peace I feel at this moment.

I need to go home soon but have been putting it off. I dread leaving. It's hard to separate myself from Olivia, but the other looming thought is that I have to get in a car, the Saturn Mike drove to the hospital earlier today, and drive myself home. I put it off as long as possible and finally say my goodbyes. On the way to the parking garage, each step becomes more and more difficult to take. It takes a few minutes for me to recognize the overwhelming sense of terror that has risen inside me. I'm terrified of driving again. The last time I got behind the wheel, we ended up in a horrific accident.

I find the car and slowly unlock the door and put my things in the back seat. My whole body shakes as I get into the driver's seat. I stop for a moment frozen in time. Finally, I take a big breath and place the key in the ignition. My panic intensifies. I can't recall ever feeling so fearful.

As I sit in anticipation of the drive, I only consider two routes to get home from the hospital. I choose the one that doesn't take me on the road where our accident occurred. I'm not ready to face that yet. Another deep breath before putting the car in reverse to leave the garage.

Halfway home, still shaking, I realize I've been driving at least ten miles below the speed limit and might cause an accident from being overly cautious, but I don't care. My knuckles are white, and they stay that way the entire thirty miles home. I finally turn on our street and pull into the driveway, let out a huge sigh, and relief washes over me. I made it home.

Tell Them You Love Them
Mike, Morning

As luck would have it, I find Olivia's four prized *101 Dalmatian* figurines. It's her favorite movie. Her Pongo and Perdy dogs and two puppies are everything to her; she carries them everywhere, clutching all four in her hand. It's a strange, bittersweet feeling. I make sure to not leave a single one behind. Having all of them with me brings a sense of completion.

I find a Disney princess tote bag, but since there's blood on it, I leave it behind. There's blood on the van's carpeting. The numbness kicks in as I methodically look through the wreckage for the tossed belongings. I must get as much as I can. I want to bring a piece of my family back together. Each item I grab will help accomplish that, at least in my mind.

Through the broken glass, I gather some of the books, coloring books, crayons, etc. I find a portable CD player and a Dalmatian (of course!) cake mold that we borrowed for Olivia's third birthday party. Each item I gather is such a treasure, as valuable as gold. They make me think of happier times—of family, love, and unity.

Both kids' car seats are intact. I see Olivia's blue winter coat, but I can't pull it out because it's wedged between the back of her van seat and the part of the van that was formerly the rear/trunk area. I find another worker at the yard, who helps me by pushing the seat forward so I can retrieve the coat. He says that his boss told him this is the worst vehicle crash he has ever seen. The worker seems genuinely sorry when I tell him who I am and what has happened. He mentions that he has a young child also. I tell him to tell his child every night at bedtime that he loves him because you don't know what the next day will bring.

Dreaded Conversations
Kelly, Late Afternoon

Hannah is ecstatic to see me when I walk into the house. She excitedly shows me the sneakers her grandparents bought her to replace the ones she lost in the accident. She asks how Olivia is and if she likes the pictures she drew. Hannah has always liked receiving praise, especially for her drawings. I don't know how to respond, so I tell her Olivia was sleeping when I left the hospital room. Hannah's instant response is that Olivia is spending a lot of time asleep. I realize that we've all been taking turns telling her that Olivia is sleeping. None of us know how else to explain her condition to a five-year-old.

Hannah's school and teachers have sent home a gift basket of books, coloring items, and trinkets for her. She's thrilled to show me all the fun things she received.

Before we leave the house for the *Nutcracker* rehearsal, the phone rings. I don't recognize the caller ID number, but with Olivia lying in the PICU at a hospital, I answer every call. The caller is a parent volunteer from Hannah's elementary school, asking if I'd like to volunteer at the upcoming holiday breakfast at school. I explain what's happened with Olivia and that I can't commit to anything at this time. From the woman's voice, I know she feels horrible. She responds, "Oh, you're the lady with the two girls I used to see at our bus stop. I am so sorry to bother you, and I hope your daughter recovers." It's so hard to keep explaining what happened. For that reason, I'm dreading tonight—taking Hannah to rehearsal. My eye still has some bruising, so I'm sure people will ask me what happened. How do I avoid talking about it?

When we get to the school where the show will be held, I get Hannah ready for her dress rehearsal. She must be dressed in her tights and leotard, which will be exchanged for the costume at showtime. Her hair must be done in a very tight bun, and of course the makeup artist will be doing her makeup. All the fuss over preparation keeps me distracted from what's happening at the hospital. Which is a good thing.

I try to avoid eye contact with many for fear they will ask what happened to my eye. Then it dawns on me that they may not ask for fear that I'm a victim of abuse. Well, that doesn't make the situation or my uneasiness any better.

Some of the parents who know us from dance approach me and ask how Olivia and I are doing. They mention they are praying for her and our family. Another woman, whom I've never met before, approaches and gives me a warm embrace, telling me that I'm such a "hero." It means so much to have her say that. I can only guess that she heard our story through the dance moms' grapevine—about the family who was in a horrific accident on the way to stage rehearsal. Not knowing me at all, she has taken the time to offer those few words that mean the world to me.

One of the other moms I know tells me the prayer circle she's in is keeping Olivia in prayer. To be honest, I didn't understand the power of a prayer circle until now. Until this accident that has changed our family forever. Growing up Catholic and going to what we called CCD back in those days, I heard priests and laypeople talk about prayer and the power it can bring to any situation. But I never understood. I've always worried about doing it wrong, so I really haven't done it at all. My mother didn't have conversations with me about what we were learning, so I didn't have a "safe place" to ask these questions.

Four nights ago, on the night of the accident, I started praying. Even though I'm very unsure my words are being heard.

Some people ask about my black eye. I tell them about the accident, but one woman responds, "Oh, she'll be fine. My neighbor's daughter fell out of a window, and she walked away from it." Does she really think that will make me feel better? Other people don't bother to ask. I wonder whether they figure that if they don't say anything, they won't have to care.

My mind keeps going back to the terrifying thought that Olivia may regain consciousness while I'm not there, and she'll think I've abandoned her. I call Mike at the hospital constantly to check on her status, but nothing changes. I feel guilty sitting in the audience, enjoying the show, while Olivia fights for her life in the hospital.

Hannah is so happy to have me there and home for the evening, which makes the pain easier to bear. She appears to be handling all this well, especially for a five-year-old. She's been through a lot over the past four days, and Mike and I always have her on our minds. We aren't sure what she saw or heard before the EMTs responded to the accident or of the fear she might be holding inside.

WEEK ONE, DAY FOUR

Please bring her back to us. I worked so hard to bring her into this world; please don't take her away from us now.

—Saturday, December 1, 2001

The Holiday Breakfast
Kelly, Morning

Last night's sleep was restless. I get up and get dressed to take Hannah to the holiday breakfast and book sale at her school. This is our first year, with Hannah coming in as a kindergartener, and we don't know a lot of the traditions. Many people are in attendance, but we know only a few of them. I'm bombarded with questions. Hannah and her friend Katherine stick close together, having their picture taken with Santa and eating donuts. We decide to visit the book fair as well. I'm completely overwhelmed, and my mind is elsewhere. It feels like I'm walking in a trance.

A few moms I've met through the school comment that I must

have had enough time to unpack after the move because I've managed to find our holiday shirts for the breakfast. I don't mention that I've spent the past five days at the hospital.

While looking around the book fair, Hannah finds an art stencil book she wants to get. I'm unsure about purchasing anything since we still aren't sure of our financial outlook, but Mary insists on buying it for her. Hannah is thrilled. I'm eternally grateful for the joy Mary is bringing into Hannah's immediate world during this terrible time.

Torn Between Two Who Need Us
Kelly, Late Morning

When the holiday breakfast is over, we return home. Sam and Estelle, Mike's parents, are eager to hear about our morning. Estelle makes sure to give us healthy food, as she always does, and keep the laundry in the house down to a minimum. It's wonderful not having to worry about those details. Hannah asks again when she'll be able to see Olivia. We tell her once Olivia stays awake for a greater amount of time, we'll make sure Hannah has plenty of time to visit. I leave as she's getting ready for the first official *Nutcracker* show.

She's on cloud nine from the previous evening's rehearsal and is looking forward to the performances this weekend. Estelle has already learned the nuances of being a dancer's assistant. The other moms are helping her get Hannah's hair tight in a bun without any flyaways. She has also learned what should and should not be worn under the tights and makes sure Hannah has plenty of items to keep herself entertained during downtime.

I'm feeling so torn. I have two children who really need me, and I don't know how to provide for both. Mike and I are thankful for his parents filling in when we can't be in two places at once, which takes some of the burden.

I say goodbye to Hannah and leave for the hospital. Getting into the driver's seat, I can't help feeling terribly shaky again. It's the first time I've had to drive from the house since the accident. The events of that evening still play in my mind. I must reverse my route and try to make it back to the hospital safely.

It's gray outside. It's not raining or snowing, but the sky is very dark, as if winter is settling in for a long nap. Rather than take the route I normally would past the scene of the accident, I choose a different way. It is quicker but involves paying a toll. I rationalize that it's worth it.

When I arrive, Mike is sitting quietly in Olivia's room, and everything looks exactly as it did yesterday. The color of the sky mimics the aura of the room. He updates me on the comings and goings of doctors and nurses. We sit quietly in the room for a while. All the testing they're doing shows that while Olivia's condition hasn't gotten any worse, it also hasn't gotten any better. But her lungs seem to be improving since the respiratory therapy started, and the treatments continue throughout the day and evening.

A Bath for My Baby
Kelly, Early Evening

Mike leaves in the afternoon, and there is a nursing shift change soon after. The nurse assigned to Olivia tonight is Meg; she's been with us previously. She's attentive and caring, which brings immediate relief. I ask her if we can do a sponge bath, and she tells me that if the doctor approves, she thinks it's a great idea. She returns a short time later with a basin, washcloths, towels, and baby shampoo and soap. I let her guide me and tell me which areas we can clean around.

The intracranial pressure monitor is still attached to the side of Olivia's head, monitoring the pressure in her brain. She's still in the C-spine collar since we aren't sure whether she has a neck injury; and of course, the ventilator is still attached. There are a lot of areas we can't clean yet. Meg is so gentle with Olivia, taking care not to pull or force her into a position. I can tell she is a mom. We end up talking about her daughter. I hope so much to observe some facial expressions or get a reaction from Olivia during the bath. But we don't.

My mind immediately goes back to the many times Mike and I have bathed Olivia in the past three years. She's never been a huge fan of the water, but she does love to play. If we distract her long enough with some toys, we can get her clean, but washing her hair is another issue. She has never liked water near her face, so we delicately wash and rinse her hair. She didn't have a lot of hair her first year of life, luckily, but it quickly grew in and became more challenging.

I'm disappointed that we don't get a reaction from Olivia but cannot fully express my thankfulness for this simple bathing gesture. I'm amazed that up until that moment, no one could see how important this is to me.

When the bath is done, I sit by Olivia's side and read quietly to her. We are allowed to speak softly but still can't hold her. The only skin-to-skin contact permitted is to touch her hand or leg, but I'm thrilled to have this. It's funny; once you are told that you can't hold your child or touch her, that's all you want to do.

WEEK ONE, DAY FIVE

It's the first step forward we've had in five days.
    —Sunday, December 2, 2001

Pointing through Glass
Kelly Morning/Afternoon

I'm up early again this morning. The day isn't looking any brighter than the previous ones, but I get coffee, shower, and dress quickly so I can return to Olivia's room. I can't shake the fear that she'll wake up and I won't be there. I don't know why this plays over and over in my mind.

The caregiver shower is on the same floor but outside the intensive care unit. There aren't many windows in this area of the hospital. The hallways always look dark and gloomy, which doesn't help my ongoing mood.

When I return to the room, doctors and residents are already there, doing rounds and checking on their patients. They've arrived much earlier than previous days, which I find interesting.

We aren't allowed in the room while they discuss our daughter's case during daily rounds, and no one meets with us afterward to go over the plan of action. Mike and I are frustrated by these events and the lack of communication. The glass wall makes it worse. We normally watch as the group of doctors, residents, and interns discuss her case, point at her, etc. This really upsets us. We understand it's a teaching hospital, but we do not want our daughter to become a "test case."

The rounds are a bit different this time. The curtains on the window are pulled shut, and I walk into the room during the examination, not realizing anyone else is here. One of the interns or residents starts questioning me about the accident. I don't understand why he is so interested—he wants to know what brand and category car seat she was using and whether it had been installed properly. I become incensed. His line of questioning serves no purpose. His job is to figure out how to help my daughter, determine whether she will wake up, and if not, why. I ask why this information is any concern of his since I have already been interviewed by the police. He doesn't have a reply.

What an awesome way to start my day.

The doctors later decide to remove Olivia's ventilator. The tests indicate she will be able to breathe on her own. She'll remain in the C-spine collar, as it's still unknown whether there are any neck or back injuries. The doctors explain the procedure will take place in her room and I'll be asked to leave during the removal.

There's nowhere to sit directly outside her room or in the immediate hallway, so I go to the waiting room, which is opposite the caregiver shower. I'm so anxious. What if the removal doesn't go as planned? What if she stops breathing? My fears of all that can go wrong consume me.

It takes such a long time before the doctors come to update me on Olivia's condition. When they finally arrive, they tell me the ventilator has been removed successfully and Olivia is now breathing on her own. It's the first step forward we've had in five days. They also explain the sedative dosage she receives through the IV is being reduced to determine whether she can be woken during the night. The doctors explain that when a patient comes out of the coma, it's not like the movies. You know . . . the comatose patient finally wakes up with a smile or witty line, and everyone breathes a sigh of relief. They are back to normal! The doctors tell me most patients may "wake" up for a minute and fall unconscious again. They may arouse and perhaps have facial movements or expressions but return to altered sleep. This could include waking in fits, flailing limbs, eyes opening but not focusing on anything.

We are prepared for both scenarios of not waking up but hope for a gradual process of regaining consciousness.

I go back to her room. I can't express how wonderful it is to see her without the ventilator. She's still hooked up to a bunch of other machines, but at least she doesn't have a tube coming out of her mouth. She is sound asleep, but my little girl is slowly coming back.

Yearning for Human Connection
Kelly, Evening

Kristin comes by the hospital, bringing me one of her delicious dinners. She insists that I go and eat elsewhere to take a break while she visits with Olivia. She's a lifesaver, once again. Kristin really has a gift for making even the worst situation a little better. The meal is on a real plate, not a paper or Styrofoam one, and with real silverware. I can't tell you how much that extra step means to me. After eating off paper plates or having a snack here or there, it's lovely to eat like a human being.

When I come back, we sit and talk. Kristin talks *to* Olivia, not *at* Olivia. She acts as though Olivia is conscious and having a conversation with us.

Olivia begins thrashing in the bed but still doesn't wake up. The doctor comes to check on her and, due to all her movement, decides she needs a sedative to calm down. They fear she'll harm herself. Once the sedative takes effect, she lies still the remainder of the evening.

A hospital can be such a lonely place in the evenings. The irony is there are so many people in the building, but everyone is hurriedly doing their jobs or visiting loved ones. When your child is in a coma, you feel the need to protect them, and yet you also yearn for human connection. I am so grateful for all the people who have been coming to visit us.

WEEK ONE, DAY SIX

"Mrs. Lang, the little girl you had on the afternoon of November 27 will not be the same little girl who wakes up."
—Monday, December 3, 2001

So Many Questions
Kelly, Morning

A hospital room on a Monday morning in December is not the cheeriest of places. I sit next to Olivia's bed; the scent of disinfectant lingers in the air. We have been told to keep the room dark and quiet since the intracranial pressure monitor is still in place.

A young woman walks into the room. She looks at Olivia and then asks if I'm her mother. She isn't wearing scrubs or the white coat of a doctor, but she has a badge that indicates she's hospital staff. She introduces herself as the assistant to the trauma surgery team. Why does she need to speak with me? No one has mentioned Olivia needs surgery.

The woman tells me there's nothing else the medical team can do for Olivia and that she must be transferred to a pediatric rehabilitation center. I am incredulous.

As she continues, I ask her where the inpatient rehabilitation is. She coughs and tells me there are perhaps two to consider; neither are in our area. One is two hours south in Charlottesville, Virginia, and the other about seventy-five minutes north in Baltimore, Maryland. The fragile floor I'm tiptoeing on falls and shatters into a billion pieces.

I throw a line of questions at her. How can a three-year-old child who's in a coma and connected to a brain monitor be so casually dismissed and moved close to a hundred miles away? Won't that impose a risk to her already fragile state? She still needs intensive care. Her lungs are still filling with liquid and need aspiration on a regular basis, and we have a five-year-old daughter at home who desperately needs both her parents. We are trying to make it work, but it's difficult, and we're only twenty-seven miles apart at this moment. To top that off, Mike was laid off not even four weeks ago and is earnestly looking for employment. What are we supposed to do? How are we supposed to do all of this?

I don't hear any of her answers to these questions. I'm not sure she's even giving me any.

She continues, saying that we don't have to decide today but that the hospital needs an answer within the next couple days. I ask if I can speak to someone else about this decision. She nods. She also informs me that physical, occupational, and speech therapies will begin. Almost on cue, the physical therapist walks in, allowing the surgical assistant to exit the room quickly.

I'm bewildered. Why are all three therapies being started on an unconscious child? The therapist explains that the speech and occupational therapists won't work with Olivia until she is awake. The main objective at this point is to get Olivia's limbs moving so her muscles don't atrophy. I'm given instructions on which exercises to do with her; then the therapist goes on her way. I'm positive by this time I have a huge sign on my forehead that reads, "Irate Mom, Do Not Engage." I don't know what an occupational therapist is, and I don't care to ask right now. I have more important issues to address.

I immediately get on the phone to Mike. His voice is calm and helps me relax a little, but I'm still irate.

My Knees Buckle
Mike, Late Morning

Kelly calls me at home. It's about 10 a.m. She's fraught and emotional, saying a clinical nurse has told her Olivia has to be transferred to another hospital by this Friday. Did I hear correctly? Four days from now? She says they want to send her to a rehab facility like Kennedy Krieger Institute in Baltimore or Kluge Children's Rehabilitation Center in Charlottesville, Virginia. The doctors tell Kelly they feel Olivia has progressed as far as she can and not much more can be done medically.

On one hand, yes, I understand that she is off the ventilator and breathing on her own. However, in my mind, she has not progressed. What does that even mean—when she can't speak, move, or open her eyes? How can we move Olivia into the next phase? How can she begin rehab?

Kelly is distraught. To make matters worse, we must decide by Wednesday. That's in just two days! The head nurse estimates that Olivia will be at a rehab facility for at least two to four weeks. I feel my eyes welling up as she tells me this.

Standing in the kitchen, I hang up, gasp, and sob at the same time, in a "dry cry." My mom tries to comfort me as my knees buckle. A tidal wave engulfs me. I grab the edge of the counter for support, struggling to understand everything at once.

- Olivia in a coma

- Uncertainty about whether she will ever wake up
- And if she does, what will that be like?
- A divided family
- Caring for Olivia and Hannah in two different cities and possibly states

So many questions: How do we choose a rehab facility? How do we navigate unemployment? Do we sell our house and move? How do I protect Kelly from all of this? Kelly and I are partners in pretty much everything we do, but Kelly is still dealing with the trauma of that awful night. This decision is all on me. How do I figure this out in two days?

Stop, steady, and focus. I simply have to shut down the swirl of emotions. Get to the hospital first and figure things out later.

When I arrive at the hospital, the story changes, but not for the better.

Potential
Kelly, Late Morning

As soon as I'm off the phone, Dr. Lee walks into the room. He motions for me to sit, then sits next to me and reintroduces himself as the chief neurosurgeon.

He begins the conversation by trying to explain why the hospital staff wants to move Olivia. I realize he has drawn the short straw, having to come in and explain the decision. I don't retain most of the conversation, but what does come through is that the staff wants to move her out of intensive care and into the pediatric wing until the next decision is made.

My next question is a dreaded one. I ask how Olivia will be once she wakes up. Will her memories of us come rushing back, will she be able to eat, walk, etc.? He looks me straight in the eye and says, "Mrs. Lang, the little girl you had on the afternoon of November 27 will not be the same little girl who wakes up. Any potential she had is erased. I cannot tell you what potential she will have, but it won't be the same."

I try so hard to contain my emotions but can't. The tears start rolling down my cheeks. This nightmare continues to get worse and worse. All I can think about is my daughter's face—the smiling, happy-go-lucky little girl who came bouncing out of preschool less than a week ago.

The doctor politely bids me farewell, and I'm left with a huge hole in my heart and too much information to process.

Increasingly, nursing staff come in and out, trying to explain why they think the move is in Olivia's best interest. I can't believe all these people feel they know what's in her best interest. We, her parents, know what her best interests are. It's time for us to step up and start advocating. To fight for our little girl.

Lemon Bars
Mike, Afternoon

The social worker tries to say in a soothing and calm manner over her homemade lemon bars that there's no hurry to have her transferred; we have a few more days to decide. But we should plan for six to nine months in rehab, and not the two to three weeks we were told earlier.

Kelly and I are dumbfounded. First, and most importantly, our child is coming out of a coma. Second, do we consider moving, or does Kelly move temporarily to be closer to Olivia during rehabilitation therapy? It is all so difficult to comprehend. Should we pack up our things again, after less than a month in our new house, to move to another city that we have never even thought about before? To top things off, I'm in my fourth week of unemployment. Maybe I need to consider how fortunate we are that I don't have a job to tie us down!

How will we even begin to explain all this to Hannah? At five years old, she will need to grow up in a hurry. We try so hard to wear a smile when we're with her and provide some sense of normalcy.

Left in Limbo
Kelly, Afternoon

We ask to speak to the doctors assigned to the unit who see her daily. While we wait, Mike gets to work on the phones. Several friends and family members have called these past five days to give us names of neurologists we should bring in for consultations. Mike calls and leaves messages asking for consults as soon as possible. He tells me he wants to research other rehab facilities in Baltimore, Delaware, Pittsburgh, Philadelphia, Richmond, and Charlottesville. We both simply want to figure out how to keep our family together. We're handed brochures about both facilities the doctors have recommended. We look them over but can't know about a place unless we visit. We ask for a tour of each one.

The doctor enters the room amid all this. He explains that once a patient is off a ventilator and breathing on their own, they are no longer in acute care. A patient with an intracranial monitor can be transferred safely, and in fact, the hospital has done many of these. We ask why she isn't waking up and what we can expect once she does. He explains that there isn't any way to determine when. He compares her injury to shaken baby syndrome. There is significant shearing in her brain, which complicates her prognosis. There could be a brain stem injury that isn't showing up on the CAT scans, and if that is the case, she most likely will never wake up.

Mike and I are devastated. No one has ever told us in such a clear and unwavering way that she may not wake up. How could this be happening?

I think about the case of Karen Ann Quinlan. Karen was a young lady who, at the age of twenty-one, slipped into a coma after consuming pills and alcohol while on a crash diet. She continued to live in a vegetative state until the Supreme Court ruled her parents could discontinue life support. Once her ventilator was removed, Karen lived for ten additional years before dying of respiratory failure.

I pray for answers while thinking about that case. How did those parents cope; how did they continue their vigil for ten years? Are there other parents who have gone through similar experiences? Where are they? Can we speak to them?

The rocking chair in our room, just as those in every other room, has an engraved plate that indicates it was a gift in memory of a child. I think about the family who donated money for the engraved plate. What was their family story? How young was their child? Did they advocate for that child the way we need to for Olivia? Are there resources for families such as ours?

WEEK TWO, DAY ONE

One young resident leans over Olivia so that his stethoscope dangles near her. She raises her arm a bit . . .

—Tuesday, December 4, 2001

Restless
Mike, Morning

Olivia has had a very restless night. Just as the doctors predicted, waking from the coma is a slow process. She falls asleep, literally for just a few minutes, and then wakes up. Valium doesn't help. I spend a couple of hours lying next to her. My back starts to hurt from squeezing into the bed with Olivia in a way that gives her ample room. I want to be close to her and hold her, but I refrain; I don't want to disturb her as she battles to rest.

Her eyes open a bit, but I'm not sure whether she can focus on me. It appears that she desperately wants to turn over and sleep on her stomach, but the collar and arm restraints make that impossible.

The CAT scan is scheduled for today, so hopefully they will allow the cervical collar to come off. That will be a victory for her, and for us. Kelly and I are desperately looking for signs of increased recognition during her conscious periods . . . any clue, and any sign of hope.

Later in the morning, a trauma team of about ten doctors and residents makes its rounds. I believe everyone is pulling for our little girl, but I'm a bit uptight about the show. This time when they come around, it's different. One young resident leans over Olivia so that his stethoscope dangles near her. She raises her arm a bit, then raises it higher, and then actually reaches for the stethoscope. I can't believe it! It's the first time she has reached for anything! The resident is thrilled, but not as much as we are.

After the doctors leave, I continue to encourage her to reach for things. I hold out her green stuffed dog, and she reaches for it, too. What an awesome day! Olivia's little stride energizes Kelly and me.

A Long Sigh of Relief
Kelly, Afternoon

Due to Mike's diligence, we're finally able to get the second opinions we so desperately need. Both doctors come and look over her records and status reports. They agree Olivia will eventually need to go to inpatient rehabilitation, specifically for the pediatric population; however, they say it's not the right time to make a transfer. Both doctors are concerned with the fever and aspiration in her lungs. They recommend holding off any transfer until further notice.

We breathe a long sigh of relief. Now we have two outside doctors recommending what we have been advocating for. With the transfer date pushed out, we have time and opportunity to visit both facilities prior to transfer. I don't feel comfortable leaving Olivia for such a long period of time, so I encourage Mike to visit them without me, but he stresses we should both attend the tours.

We schedule our first appointment, which is in Charlottesville, at 1 p.m. It will take a little over two hours to drive there without traffic. Mike's mom agrees to come back the next morning with Mike so we can get an early start. His dad is staying at our house to assist with Hannah.

Not Quite Home
Mike, Late Afternoon

Kelly and I say goodbye, and I drive home to be with Hannah.

Tonight has been difficult. Restless for all of us. Though I'm sleeping in our house, the guest room has no furniture, and the only light comes from the bulb of a small broken lamp. My bed is simply a mattress on the floor. A pile of clothes is the only decorative touch in the room as there's nothing on the walls. Besides Hannah's room, which we took care of first, decorating rooms and establishing our new house has stalled. We moved here just a month ago. I'm unemployed, and our daughter is in a coma. This house will not be our home for quite some time. I'm not convinced on what "home" even means now, or in our future.

People continue to stop by to see us, but we don't want anyone to see Olivia in her current state. We want everyone to remember her as the sweet, adorable three-year-old with a constant smile on her face. So, our visitors stay with us for a time, which I imagine is difficult enough for them since we aren't much for conversation. Kelly and I are of course haggard looking.

Our updates on Olivia's condition are somewhat limited because not much has changed. Mostly, people just try to give words of encouragement; unfortunately, there are not many to share. But their presence has been touching: my parents; my brother Jeff; Kristin and David Campbell; Susan Campbell; our former neighbors, Steve and Sue Garnier, and Carol Dupuis; Father John; and Michele Zuckerman, Sherri Brown, Laurie Mangold, and Mike and Jackie Simon, all members of the Loudoun Jewish Congregation.

We want to provide an update for the many people calling us and for my parents. One of the hardest parts is figuring out how to put it all into words.

Planning Hospital Visits
Kelly, Evening

Mike leaves the hospital in the late afternoon to spend time with Hannah and get a good night's sleep prior to our long-awaited tour. Dr. Keller comes in to check on Olivia and inquire whether we have decided regarding the transfer. I tell him we're visiting Kluge in the morning and have set up a tour of Kennedy Krieger for Friday. He seems surprised we're visiting Kennedy Krieger since it's in a very rough area of Baltimore. I respond that we want to see all our options before making a final decision.

Mike's older brother, Jeff, has been in constant contact with Mike and their mom since the accident. He's feeling helpless in New York City and wants to visit, so he takes the train down from New York after work today and arrives around eight in the evening.

He comes to the hospital and wants to sit with us and spend the night. He offers to let me go home, but I can't bear leaving. I am, once again, so grateful to have the company. Jeff and I don't know each other very well; we've only spent time together at family functions such as weddings, funerals, naming ceremonies, and Thanksgiving dinners. So this has turned out to be a unique time to know him better! I am so awed by the gesture—taking time off work to travel to Virginia to spend time with his niece. I also speak to his wife, Leslie, who is home with their three boys. We saw them over Thanksgiving while in Pittsburgh. I recall the kids sitting on the couch in the morning, watching the Macy's Thanksgiving Day parade, still in pajamas. They all get along so well. How will our holidays look after this tragedy?

The doctors decide to remove the ICP monitor and the C-spine collar after a CAT scan reveals reduced swelling and that her neck is stable.

Tonight, I finally get to lie down on the bed with her and hold her. I'm thrilled! While I sleep on the bed with Olivia, Jeff stays to keep us company.

The Email
Mike, Evening

I decide to send an email to update friends, family, and others who simply want to know what's happening and how they can help. Not only do I feel obligated to try to present the facts of our situation, but I realize, regardless of what happens, I need to provide for my family. Even in this dark hour, I need to start concentrating on bringing an income. Our health insurance through COBRA is costing us a small fortune. How will I conduct a job search, as well as actively interview? It seems like an impossible task.

The following is the email I'm sending tonight to quite a few people—family, friends, acquaintances, neighbors, and friends of friends. It's rather blunt, but in this instance, I don't feel the need nor take the time for eloquence.

Email message:

No words can express our deep gratitude and thanks for the support of many friends, neighbors, families, and even strangers. We appreciate the flowers and food but please continue to read this so you can see what we could really use. Also, we don't have e-mail addresses for many people, so please forward this to others who may be interested in Olivia's progress and apologize for us that we didn't have their e-mail address.

On Tuesday, November 27 in Leesburg, a Toyota 4-Runner hit 4 cars, then went through an intersection and rear-ended our minivan. The van went to the left, 3 lanes over, and hit a guardrail. The van ended up perpendicular to the ground with the other vehicle under it. The paramedics came to the scene 2-3 minutes later from the dispatch. Hannah, although scared, as any 5-year-old should be, was remarkably unhurt. Kelly was slipping in and out of consciousness but woke up at one point to hear Hannah screaming. Kelly suffered a concussion and bumps and bruises. She was treated and released that night.

Olivia was taken to Inova Fairfax Hospital, one of only two facilities in the DC area for severe pediatric head trauma cases. She was in a coma for 6 days and now is in a "semi-coma." She can open her eyes but cannot consistently track objects. She is also inconsistent with simple commands, such as "grab my finger," and cannot speak. She is now breathing on her own but requires a tube for feeding. She will probably go to a rehab facility either in Charlottesville or Baltimore. How long? As with many questions, we simply do not know; it could be weeks or months. Kelly will be staying with her mostly, but we will alternate days when possible. Hannah will stay in Leesburg where my mother has temporarily "relocated."

Where do we go on from here? Again, not many answers yet. We will try to have Hannah lead as normal a life as possible. We will make many changes, especially since I was laid off 3 weeks before the incident.

Again, we are grateful for the support of so many. People keep asking what they can do for us? When Olivia's rehab begins, we may need assistance, but we really don't know what that will be. Please no more flowers or food. Simply put, we are maxed out! There are a few ways now that people can assist us. Please send e-mail addresses of people who want to be updated. It is too difficult to contact each person by phone. Secondly, and most importantly, I have attached my resume to this e-mail. If everyone could pass the resume to at least 3 people, no matter what industry, discipline, etc., we would greatly appreciate it. My background is marketing, advertising, sales, and publishing, and we are trying to stay in the DC, Maryland, and

Virginia area. The economy is still rather slow, this time of the year is notoriously light for hiring, and with our current situation, it has been difficult finding a job. However, this is the area that we need the most help.

No matter what happens, our family will be stronger than ever due to the love we share for each other. Your love and support are well appreciated, but even more importantly, it has strengthened our resolve and commitment.

Lastly, please pray for Olivia. No person should go through what she went through and the challenges that will confront her. We pray that our 3-year-old will have a full childhood and when she becomes an adult, we hope that her dreams and aspirations will come true. With the support of wonderful people like you, she stands a good chance.

As I press the "send" button, a feeling of relief comes over me. It's so much easier to provide one email update without going over the situation repeatedly to a variety of people. It also means I won't need to see the shock and helplessness from the people who haven't been apprised of the crash and the resulting fracture of our family.

WEEK TWO, DAY TWO

Her eyes glow like the blue robe she's wearing, but there's also a look of frustration on her face.

—Wednesday, December 5, 2001

In Her Arms
Mike, Early Morning

My mom and I drive to the hospital and walk into the room to find Olivia in Kelly's arms. Olivia has been bathed and has her hair in a ponytail. Her eyes glow like the blue robe she's wearing, but there's also a look of frustration on her face. Still, it's touching to see mother holding daughter again. Kelly seems to be more content now that she's holding her baby again. Olivia's not much older than in those much happier times.

An MRI is scheduled in the next two or three days. There are some controversies over sedating her again, since she's just starting to come out of the coma, and whether her CO_2 rate will be too high.

We decide to go ahead because we want to have as much information as possible. Kelly says Olivia nodded to the question, "Do you want to see Hannah?"

A Prison of Limited Opportunities
Mike, Morning

Today is a key day. Kelly and I are taking the first step in Olivia's long road to recovery—whatever that means. We discussed the pros and cons of the inpatient facilities that might be best suited for Olivia. We've narrowed the list to what we think is feasible given our circumstances and our desire to be at least somewhat close to our home. Now, Kelly and I drive, without too many words, to Kluge Children's Rehabilitation Center in Charlottesville, Virginia. Charlottesville is a beautiful area tucked into the Blue Ridge Mountains of Virginia, but the rehab center is like a clean . . . prison. A fifty-year-old, worn-down, prison-like facility in a remote and wooded area.

A quick assessment of Kluge: It's in a quiet and peaceful town with a true "campus" appearance. However, inside the facility is a different story—a dated building with dimly lit hallways. The staff seems somewhat friendly, and I'm impressed that Kluge has a greenhouse and pool for the patients, but . . . there is no joy in the hallways; it is rather lifeless. Walking through the residence halls, we see a few room doors with small wreaths about six inches tall. The housing for parents is about one hundred yards from the facility. The patients have limited opportunities to see or go outdoors, mainly due to the liability issues, we're told. In one patient room, I see a young boy sitting in a chair, staring blankly at the wall. It seems he simply has nothing else to do.

The case manager greets us, and our first impressions persist. She's wearing a dark business suit and carrying a clipboard. The facility is so very sterile. Despite the friendly staff, the space feels confining. Olivia would be sharing a room with up to three other patients. There are many limitations for her and for us as parents due to, again, liability concerns. To this point, Kelly and I just assumed we would be able to put Olivia in a stroller and walk her around the premises. Well, we can't do that unless we have a doctor's note, and we're even unlikely to get permission that way. That means Olivia won't get to go to the housing areas for the parents just a hundred yards away. If we have a family gathering, it will have to be in the facility. No privacy there. Though everyone has mentioned the beautiful setting of Kluge, what good is it to see the squirrels through a window when you are held captive in a dark and dated facility?

Uncontrollable Tears

Kelly, Morning

As we walk around, touring the swimming pool for aquatic therapy and the occupational and speech therapy rooms, I cry the entire time. I can't stop the tears. I can't picture us in this dark and dreary building.

While observing the therapy rooms, I ask whether the parents participate in the therapies and am told that caregivers are not allowed in the therapy rooms with the child. The facility believes the caregiver will only be a distraction. Instead, they wait outside, sitting and observing from a windowed area while the session takes place.

I'm a bit surprised but figure if this is the policy, I can't do anything to change it. But our decision is cemented when we enter the patient room area. I'm struck by its starkness and a feeling of loneliness and despair. There are four patients to a room. A few of them sit on their beds, zoning out. There are no decorative touches at all. Each bed is assigned a bulletin board, but there aren't any personal notes, cards, or pictures. I ask whether these things are allowed, and the administrator says yes, but they are limited to whatever can be pinned within the parameters of the bulletin board. Nothing can be taped to the walls. I'm not quite sure why this makes me so upset, but it does.

The last straw is when I ask whether the caregiver can sleep in the room on a cot beside the patient. I'm told that caregivers are prohibited from sleeping in patient rooms; any caregivers who don't live in the immediate area are housed in a separate building. I repeatedly ask the same question and remind her that our daughter is only three years old. I understand a teenager would not want a caregiver in such proximity, but this is different. She counters that it doesn't matter how old the child is. Each evening at eight, the caregivers are told to leave.

The tears come gushing out like a waterfall. I try my best to stop the flow, but they just keep coming. Mike seems distressed because he doesn't know how to help me. He thanks her for her time, and she tells us that we need to decide quickly to ensure a bed is available for Olivia.

The Tears Keep Coming
Mike, Afternoon

We rush to the car and hug and console one another.

Kelly cries on the way back to Fairfax, stopping intermittently. We decide to continue our search and will tour Kennedy Krieger next. Once we do, a final decision can be made.

We have been so worried that Olivia will fully wake up while we're gone. Kelly calls my mom to get an update, but there haven't been any changes since we left this morning.

When we arrive back at the hospital room, my mom is holding Olivia in the rocking chair. We decide Kelly will leave with my mom and go home for the night to spend time with Hannah. Our visit to Kennedy Krieger is in two days, so we have something to strive for.

Holding to Hope
Kelly, Evening

I'm exhausted by the time we arrive at home but manage to have a nice time with Hannah. She has been busy making cards and pictures for Olivia. I tell her I'll talk to the hospital staff and determine when she can come visit. She's excited.

The doctors have suggested we start playing music in Olivia's room—specifically, any music she may remember, so anything she heard prior to the accident. I gather up all the CDs we have. They have also suggested that when she starts waking up, we put pictures of family members on her bed rails and walls to jolt her memory. So I gather the most recent photos I can find.

I've taken all of this as a good sign, giving us hope that she will fully wake up; otherwise, why would they want music and pictures? I go to bed and sleep a little better, holding tight to that hope.

WEEK TWO, DAY THREE

The tube goes into one nostril and is held to her face by medical tape. All I can think about is how they will remove that tape once she's awake.

—Thursday, December 6, 2001

Reminders of Home
Kelly, Morning

Mike and I set up a portable CD player and start playing the CDs I brought from home. We hang up the pictures as well. Already, the room is looking more cheerful. ICU patients cannot have flowers in their rooms, so those have to be placed elsewhere, but all the photos, along with Hannah's drawings, really brighten things up.

Kristin stopped by the house before I left and dropped off a CD she purchased at Target. They were selling a collection of CDs for kids that centered on their names. She found one for Olivia. It's perfect.

Olivia's lung has healed, and she no longer requires the assistance of a respiratory therapist. Her temperature has also stabilized, so we're prepared when the doctors approach and tell us a room has opened for her in the pediatric wing.

A Room in Pediatric Oncology
Kelly, Late Morning

It is amazing how much work it takes to move a three-year-old girl. We pack up all her gifts, cards, photos, and other things and head over to her new room.

We're placed on the children's oncology floor. The new room is larger and has a private bathroom with shower, which is fantastic. No more walking down the hall to take a shower. Once the room is filled with pictures and our own special touches, it starts to feel more comfortable.

Olivia still has not woken up fully, but she moves around and thrashes a bit, her legs and arms uncoordinated in the bed. Her eyes partially open but do not focus. A sound comes from her that is neither a cry nor a moan, but I hope it shows she has some use of her vocal area. There are still so many unanswered questions. We have repeatedly been told a full assessment will not occur until she is totally awake and responding to stimuli. So far, that is not happening, and I am impatient.

The physical therapist comes to the room and moves Olivia's limbs to keep the muscles flexible. An occupational therapist comes by and, once she realizes Olivia is not able to sit up, says she can't do much work with her yet.

The goal for the occupational team is to determine whether Olivia can swallow properly so she can be taken off the feeding tube. The tube goes into one nostril and is held to her face by medical tape. All I can think about is how they will remove that tape once she's awake. Olivia has never liked taking bandages off. It's always been a big ordeal. Plenty of times, she's refused to take it off or allow us to take it off. She slathers hand lotion or Vaseline on to try and take the sting out. Finally getting that bandage removed takes an exceptionally long time.

After the occupational therapist leaves, Mike and I discuss our plans for the following day—our tour of Kennedy Krieger Institute in Baltimore. We find out that my sister-in-law, Carrie, has a family friend who works there as a recreational therapist. We are happy to have a connection.

Kristin comes by later that evening and brings me a home-cooked meal. What a delight, again.

Apprehensions
Mike, Early Evening

At home, I try to keep myself focused on Hannah and not think too much about the monumental choice that Kelly and I are facing. I'm afraid that our ultimate selection of a facility will be about as important a decision as we will ever make. I can't shake the dark cloud hanging over me as I play with Hannah. I don't know what the following day will bring us, and the anxiety suffocates me. All I know about Kennedy Krieger is that it isn't in the safest part of Baltimore, so it's hard to look forward to our tour tomorrow. Our visit to Kluge set the stage for me; I feel that we have so few feasible rehab facilities to choose from. Despite our impression of the place, Kluge has a great reputation, and the surrounding area doesn't have the hustle and bustle of a major metropolitan city. I'm resigned to ultimately choosing Kluge.

WEEK TWO, DAY FOUR

I expected that when her eyes opened, she would look at us and immediately brighten up. But when they finally did, that was not the case.

—Friday, December 7, 2001

The Kennedy Krieger Tour
Kelly, Early Morning

Mike and I drive to Baltimore in the early hours. Once again, the sky is overcast. For obvious reasons, these past days have felt like a big cloud has been hanging over us, and the weather just cements the grim mood.

When we pull up to Kennedy Krieger, the parking area looks a bit run down, but the building itself appears fine. It's connected via a walkway to Johns Hopkins Hospital. What a relief to have a world-class hospital right next door.

We enter the building and are a little surprised to see a security guard standing next to the reception desk, but it does make us feel more protected. We're directed to the administrator's office and ride the elevator to the designated floor. I'm already feeling a very different energy here. It seems much more cheery, upbeat. Children are in the hallways, talking to staff, and there are holiday decorations everywhere we turn.

As our tour begins, we know that this is the place. Vitality seems to permeate the facility. Maybe it's that Kennedy Krieger has more foot traffic, and the extra hustle and bustle of the people gives off a certain sense of energy. Maybe I judge the facilities too much by the holiday decorations, but Kennedy Krieger clearly embraces the season more than Kluge and feels brighter and bigger. Here, Olivia will be in a room with only one other patient, and the room, although a typical hospital room, is more open and inviting. At Kluge, inpatients are in a relatively small wing. Kennedy Krieger has an entire floor for rehab sessions.

I ask if the caregiver can stay in the room with the child, and I'm assured that most caregivers do stay, especially since the facility primarily has children in the inpatient section. We're shown the parent lounge where we can keep food, microwave meals, relax with other parents, use the computer, and shower. The only drawback: I'll have to get used to going down the hall again to shower.

Olivia will wear clothes, not hospital gowns, while a patient. It makes it easier to conduct all the therapies when the patient is dressed appropriately. There's even a laundry facility for us to use. We are instructed not to go in the neighborhood unescorted, but I'm not worried about that since I don't plan to ever leave the building with Olivia.

The doctors estimate her rehabilitation will take six to nine months, but we are expecting that since Kluge projected the same. They also mention that once a patient progresses to a certain level, they and their caregiver are invited to participate in various field trips like bowling and going to the movies, arranged through the recreational staff. These trips are both therapeutic and fun. The staff explains to patients and caregivers how to handle accessibility issues in public areas once they're discharged and how they will acclimate them to this new level of care. We are also told that patients can leave the hospital with a caregiver for a few hours a day for a holiday or other event. This, too, sounds great since the holiday season is closing in.

Mike and I leave feeling much better than we did two days ago after our Kluge tour, confident Olivia will be cared for properly and that whoever is with her will be able to participate in all her therapies. Finally, some of the gray clouds lift.

We are also excited because Hannah is coming to the hospital this afternoon; we hope it brings a smile to Olivia's face. Since she's "woken up," her eyes have looked blank. We're not sure she knows who we are. She hasn't uttered a sound. She just lies in the bed, looking extremely confused.

I expected that when her eyes opened, she would look at us and immediately brighten up. But when they finally did, that was not the case. I was devastated at this development. I'm very concerned that there is more damage to her brain than we originally thought.

A Day of Firsts
Mike, Afternoon

Back at Fairfax Hospital, we enter the room a bit cheerier. Of course, it is a different experience to walk off the elevator onto the children's floor versus walking into the Pediatric Intensive Care Unit. There are more windows, and colorful pictures adorn the walls. The sound of children playing nearby is unmistakable.

My mom sits with Olivia in her room. Dad arrives shortly afterward and brings Hannah to the child life specialist's office. A child life specialist is a healthcare professional who works with children and families in hospitals and other settings to help them cope with the challenges of hospitalization, illness, and disability. The doctors and nurses feel the specialist will help Hannah process her feelings from the incident and learn what to expect when she finally sees Olivia. Olivia isn't the same little girl Hannah sang *Blue's Clues* songs with the night of our incident. We want her to be prepared for this.

My dad leans a bit over the bed. Slightly louder than a whisper, Olivia says, "Gran-pa."

Silence in the room. We can't believe she has just spoken for the first time. We are elated, but perhaps no more than my dad, who is the recipient of the greatest gift. His is the first name she has called out!

When Hannah enters the room, she has a look of pure delight. She holds the specialist's hand and has a book in her other hand. Kelly sits across the room, holding Olivia on her lap. All the IVs and other equipment have already been removed except for the feeding tube. The hair on the left side of Olivia's head, where the ICP monitor was implanted, looks as if she has played with scissors and tried to cut her own hair, but otherwise, she looks the same. There aren't any bruises or abrasions on her body.

This is only Hannah's second or third time inside a hospital; the other two times were to meet her sister when she was born and when Kristin's daughter, Logan, was born. Both of those occasions were happy ones, whereas this one is still undetermined at this point. Hannah approaches us, and we immediately see recognition in Olivia's eyes. Hannah tries to engage her by holding her hands and swaying to the music on the CD player, but Olivia only stares at her. We all try to explain that Olivia may not understand what Hannah is trying to do, but she continues talking to her softly, not boisterous. Suddenly, Hannah starts making goofy faces and telling silly jokes, and Olivia's eyes light up again.

Then it's like the sun has come out. Olivia starts to laugh. My heart swells, and I see the tears rolling down Kelly's cheeks. I think Kelly is trying to hide them, but Hannah smiles at her and continues entertaining Olivia. My first thought is *There's a voice in there.* Eventually, she'll regain her voice and words!

We should have known that it would take a child to bring another child out of her stupor. We are thrilled! Hannah shows us the book she worked on with the child life specialist and the pictures she drew inside, depicting what she remembers from the incident. They're hard for us to see. We don't fully comprehend what Hannah remembers, and it plagues us.

Olivia tires very quickly after her session with Hannah, so we lay her down in her bed for rest. Hannah and my parents stay a bit longer and then leave to have dinner and head home to take care of our dog and cat. It's a Friday night, so Hannah doesn't have to get up early tomorrow, but true to Hannah, she will probably be awake even earlier.

Kelly and I feel this has been the best day since before November 27. We found a place for her inpatient rehabilitation, her sister came to visit, *and* Olivia was able to laugh at Hannah, proving that no matter what, her brain is processing things, and there is a voice waiting to be heard.

WEEK TWO, DAY FIVE

Out of the blue, she starts to spell "O-L-I-B-I-A."
—Saturday, December 8, 2001

A Time to Play

Kelly, Late Morning

Now that Olivia has transferred to the new wing, she seems to be progressing every day. We have a lot of privacy in our new room, which is nice. I don't have to worry about anyone staring at her through a wall of windows or pointing at her like she's in a shop display. The occupational, speech, and physical therapists start visiting more frequently. Olivia can't walk, but she can sit and hold her head up.

The occupational therapist stops by to see if Olivia can drink water from a straw. This is a very laborious task and fatigues and frustrates her very quickly. I never realized how much effort it takes to drink from a straw.

One thing is very apparent—her frustration level is high. She tires easily, and if we don't watch her closely, she just starts sobbing. She's also a bit cautious around many of the medical staff. She seems frightened when they enter the room and try to touch her. I have to sit on her bed and hold her hand and talk softly so she feels more comfortable.

Olivia is still little enough to be carried wherever she needs to go. She seems to have lost some weight in the ten days we've been here, but it's difficult to tell since she has only worn a hospital gown. There's a play area in one part of the wing that's covered with pictures of Winnie the Pooh characters. We can use any games, books, coloring books, or movies, and we are encouraged to bring them to our room if the area becomes too busy.

Olivia has always loved to play, and she especially enjoys figurines. Her favorite books and movies are *101 Dalmatians* and *Beauty and the Beast*. She can watch these over and over. We get a copy of each for her to watch. It's amazing to see the recognition on her face.

It's Starting to Come Back
Mike, Afternoon

I bring out Olivia's four Dalmatian figurines to play with (the same ones rescued from the wrecked van), and something clicks. She begins to react to them and play. She's very alert. Out of the blue, she starts to spell "O-L-I-B-I-A." She always had trouble with the *V*. Later, I hear her saying something and I recognize a "seven"—she is counting out loud. She counts to twenty with me.

So many things seem to be going on in her mind, her brain quickly processing all the information as if from the floodgates. It's like a rebirth. It has been an enjoyable day with her (and me!) laughing quite a bit. Our little girl is coming back.

WEEK TWO, DAY SIX

I am uncomfortable. I don't feel whole. Having only part of my family at the celebration is an awkward and uncomfortable feeling.
  —Sunday, December 9, 2001

Dancing at the Party
Mike, Afternoon/Evening

My parents, Hannah, and I attend the Hanukkah party at the Loudoun Jewish Congregation in Leesburg. Hannah has a great time and, of course, dances up a storm. My parents watch the festivities and Hannah, red faced from her exertion and beaming at them. My parents are putting up a good front of enjoyment, but I wonder what's going on in their minds. I know they're loving the time with Hannah, but are they feeling that the day is . . . incomplete since her sister is not there? I know I am uncomfortable. I don't feel whole. Having only part of my family at the celebration is awkward.

I find it difficult to socialize because I don't want to go into the details of my missing family members. Everyone is having a fun time, so how can I transform their happiness into looks of shock and shuffling feet? Finally, after what seems like an eternity to me, I motion to Hannah that it's time to leave. Although a part of her doesn't want to go, she's looking forward to seeing Olivia and celebrating Hanukkah with her.

Beanie Babies
Kelly, Evening

While Mike, Hannah, and his parents are at the party, Olivia and I play with figurines, I read her some books, and she watches a bit of *Beauty and the Beast.* She loves Belle. This past Halloween, she dressed up as Belle. She was so adorable trick-or-treating in her gold dress and wearing the Belle dress-up shoes. We were concerned she might fall and get a cut or bruise. It is almost ironic thinking about that now as I sit in this room, unsure of how severe or long-lasting her injuries are.

The group bustles into the room, and Hannah is bursting with energy. She tells us all about the fun time she had at the party. One of the members gave her some Beanie Babies and included some for Olivia. I think, *What a sweet gesture.* Mike Simon has a daughter a little younger than Olivia. We have only known him and his wife Jackie a brief time, but they have been so supportive through this awful period.

Mike and I had bought the girls a few gifts before all this, so we have them open one each. Olivia's gift is a Barbie dressed in an electric-blue outfit. Her hair is blond and piled on her head in an updo. There is a button on her, and once it is pressed, Barbie spins around. Watching Olivia's reaction to the Barbie is magical. She is transfixed. She has always loved anything girly, so it isn't a surprise, yet the attention she gives it is amazing.

Sisters

Mike, Evening

Hannah bounds into Olivia's room, full of excitement. Our five-year-old was already having a wonderful day, and now she is with her little sister, bearing gifts and a huge smile. As we open the gifts in Olivia's hospital room, it gets crowded with all the toys and wrapping paper strewn everywhere. Hannah giggles, and her energy is infectious. Olivia takes in everything with a slight smile, but I think the smile is directed at Hannah more than the presents. We hand Olivia a doll, and she runs her fingers through the doll's hair but only looks at Hannah. After a while, all the stimulation is wearing Olivia down, so we end early. Watching Hannah say goodnight and kiss her sister is a sweet moment. The atmosphere of the room changes within seconds of everyone leaving, but the quietness and stillness feel good. I realize I am probably overstimulated like Olivia and need a break from the long day.

Olivia is exhausted, so we get ready for bed. Olivia falls fast asleep. As tired as I am, I wake up frequently to the feeding tube alarms, which are false alarms as everything is secured and in place. I toss and turn on the room's recliner. The only satisfaction I have is looking at Olivia, who sleeps well.

WEEK TWO, DAY SEVEN

Now that we've decided, it's hard to sit back and wait. We want to get busy rehabilitating our girl so we can go back to our "normal" life. Though we don't know what that will be.
—Monday, December 10, 2001

Nothing More Important
Mike, Morning

Olivia wakes up very serene and peaceful looking this morning. She gives me a "Hi, Daddy." I love hearing her voice. I get emotional over this most basic aspect of life—my little girl simply saying hello to me. Nothing seems to be as important, at least at that moment. I've realized lately how much I have taken for granted.

Today is Olivia's last day at the hospital. Tomorrow, we transfer her to Kennedy Krieger. Olivia is enormously proud of herself when she walks to the playroom with Kelly and me. She glows as she sits and looks at herself in the playroom mirror.

After she plays for a while, she watches one of her favorite videos, *Beauty and the Beast.*

The First Picture
Kelly, Morning

After so much activity over the weekend, the hospital seems eerily quiet for a Monday morning in December. All the patient room doors are decorated for the holidays, and Christmas trees are displayed on every floor of the hospital—each one different, but all are beautiful and cheery.

Mike and I sit and play with Olivia, awaiting the arrival of the therapists and doctors to tell us when Olivia will be transferred to Kennedy Krieger. Now that we've decided, it's hard to sit back and wait. We want to get busy rehabilitating our girl so we can go back to our "normal" life. Though we don't know what that will be.

Charities and other groups do a tremendous job of showering children with a lot of love and attention during this time. A few airline pilots come down the hall with gifts for the children. They're escorted by a hospital employee, and they kindly ask if they can come to say hello. Of course, we say yes. They speak to Olivia, and she just stares. She may be overwhelmed with all the attention and confused by their uniforms.

They present her with two gifts, a stuffed brown bear and a children's book. One of the staff members has a Polaroid camera and asks if they can take a picture with us. We haven't permitted any pictures of Olivia since the incident, but how can we say no? This is the first photo taken during her stay at Fairfax. Though I wonder if I'll regret the lack of photos, my need to preserve and protect Olivia has largely won out.

Gearing Up for a Long Road
Kelly, Late Morning

The doctors come by for rounds and inform us that Olivia's transfer has been arranged for the following day. They explain she will be transferred via ambulance and one parent can ride with her. Mike offers that position to me and says he will follow us in his car.

We have continually asked for Olivia to have the MRI we were told she was scheduled for. The hospital has completed several CT scans, but we want the MRI to give us a more complete picture of the location and extent of her injuries. Every time we ask for this, we're denied. The staff tells us that because she's progressing, there isn't a need to do such an invasive test. Mike and I are no longer in agreement with their assessment. We finally ask that the trauma surgeon review our request.

The remainder of the day is spent visiting with the therapists so they can complete reports to send along with us. We also gather up all the gifts and toys and pictures. Mike goes home to pack up clothes, toiletries, and personal belongings for Olivia and me so we'll have them once she's admitted. We decide to try switching off every two or three days since the travel time will be longer. Though we're gearing ourselves up for a long road ahead, it's starting to look brighter.

PART 2
FIRST STEPS TOWARD NORMAL

WEEK THREE, DAY ONE

I feel extremely guilty leaving her alone. I say hello as I enter, but there isn't any sign of recognition.

—Tuesday, December 11, 2001

The Transfer
Kelly, Morning

So, this is the day, finally. It's a bit scary. We don't know exactly what will happen or how long we'll be in Baltimore. We figure the first few weeks will give us time to figure out how this is all going to work—especially once January rolls around, Hannah returns to school after her winter break, and Mike starts picking up the pace on his job hunt.

It has been so wonderful hearing Olivia's sweet little-girl voice again. She knows who we are but still has difficulty retrieving words and communicating her wants and needs.

We pack up all of Olivia's belongings, which have grown quickly in the fleeting time we've been in this room. We're planning to bring it all with us, and whatever isn't needed will go back with Mike later today.

The transport team arrives, introduces themselves to us, and explains how Olivia will be transferred into the waiting ambulance through the emergency room bay. Then they leave to check with the nurses about the final doctor orders allowing the transfer to move forward.

We sit in eager anticipation, again not knowing what to expect but also knowing this is the right decision for Olivia. As we wait, a doctor and a few residents enter her room and introduce themselves as the trauma team who have looked over our request for an MRI. They agree an MRI can be done, but if we choose to do so, it will delay the transfer by one day.

Mike and I are incredulous. We have been asking about this test for days, and now, as we are about to get discharged, they agree to allow it. Our first thoughts are, *Wow, isn't that convenient on their part?*

The nurses enter with the final discharge orders, so we tell the trauma team we're going ahead with the transfer. We hope this MRI issue will resolve once we arrive in Baltimore.

I walk beside the gurney with Olivia. Mike goes to the car and pulls up in the bay to follow us to Baltimore. Olivia is loaded in, and the EMT gets her gurney locked in and makes sure all her vitals are monitored during the ride. I sit on the bench next to the gurney. Olivia keeps asking where Daddy is. I try to point out the car right behind us, but she can't see it.

As soon as the ambulance starts the journey, Olivia falls asleep. Well, this is like old times. Olivia always sleeps in the car. Anytime we take a trip to visit Mike's parents in Pittsburgh or are in the car for more than an hour, she falls fast asleep.

This is my first ambulance ride—at least, the first that I remember clearly. The cold of the metal bench shoots through me, giving me the chills. The EMT and I speak a bit, and she mentions she has a child a little younger than Olivia. She records Olivia's vital signs, and I realize she has the entire medical chart in her hands. I ask if I can look at it, and she agrees but tells me we aren't following protocol. I really appreciate her kindness in trying to help us in any way she can.

As I start reading all the reports, I find some very startling information. It is interesting what medical providers tell you versus what is indicated in the patient chart. Apparently, when the rescue personnel arrived at the scene of the accident, Olivia was code blue. *What?!* How did I not know this? Finally, I understand why I instinctively felt she was in danger. I also discover that Hannah, Olivia, and I had all traveled to the hospital in separate ambulances. I assumed we were all put in the same one. When I look around the one I'm currently riding in, I realize that would not have been possible. There isn't enough room for three gurneys.

I keep thinking about Hannah. She was conscious and had to ride all the way to the hospital all alone. How scary that must have been for a five-year-old girl. I wonder if she saw Olivia and I taken first or if she went first.

All this information swirls around in my mind. I try to read as much of the file as possible, but it is so extensive. I can't finish it. I'm stunned. I really need to share all this information with Mike, but first we have to get Olivia out of the ambulance and settled in her new room.

We are escorted to her patient room by a staff member. As we step off the elevator, a cheery greeting comes from the nurses' station, and I notice that all the patient room doors are wrapped in holiday paper, looking like gifts. How appropriate, even heartwarming. Children are gifts, and the children here are special gifts indeed.

The EMTs transfer Olivia from the gurney to the patient bed and pull up the safety bars on the sides.

Settling In
Mike, Late Morning

Olivia is sharing her room with a sixteen-month-old, Kara, who is also connected to a feeding tube. Kara is by herself, which seems sad, but I suppose her parents just stepped out for a bit. Olivia seems content in her bed with the side bed rails.

Her bed is the closest to the doorway. Another bed is next to a window. There's a private bathroom with another sink outside the bathroom and a large mirror hanging on the bathroom door. The bottom third of the walls are painted a medium blue, and then sky blue colors the rest of the walls. Two curtains act as a divider between the beds. Over each bed is a single recessed light that has a dimmer switch. On the wall between the beds is a wall clock. There is an overhead TV between the two beds. I doubt we'll ever turn it on. Not much furniture to claim during our stay. There is one four-drawer dresser and one small, three-drawer nightstand per patient. Short of storage space, we stuff many things under the bed.

Olivia is playful but a bit confused with all the doctors and nurses coming to see her. I probably don't help things since I am anxious to head home before rush hour and see Hannah because I haven't seen her since Sunday.

The Trouble with Multitasking
Kelly, Late Morning

Mike and I start putting her things away, hanging the cards, photos, and posters we received to brighten up the room. A white curtain separates Olivia from the window side of the room. We peek over and see her roommate asleep in the bed. She's hooked up to a lot of machinery, but I don't see anyone else with her.

As we wait for the doctor to arrive, Olivia suddenly rolls over in the bed. Mike and I are thrilled. She hasn't done this since the accident. Wow, she's making progress already.

Finally, the doctor arrives. Olivia has already worn herself out and is asleep. She only wakes up briefly when he examines her and takes her vital signs. While the doctor continues his exam, another woman enters the room and introduces herself to us as Patty, the educational consultant. She pulls me aside to answer some questions. I'm a bit annoyed as I don't want to miss anything the doctor might say, but I follow her anyway. She confirms that we live in Leesburg, Virginia, and explains she wants me to sign some papers so the process of applying for special education services can begin.

I'm so confused. Special education services? Why would we need these? Olivia isn't old enough to be in school yet. I am distracted between listening to her and trying to keep my ear on what the doctor is saying. My multitasking skills are usually much better than this. I easily handle making dinner, talking on the phone, and refereeing my children at the same time.

Patty's questions primarily concern Olivia's skill level prior to the accident. Her presence and ongoing questions are overwhelming. I don't understand why we have to do this right now. She keeps telling me she wants to file paperwork with our school division as quickly as possible to get Olivia some special education services once she is discharged. I keep telling her that Olivia did go to preschool before the accident, but I have already told the school she won't be returning due to the extent of her injuries. Patty doesn't care and persists in asking if Olivia knew how to cut, color, sort shapes, etc., prior to the accident. Many of my answers are pure guesses since I can't recall everything. I am so glad when she finally leaves the room.

Mike heads for home soon afterward. He has an hour-plus drive back, and we decide Hannah could use some one-on-one time. There is nothing like the guilt a parent feels when they are unable to split themselves in two and give each child equal time and attention.

A String of Therapists

Kelly, Afternoon

A brief time later, a band of therapists come to assess Olivia and determine the level of care she will need. The occupational therapist arrives first and tries to have Olivia eat and swallow some applesauce. It is a terribly slow process, and Olivia ends up too frustrated, refusing to open her mouth. The therapist isn't the most patient person, and rather than give her a break and then resume, she immediately suggests we schedule a barium swallowing test to determine whether she is aspirating in her lungs.

She gives me a brief description of the test and schedules it for Thursday. Olivia can't eat or drink anything Thursday morning until after the study is complete, but she's still getting all her hydration and nutritional needs through the feeding tube, so that isn't going to be an issue.

When Betty, the physical therapist, arrives, she gets Olivia out of the bed and helps her walk a few steps in the room. Olivia then stands on the side of the bed and plays with her *Lion King* figurines while Betty continues her evaluation of her gait. *The Lion King* is yet another beloved movie, so these are the perfect toys for her right now.

The recreational therapist, Brenda, stops by next. This is the woman my sister-in-law knows—their parents are friends. Brenda brings along some bubbles and blows them over Olivia's bed, which fascinates her. It's nice to have a connection with someone in the facility. And Brenda also has children, so she can relate to how I'm feeling as a mother and thus far has been the only person to address it.

A neuropsychologist is the final one to enter. She tries to interact with Olivia but doesn't get very far. She keeps asking Olivia who I am, where we are, whether she has a sibling, and how old she is but isn't getting any responses. She has a pen with a Big Bird figurine on the top and repeatedly asks who the character is. I tell her that Olivia may not recognize it since she doesn't watch *Sesame Street* and we haven't read any of their books in a while. This does not stop the question.

After all the visits, Olivia and I read lots of books, and I finish decorating her room with the pictures, cards, and letters we brought with us. I read two more books and sing "Rock-A-Bye Baby" to her; this has always been our nighttime routine.

She is asleep within five minutes.

I wait for about fifteen minutes to make sure she stays asleep and then go to the parents' lounge to send emails to Hannah and Mike, letting them know how the rest of our day was. I also quickly eat something. Mike and I have been trying not to eat in front of Olivia. We don't want to have to say no if she asks for some. It reminds me of the time when both my girls were younger and loved to eat lots of fresh fruit in the summertime. They would both get an awful diaper rash, and we'd keep them away from the fruit for a few days until they healed. Mike and I would hide so they would not see us while we enjoyed an occasional peach.

When I get back to the room, Olivia is lying in bed with her eyes wide open. I feel extremely guilty leaving her alone. I say hello as I enter, but there is no sign of recognition, only a glazed stare. I lean over the bed and give her a kiss, telling her it's Mommy, but she still looks at me blankly. Does she know me? Remember me? I am filled with anxiety that we may have lost our bond.

WEEK THREE, DAY TWO

As soon as I hear her scream there in her hospital bed, I worry she's having a flashback of the night of the accident.

—Wednesday, December 12, 2001

Tears I Can't Console

Kelly, Morning

Olivia and I have a long night, or at least I do. Her feeding tube alarm goes off every hour, which I don't understand since this isn't happening during the daytime hours. I lie awake for the nurses to enter and fix the problem, but no one comes until I press the nurse call button repeatedly.

At 5 a.m., Olivia wakes up screaming. It's the first time she has screamed in the past two weeks. When she was younger, instead of trying to tell us what she needed, she would scream or point angrily at whatever she wanted. The screaming wasn't a behavior we were used to; Hannah was verbal at a very young age.

When Olivia was around a year old, I had to run an errand one day, so I dropped the two girls off with Kristin, who lived about twenty minutes from us at this time. She told me Olivia kept screaming whenever she looked around and realized I was no longer there. Kristin eventually retrieved her backpack carrier and put Olivia in it so she could go around the house. Olivia was incredibly happy until they passed by a mirror and she saw their reflection. She then remembered, again, that I was not there.

As soon as I hear her screaming in her hospital bed, I worry she's having a flashback of the night of the accident. Once she's fully awake, she shifts quickly to a chatty mood, though I can't understand all she says. We talk about the pictures I've put up around her bed, and she points out who Mommy, Daddy, and Hannah are. We read some books, and then she asks me where Hannah is. I explain that Hannah is at home and will come visit in a few days. I am relieved that she remembers us and has more brightness in her eyes.

When the nurse comes to check on us, I ask if I can take a shower in Olivia's room since neither Olivia nor the other girl in her room are using it. She instructs me to use the shower in the parents' lounge. Once Olivia falls back to sleep, I quickly gather my things and head to the other side of the patient floor. The lounge isn't anything fancy. There is a small refrigerator, a coffee machine, and a computer. The shower is in a small room on the other side of the lounge, resembling the ones in the patients' rooms. Since it's still early, I don't have to wait to use it, and the shower is extremely quick since there's no hot water. I wonder how the water could already be frigid. I can't imagine what it will be like later in the day.

When I arrive back at the room, Olivia is awake and tells me she has pooped in her diaper (another first in communication!). I change her and start getting her dressed. She begins to cry, especially when I try to put her shirt over her head. Tears stream out of her eyes. I can't seem to console her, which is heartbreaking to me as a mom. Once she is dressed again, she lies down defeated on the bed, and I gently stroke her back until she falls back asleep. I can't help but wonder if her head hurts when someone touches it or if some distant memory has come back into her consciousness. I worry that she somehow blames me for what happened since I was the parent present and couldn't protect her. My only consolation is that she has always been responsive when someone rubs her back, even when she was a newborn. I'm relieved that at least one old comforting mechanism has returned.

Keeping the Checklist Full
Mike, Morning

Lots of errands to run today at home, including a stop at the Leesburg government office for car registration and at the police department for a copy of the incident report. I also must concentrate on job hunting. I have an upcoming interview, calls to make, and emails to check. I really don't have a specific type of job in mind, other than needing one quickly and hopefully in a location somewhat close to home or Kennedy Krieger. I used to be very career motivated and work long hours, but that is not so important anymore. Yet good healthcare is more critical now than we could have ever imagined. I'm thankful that, at least for the time being, we have COBRA, although I'm not sure how much longer I can afford the $1,000-per-month premium.

I think I am at my best when I'm busy. I set myself on autopilot and just check things off my list. Food shopping, check. Laundry, check. Cleaning up the kitchen, check. Running through these items also keeps my mind off what's happening in Baltimore now with Kelly and Olivia. However, as soon as I have a slight break in any activity, my thoughts wander to Olivia and whether she is improving.

We are quick to claim a victory when we understand something she is communicating to us. However, most of the time she becomes frustrated because we can't understand her grunts or what she wants when pointing to objects.

I can't imagine how our lives are going to change and what that will mean for our family as a whole. As for Kelly, I am more than just worried about how she is faring through all of this. The mother–daughter bond is like no other, and I fear how it will affect Kelly if Olivia doesn't improve. In some ways, both Kelly and Olivia are equally fragile and could be at the breaking point.

Activities with No End
Kelly, Late Morning

The nurses give me a schedule for the day, indicating when and where all of Olivia's appointments are. I'm also given a brief explanation of where each department is located. Kennedy Krieger isn't nearly as large as Fairfax Hospital, but I still manage to get lost numerous times.

We leave the room early since I know we will get lost. The nurses' station is a hive of activity. A few patients sit around in wheelchairs and on hospital beds. I assume they are there because there isn't a caregiver to keep them company or care for them. Some parents need to work, but it seems very strange. The little girl in Olivia's room did not have any visitors last night, and it broke my heart. Doesn't anyone care that she is all alone? She is only about eighteen months old.

We get into the elevator and go to the floor that houses the Speech and Language Department. The walkway leading to the department shows its age, though they do try to make it cheerier with holiday decorations. Rachel reintroduces herself to Olivia. She tells me she is the therapist assigned to us and will be the only one in the department working with Olivia. She asks Olivia to touch her tongue to a lollipop and gives her a minuscule amount of applesauce to try. She explains that eating and drinking involve both occupational and speech skills, so some skills and exercises will overlap between therapies. The process is long, so our session ends after those two skill assessments. We are then told that her barium swallowing test has been moved to Friday.

Immediately after speech, we continue to physical therapy. The department is quite large in order to hold all the equipment they house for older patients. Betty greets Olivia with great enthusiasm, and Olivia seems to enjoy the greeting. I am struck by how much Betty enjoys her job. I feel so lucky to have her working with us. We are led to a back room that has mats like those stacked on top of each other in a gymnastics class, as well as a few child-sized tables. She measures Olivia's range of movement and directs Olivia to stand at the small table. To distract Olivia, she gives her a few dog figurines to play with and eventually gets her to walk around the table. I don't think Olivia realizes she has moved. At least she hasn't lost her love of imaginary play.

They end with a few stretching exercises. Betty recommends we bring Olivia's stroller from home for transport rather than using a wheelchair that is too big for her. It is odd that a pediatric rehabilitation hospital doesn't have any child-sized wheelchairs. Olivia has always loved the stroller, though, so hopefully it won't be an issue.

The thirty minutes go by quickly, and it's time to move on to occupational therapy with Cindy. This area is small in comparison to the others. There are a bunch of little rooms that look more like office cubicles. I don't notice many patients here and wonder if everyone receives this service. I notice Olivia is already fatigued and don't know how cooperative she is going to be. Cindy gives her a spoonful of chocolate pudding. She takes it slowly, but it goes down easier than the applesauce. I assume it is because it's sweeter but then learn it's the texture that makes it easier.

Olivia stacks rings on a cylinder (a common baby toy) and builds a tower with blocks. This last task frustrates her; she can only stack four. Each time she tries to do more, the frustration builds. Finally, she refuses to cooperate. Cindy gives her some markers and tries to show her how to hold them. Olivia can draw a vertical line and a circle but not a horizontal line. I am fascinated by what all these clues mean as to her cognitive processing and ultimately her prognosis.

With these therapies complete, we have three hours of much needed rest time. We return to her room and read some books. She is getting tired and asks if I can play the *Beauty and the Beast* video we have. Her preschool teacher heard it was one of her favorites and sent her personal video to us. While at Fairfax Hospital, we had access to some children's videos, but not here. I go to the nurses' station and speak to two technicians, but they don't know how I can get a TV/VCR for the room. I then ask for the charge nurse, and she tells me that I can look around the hallways to see if I can find one. She says if I do, I should grab it before it disappears. I inquire about a sign-up sheet to request one, thinking this would be a more democratic system, but receive an emphatic no.

I decide to go on the hunt and am surprised to find one. I bring it to the room and, wouldn't you know, I can't get it to work. I ask two nurses to help and neither of them can get it to work, either. They suggest I find another one and abruptly exit, leaving the broken TV/VCR in Olivia's room. Defeated, I turn to the local PBS station, and Olivia watches something and falls asleep, taking an hour-long nap.

Dr. Nina, the neuropsychology resident, comes into the room soon after Olivia wakes up and tries to get Olivia to recall her name from the previous day. Olivia cannot come up with her name, but when given choices, she selects the right one. Dr. Nina asks her some questions about *Beauty and the Beast*, but Olivia can't recall Gaston's name. The doctor then brings out some shape blocks and asks her to match the alike ones. The only shape she can match correctly is the circle. I feel defeated, once again, and I'm not even the one being tested.

Betty, our physical therapist, brings another wheelchair to the room for Olivia to try; but when she puts her in, Olivia resists, crying and saying no repeatedly. Betty steps out of the room and returns holding a walker with wheels. Olivia agrees to try this new toy with which she can walk while gripping tightly. Afterward, she sits in the wheelchair while Betty blows bubbles and asks her to pop them with her fingers and feet. We both demonstrate for her in case she doesn't understand. She tries but can't coordinate the movements with her body. She does enjoy seeing the bubbles, though, which is encouraging.

Our next appointment is audiology. The doctors want to conduct hearing tests to determine whether any hearing loss occurred during the accident. I hadn't considered this before now. I can't imagine how the tests will be conducted since she doesn't always understand directions and isn't willing to cooperate. I'm in a separate room but can observe everything through a window. Thankfully, there isn't any hearing loss. At least we can knock one potential problem off our list.

We have thirty minutes before the afternoon occupational therapy session, so rather than go to her room, I take her to the recreational therapy room. Mike and I visited there when we toured last week, but Olivia has not been here yet. We see the head of the department. She welcomes us and leads a tour of the room. There are lots of toys, games, and arts and crafts materials. We play a bit before our next appointment. We arrive at occupational therapy, and much to my disappointment, the area isn't any more cheerful than I remember. Cindy allows Olivia to try some Cheerios. Prior to the accident, Olivia loved Cheerios. If she was hungry, all we had to do was put some in front of her until the rest of her meal was ready. One day, when we were visiting the mall at a busy time of day, a child dropped some on the floor, and Olivia darted over and grabbed them to eat them. Luckily, I got to her in time.

Cindy begins the exercise by placing one Cheerio in Olivia's mouth at a time. Olivia can maneuver each one and swallow without choking. Cindy then tries to get her to pick up a Cheerio from her open-palmed hand. Olivia can't pick up any Cheerios with her right hand, which had been her dominant hand. However, she's able to pick one up with her left hand and "fist" it up to her mouth.

Their next activity is catching and throwing a ball at a short distance. Then the final activity of the day is trying a puzzle. After Cindy takes the puzzle pieces out one by one, Olivia can put the pieces back where they belong. As was the case with the stacking toy, the puzzle activity is a quite simple one designed for a child under the age of one.

We venture back to the room following therapy. Olivia is thoroughly exhausted. This has been the most activity she's had in over two weeks.

I plan to take her to a magic show the recreational therapist told us they are hosting later this evening. Every weeknight there are planned events. It's important for both of us to attend. A change of scenery outside of her sterile room will be beneficial.

We have some time before the show, so I entertain her with books and talk to Daddy, Hannah, and Kristin as well. They are all eager to hear how our first full day in rehabilitation has gone.

The Tube of Terror
Kelly, Evening

We make our way down to the magic show, which is good but a bit over Olivia's head. A lot of kids are in attendance.

When we arrive back at the room, Edna, the technician assigned to Olivia, tells us she is ready for the bath. We take Olivia to a room with a large bathtub high off the ground, allowing for ease of transfer. As Edna lifts her out of the wheelchair, her feeding tube gets stuck on the armrest and pulls out of her nose. Olivia becomes despondent. Along with the tube comes the tape securing the tube to her.

The bath is uncomfortable for her, especially when she gets her hair washed. Afterward, I speak to the charge nurse and ask if the feeding tube can be reinserted in a treatment room rather than her bed, and she concurs with me.

We go back to the room, and I notice a cart with a TV and VCR sitting between her bed and the curtain separating the two areas. One of the staff must have put this here while we were giving her a bath. I put *Beauty and the Beast* on for her. Edna then comes to weigh Olivia. She places a mat on the bed, which Olivia lies on. As Edna lifts the mat with Olivia on it, it becomes obvious that Olivia is very unhappy about it. She has never liked sitting on a doctor's exam table, never mind being lifted in the air on a mat by a woman she does not trust. Once her weight is recorded, we proceed to the treatment room to have the feeding tube reinserted. This time, it isn't as bad as I expect, though she cries uncontrollably. We return to her room and watch the rest of the movie.

I put Olivia to bed at 9:45 p.m. I tell her I'm going to get a drink and then head to the lounge to have soup and check emails. When I return at 10:30, she's asleep.

I get myself ready for bed. I lie down on the cot, and my mind drifts through our day. Even though the facility is full of staff, patients, and some parents, it is a very lonely place. I crave connection. It is frustrating at times but also good to see how she is progressing in some areas. What all these tests show I am not fully sure, but I remain hopeful she will continue progressing so we can go home and return to our previous lives. I quickly drift off to sleep.

WEEK THREE, DAY THREE

I am constantly looking at the monitors, trying to gauge Olivia's vitals. I am always on high alert. Will the worries ever cease or relent for even a brief time?

—Thursday, December 13, 2001

Wide Awake
Kelly, Morning

Once again, it is difficult to get a good night's sleep in a hospital setting. The room is either too warm or too cold, and there are so many noises in the room and hallway. Once I do fall asleep, it doesn't feel very restful, and I'm soon woken by a nurse. I am constantly looking at the monitors, trying to gauge Olivia's vitals. I am always on high alert. Will the worries ever cease or relent for even a brief time?

I wake up at 1 a.m. to another monitor beeping and call the nurse. At 6 a.m., the night nurse wakes me to ask if she should draw blood now or ask the day shift since Olivia is still asleep. Really? She can't answer the question herself? I say to let her sleep. After that, I am wide awake. I can usually get back to sleep quickly, but this morning is different.

A short time later, Olivia wakes up startled as if she doesn't know where she is. She sits up in bed and seems relieved to see me lying next to her. Though her feeding tube is turned off during the early-evening hours each day, her sheets are still soaked. She seems upset the bed is wet, and I tell her we will get her clean clothes and change the sheets. I get her changed, talking to her the entire time to explain what we are doing and trying to stay on the small dry patch of her bed.

She is still unsteady on her feet, so I don't feel comfortable letting her stand on her own, especially on the slippery linoleum floor. I pick her up and go to the nurses' station to inquire about clean sheets. It is still early in the morning. A lot of children aren't awake yet, and the hallways aren't buzzing with activity. The nurse's response flabbergasts me. She instructs me to lay Olivia on my bed, which doesn't have any support rails, while I change the sheets. I stand there with a stunned expression as she tells me where clean sheets are kept.

Throughout my life, I have been unable to disguise my feelings and facial expressions. Many have remarked about it over the years, so I know this time is not any different.

The nurse does come to the room soon after our exchange and assists with the sheets. I appreciate the gesture, but the damage is done. I have a difficult time understanding how, in a pediatric neurological disorder facility, the staff doesn't put safety as the number one priority.

Once I have Olivia tucked back in bed, I set up a PBS program for her so I can take a shower. Mike and I have never relied on television to babysit our children, but while we're here, I decide to employ it during those rare moments I need to leave the room for short periods of time. The nurses have all the parents' cell phone information should she need me, but we are not supposed to use them in patient areas. At the same time, I wonder whether they will notice her if something happens.

She soon falls back asleep, allowing me time to gather our laundry and use the machine provided for families on the main level. When I step off the elevator on the patient floor, the nurses inform me that our morning occupational therapy session is canceled. This gives Olivia a bit more time to sleep. Every extra minute of sleep is beneficial.

Once she wakes, we gather our things and head to our 9:30 a.m. physical therapy session. The extra sleep has really helped brighten Olivia's face, and she appears more rested than ever.

Betty greets us with a very cheery hello and leads us to one of the therapy rooms with low, kid-sized tables. She explains to us that we are going to practice "coasting." Some of the therapists are skilled in explaining the activities in nonmedical terms I can understand, while others, not so much. Coasting is a pre-walking skill children between zero and fifteen months old usually achieve before learning to walk independently. Olivia really is having to relearn everything.

Olivia is easily distracted and doesn't want to walk around the table. She's happy to stand and play. Betty gathers up a play purse filled with pretend makeup to distract Olivia while working with her at the same time. I marvel at how adept she is at making children do things they don't want to do. After a few tries, Olivia can walk herself around the table without holding on. Yeah, progress!

Following the demanding work at physical therapy, we head to an appointment with our case manager, Fred. Each family is assigned a case manager at admission. The case managers oversee care plans for each patient and their family members. Fred's office is down below the main floor, and as we step off the elevator, I realize that it looks like a dungeon. The colorful holiday decorations have not made their way down here.

He asks a lot of questions regarding our family stability, living arrangements, extended family support, and other things. I express my concern for how we will manage as a family once the holiday season is over and Hannah goes back to school, Mike finds a job, and Sam and Estelle return home.

I tell him about my concerns regarding Olivia's level of functionality once she is discharged. He won't directly address my question but explains the staff can answer it during our weekly meeting. The weekly meetings with family and staff are held on Mondays, so we have four more days until we receive an assessment. The case manager also explains we will receive twenty dollars a week to cover gas expenses we incur while traveling between Leesburg and Baltimore. He offers me the use of his phone and office if I need a private place to make long-distance calls.

I discuss our dissatisfaction with some of the nursing staff, including the morning's incident, showers, and the lack of services for parents. Fred listens attentively, takes notes, and tells me he will speak with the nursing supervisor regarding our concerns. He also suggests I bring this up at Monday's meeting. I'm not certain I can wait that long. As I stand to leave his office, I look over at Olivia sitting quietly in the stroller and realize she has pulled her feeding tube out. I sigh, exasperated. Here we go again.

When our meeting is over, we go directly to speech. I sense Olivia getting tired. Rachel greets us and again tries to get Olivia to suck the lollipop, eat some applesauce, and pick up Cheerios with her fingers. She then reads some simple books to her. I ask some questions. She's not as forthcoming as Betty, but she explains this exercise assesses Olivia's receptive language skills. Receptive language is the ability to comprehend information such as understanding the words, sentences, and meaning of what others say or what is read.

Following our speech session, we head back up to the room. Olivia gets more irritable as the fatigue sets in. Once we step off the elevator, the nurses' station is a flutter of activity once again. Olivia's room is noticeably quiet. The only sound is the hum of Kara's machines; she still doesn't have any visitors, flowers, balloons, or personal items. I settle Olivia in, and we look at some books, which has always relaxed her. A few minutes later, the nutritionist knocks and enters the room. She explains the barium swallowing test will be done first thing in the morning. If the test shows Olivia is not aspirating into her lungs, the next step will be to modify what foods can be introduced. The feeding tube will remain until she can safely eat a set number of calories. The nutritionist also explains that this process will take a while and we will have to closely monitor her to ensure she is getting her nutritional needs met. I was hoping that the feeding tube would be permanently removed once the test is done, but I guess not.

As the nutritionist leaves, the phone in the room rings. It's Mike checking to see how we're both doing. I give him a very short update as a nurse arrives carrying a basket full of bandages, syringes, and needles. She explains that she has an order to draw Olivia's blood. We go down the hallway to the treatment room, the same room where Olivia had her bath and her feeding tube reinserted. Olivia cries, of course, but amazingly recovers very quickly. When we come back to the room, we pull out a few books again, one of the activities she still enjoys. I tell her I need to eat something and grab an apple from our bag of snacks. When I'm done, Olivia asks if she can have some. When I tell her that I don't have any more, she asks for chips. It tears through my heart not to be able to give her any food. On the positive side, she is interested. Hopefully, we will be able to wean her off the feeding tube quickly.

Our next appointment that day is with the neuropsychologist, who works on more memory recall. Olivia has a tough time recalling names that the doctor gives her, though she can repeat a sequence of two numbers and occasionally three numbers. She sits and plays with a stuffed bear while answering questions about *Beauty and the Beast* and *The Lion King*. Surprisingly, she is also able to complete a simple puzzle. When we are done, Dr. Nina gives her a little yo-yo as her prize.

Next, we are back at physical therapy. Betty takes out the purse and contents Olivia played with earlier in the day, and Olivia immediately remembers them. She plays with the jewelry, putting a few necklaces on and off. My girl is coming back. She loves to play dress-up, use pretend makeup, and wear jewelry.

She then walks a few steps on her own before sitting down and playing with an electronic toy. She doesn't seem to care how to play the game; all she's interested in is getting the toy to make sounds. Betty notes to me that Olivia has good trunk control, which will help her gain mobility. Betty brings over a push toy for Olivia to try holding on to while taking some more steps. Olivia notices there is a play kitchen and indicates she wants to play for a few minutes. Again, another activity she has always enjoyed is returning. I take all of this to mean she is making progress. It's slow, but I will take whatever I can get.

We arrive at speech, and for the first time I realize none of the therapy rooms have windows. The lighting is fluorescent and continually casts a dim light on us. No wonder we feel sluggish going to all these appointments. It's interesting how lighting can have such a strong effect on us. I think about the last time I was outside. It has been close to three days, and I'm feeling the deficit of natural light and fresh air. I wonder how Olivia is feeling without these things. She can't tell me. Even if she had the words, she wouldn't be able to relate it to how she's feeling.

Rachel has a shape sorter out on the table. I wonder whether Olivia recognizes it since we have the same one at home. I don't detect any recognition. Olivia is good at distinguishing between circle, triangle, and square. She's able to recall most of the colors, and when she doesn't, she's able to answer correctly when given choices. We play with some Play-Doh for a bit at the end of the session as a release. She enjoys it, I think, but doesn't really know what to do with it. I am immediately transported back home. Play-Doh has always been a popular item for my kids and their friends to play with. Mike used to get really upset if it ended up on the carpet in our family room. It was difficult, at times, to keep it all in the kitchen. The kids wanted to take their creations in the adjoining room to play. One thing we've looked forward to in our new home has been the large, mostly finished basement. We have plans for the unfinished room to become the arts and crafts room. The first thing Mike did was designate that area as the paint and Play-Doh room.

I'm shaken from my wandering mind when the therapist reminds me that we are done. I help pack up the Play-Doh, and we head to occupational therapy. I dread this therapy; it is not Olivia's favorite. I still can't figure out why. It may be because it isn't as much fun, or maybe the work is more difficult for her. I would think physical therapy would be more taxing. It's tough, but the therapist makes all the difference in the world.

Cindy asks me to feed Olivia some chocolate pudding slowly. Olivia eagerly takes to this exercise, and I keep looking for direction as to when we should stop. I'm encouraged to keep going. Olivia gurgles a bit, but once she clears her throat, she is all right. Before I know it, Olivia has eaten the entire amount—how exciting! This is the first time she has eaten an entire serving of anything. Phew, progress.

I am then instructed to give her a few small pieces of graham cracker. She sucks on these a bit before swallowing, which helps them go down easier. We encourage her to swallow them and remind her to eat slowly. I can give her two spoonsful of apple juice. She keeps smacking her lips, and I know she really likes it. This is the first time we've given her any liquid to drink. Up until this moment, whenever her lips have seemed dry, all we've been able to do is dip a small sponge attached to a stick in water and have her suck on it. It never takes care of her thirst adequately. She usually tires out before her lips are hydrated.

Cindy takes out an Oreo matching game. I can tell by the expression on Olivia's face that she is not thrilled about this next activity. She is disappointed we aren't going to have more food, and I don't blame her at all. She is given a heart, cross, and square card and instructed to get the matching cards. She can match the cross and square but not the heart. Next, Cindy takes out some blocks and asks Olivia to replicate what she has built with the blocks. It takes a few tries, but Olivia eventually builds a train. I am surprised but encouraged. The next structure is a bridge, which I know will be more difficult for her. I watch the frustration grow on her face, so we decide to end our session. Once she gets frustrated, there's not much use in continuing. We won't be able to turn it around in the short time we have allocated to each therapy.

Olivia is exhausted as I push her in the wheelchair down the long, dark hallway and into the overly bright elevator. What a contrast those two areas are. I've started noticing all the nuances of the building that I overlooked at first. We go to her room, get her settled on her bed, and play a bit until she looks as if she is going to fall over. She falls asleep, but only for about thirty minutes because the nurse enters the room, explaining we must place her feeding tube back in her nostril so she can have her nourishment. We go to the treatment room, and as soon as we enter, Olivia is wide awake and squirming to get away. She knows immediately what we're doing in here. Two nurses are required to place the tube back in, but we aren't done yet because the tube has to be taped on to her face. She keeps thrashing. I'm afraid of the tube coming out again. A second nurse comes to assist, and finally it's done. My heart breaks, hearing her cry so fiercely. The nurses give her a sheet of stickers to soothe her.

WEEK THREE, DAY FOUR

What would be considered an ordinary meal by many was a feast for my daughter and me. My heart is filled with joy after what has been one of the happiest, most memorable days of my life.

—Friday, December 14, 2001

Nurses in Hiding

Kelly, Early Morning

Overnight, the feeding tube alarm starts beeping at numerous intervals. Again, the nurses never enter the room to check on us even after I press the call button several times. I finally get up and go to the nurses' station and am surprised no one is there. The lights in the hallway are dim, and walking in my half sleepwalk, I look around but don't see anyone. I walk back to the room, hoping the alarms won't keep beeping. Sometimes, they shut off by themselves.

When the alarms start going off again, I get up and walk into the hallway. Now I'm angry. Again, no one is at the nurses' station. I hear laughter down the hall and walk toward the sound. I'm in disbelief at what I see. There's a community room at the end of the hallway with a small window in the door. I peer in and finally find where all the nurses and technicians have been hiding. They all stand around laughing and carrying on as if they are having a party.

I walk in and in the calmest voice I can muster ask if someone can help with the alarms going off. The look I receive in return is appalling. They all turn toward me and look as if I have asked them to run up and down the hallway one hundred times. One of the nurses replies that someone will be there shortly to assist. The nurse who has drawn the short straw acts as if I have asked the world of her. I am only asking her to do her job.

Intermittently, Kara's alarms start going off as well, which just makes my night. To make matters worse, the nurse keeps leaving the door ajar, and the hallway lights shine through, making sleep even more difficult.

Luckily, Olivia doesn't seem to hear all the commotion, and when the doctor enters her room at 8:30 a.m., she is still sound asleep. He asks if I want to step outside and chat. I agree, and we proceed to the hallway, which is already filled with light and lots of activity—a stark contrast to the previous evening. He asks if I have any questions regarding Olivia's progress thus far. I ask about the blood work results from the day of our admission, and he comments he needs to check, as they have not been entered into her chart yet. I discuss the memory issues she's having, and he comments that the bleeds on her brain are very similar to a stroke patient. He continues that strokes and brain injuries are extremely similar. He also mentions that he expects Olivia's inpatient recovery to take at least six months.

I'm a bit taken aback with this comment. No one has explained her injuries in this manner. One of the doctors at Fairfax compared it to shaken baby syndrome because her injuries were so widespread and there had been shearing of all the neurons and pathways. I'm not sure which explanation is worse, but I guess it doesn't really matter, as long as she recovers.

Time to Eat!
Kelly, Morning

Olivia wakes soon afterward and seems happy to see me and talks a lot. The mood quickly takes a turn when it's time to get her dressed. I can't help thinking that maybe putting things over her head is bringing up some subconscious memories. Well, hopefully physical therapy with Betty will turn her mood around.

She plays with the pull-along caterpillar toy, and Betty drops balls sporadically and asks Olivia to pick them up. When Olivia gets tired of that game, she stands at a low table and plays with a *Blue's Clues* toy radio. Betty goes to a closet and retrieves a small, child-sized walker, and she shows Olivia how to walk while holding the walker. The front two legs have wheels, making it a lot easier, and she enjoys walking. It's somewhat like a push-along toy most kids use when they learn to walk, which is precisely what she's doing. Betty gives us the walker to practice in Olivia's room whenever she feels up to it.

At occupation therapy, I do my best to distract Olivia with books while awaiting Cindy's arrival. It is time to go for the barium swallowing test, and I'm not sure what to expect. I keep waiting for Olivia to ask for food, but thankfully she never does. Cindy arrives promptly, so I put Olivia back in the wheelchair.

It's a good thing my back has recovered since the herniated disc injuries I suffered a few months after her birth. There is a lot of lifting and picking her up these days. And it's a good thing she's only three years old. If she were five, I don't know that I would be able to keep this up.

We must go next door to Johns Hopkins Hospital for the test, and Cindy directs us through the tunnel that connects the two buildings. Once we arrive in the lobby, the difference in activity level is amazing. Hordes of people run from door to door. There are doctors, nurses, and others looking to catch an elevator in a bank of eight. Luckily, Cindy knows how to get there. I don't know if I would have found my way, even with the best directions.

The technician explains that barium is used only for imaging tests for the gastrointestinal tract. A barium swallow test may be used by itself or as part of an upper series. This series looks at your esophagus, stomach, and the first part of the small intestine (duodenum). He also explains that if Olivia needs further testing, we will talk and decide how to proceed.

The barium is mixed into a small amount of chocolate pudding, and the technician feeds it to her very slowly. We can watch the monitor to track how she is swallowing and whether the food is entering her esophagus properly and without any entering her lungs. Once they are assured it is all right, they mix a little barium with some ground-up crackers, explaining that the crackers are a little harder to swallow and they will only give a few morsels at a time to see how she handles it.

Finally, they mix barium into some chocolate milk and have her take little sips. She can't get any from the straw, so they give her some on a spoon. The look on her face is pure delight. She likes her chocolate milk. She keeps licking her lips to get more of the taste and indicates with hand motions that she wants more. I keep thinking, *Oh, what a tease this must be for her.*

Once the test is complete, they inform me that she can start eating ground-up food and drinking from a cup, but we cannot use a straw. YEAH! It's another day of progress. We get Olivia back in the wheelchair, and Cindy explains the feeding tube will remain until she is able to take in enough calories to sustain her. She also mentions it can take between two days and two weeks to wean her from the tube.

We go back to her room with Cindy's help, and I feed Olivia more chocolate pudding. It feels so good to feed her again. I'm nervous she will choke, so I go very slowly. Olivia is hungry and indicates she wants me to speed up, but I don't. I also slowly give her one ounce of juice. Cindy explains we will have to write down everything Olivia eats in exact amounts so the nutritionist can evaluate how to supplement her with the feeding tube and determine when the tube can be removed.

No Time to Really Talk
Mike, Afternoon

I get to Kennedy Krieger at about 1 p.m. Unfortunately, the best-case scenario from Leesburg to Baltimore seems to be a drive of about one and a half hours. I get very impatient, so I constantly try to shave a few minutes off the drive. When I finally get to Olivia's room, my little girl gives me a big smile while seated in a wheelchair. I can't seem to kiss her enough! I really missed her.

It's also great to see Kelly, but almost immediately we must talk about the sleepover plans. We never have a chance to just talk. When we see each other, time is limited since one of us needs to get back with Hannah, who is currently staying at a friend's house, and we are constantly interrupted by doctors, nurses, and therapists.

It is difficult to take in so much information during such a limited time. I need to divert my attention from Olivia and allow Kelly to open the floodgates, spilling out the details of Olivia's days: notes about the doctors, nurses, and therapists; upcoming schedule of Olivia's treatment; and, well, pretty much anything else that has crossed her mind. I try to allow her the time to "unload," but I find myself interrupting her as I don't want to forget to ask her some questions.

I finally get to ask her how she is holding up, but we find ourselves asking this less and less. We simply don't spend time telling each other how we are doing or coping. The responses are short: "Okay," "Hanging in there," or we just ignore the question altogether and ask the other, "Who is going to spend such and such day(s) with Olivia? Did you remember to take Hannah to this place/appointment? Don't forget you have to . . ."

Sometimes, we simply plow ahead and ask each other, "What are our next steps going to be for Olivia's treatment, how are we going to afford things, how is this affecting Hannah?" and more. Usually, we just talk about next steps.

I wonder about the future of our relationship . . . not in the sense of our commitment to each other, which has never wavered, but more about what type of future we have as husband and wife, father and mother, caregivers, family, even as best friends. What sacrifices will we have to make to preserve, nurture, and grow as a family? Everything is terribly unfair, and not just to Olivia, of course(!), but to Hannah as well. Will our lives be altered to the extent that we live primarily to preserve our family rather to love and look forward to each day with each other?

I imagine that Kelly has similar thoughts, but I can't see any benefit to having this type of discussion with her. We need to somehow look forward and convince each other that things will get better.

So as Kelly tells me what Olivia's schedule looks like, I want to hold my wife and tell her that I am worried about her, too.

Mike's Turn to Learn the Ropes
Kelly, Afternoon

Mike arrives at the end of our feeding session, and Olivia looks really surprised to see him. I wonder if she has been thinking about him or questioning where he is. We've decided that Mike will stay with her over the weekend, and I will go home to spend time with Hannah.

As soon as he walks into the room, the hospital room phone rings, and it is Estelle with a message for Mike. My parents call soon afterward, making me wonder why everyone is suddenly calling here. My mother keeps asking what she can bring Olivia and Hannah for Christmas, and I tell her not to bring any gifts for Olivia since she won't be home for Christmas. My parents, along with my brother, Edward, and sister-in-law, Catherine, usually come to our house for Christmas. Edward and Catherine have been married twenty-nine years, but they don't have any children. My girls are the only grandchildren my parents have.

As my mother insists on talking about Christmas, I mention, again, that Olivia will be here for six more months. She responds by continuing to argue that Olivia will be home by Christmas. It is exactly these types of conversations that make me question why I continue speaking to her. She consistently doesn't listen and refuses to acknowledge the severity of the situation.

I tell her we need to take Olivia to physical therapy now. She hasn't once asked to speak to her granddaughter. After the call ends, the three of us go downstairs, using the stroller that Mike brought from home. Olivia seems more comfortable riding in it and is happy to see a reminder of home. Mike hasn't been to any of her therapies, so it's good for him to see the progress she is making.

Betty has her stand next to the small table and play with a toy phone that makes noises. She explains that standing at the table is slowly building strength in Olivia's legs, which she needs to walk further distances. Mike then walks with Olivia and the walker with Betty's instructions. Olivia beams as she walks alongside him. From the time of Olivia's birth, she has had Mike wrapped around her little finger. I think even more so now, given all she has been through as well as his guilt for not being there at the time of the accident.

The bonds he has developed with each girl are separate and unique, but they both adore him and look for his approval and encouragement. Olivia is serious most of the time, but when the smile comes on her face, it is contagious.

Sessions with Olivia
Mike, Afternoon

Olivia does well at physical therapy but sometimes doesn't respond when asked about particular colors or objects. I wonder whether she is listening, doesn't understand the questions, can't process the information, or simply is in some type of black hole and doesn't care to answer. At 3:30 p.m., we head to speech therapy. Her days are very regimented, almost like a school day of learning about science, math, history, and more. The difference is that her days are filled with learning to live, to exist, and to make it to the next day.

Kelly leaves about fifteen minutes early, when we are taking a break in the rec room. This is an appropriate time for her to say goodbye and not distract Olivia while she is in a therapy session. I think that, overall, this transition works well since Olivia is tired but is also in a playroom away from her "work." Kelly and I share a brief goodbye, and Olivia turns to the Play-Doh. I think she enjoys the current quietness of the room and kneading her fingers in the soft, pliable Play-Doh.

I don't say much to Olivia. I want to preserve the serenity of the moment. I watch her; her eyes seem somewhat empty as she slowly opens and closes her fingers around the soft mounds. At that moment, I allow my worries and thoughts to escape. Nothing fills my mind, and I relax as I watch the calmness of my little girl.

Time with Hannah
Kelly, Evening

After physical therapy, I go back to the room to gather my things before making the long drive back to Leesburg. Rushing. Always rushing. This mantra runs circles in my mind as I gather my things. I feel as if I have so much to share with Mike, but when we are together, we must tend to the business of the hand-off and move on.

We don't have leisure time to discuss our inner thoughts and feelings. I don't have time to dwell.

Hannah has a *Nutcracker* rehearsal this evening, and I arrive at the school just as it starts. I find Sam and Estelle in the auditorium and sit, exhaustion sweeping over me. One of the dance moms approaches me and comments that her prayer circle is saying prayers for Olivia. She ran into Kristin, who told her how well Olivia is doing. It's funny how so many people I know are connected to others. Such a small world. It also strikes me how many are praying for Olivia's recovery.

Once rehearsal is over, we go to dinner. Hannah seems so excited to see me, which, of course, delights me. I love her so much and really miss seeing her every day. Hannah has always been a happy child. I can detect her mood as soon as I lay eyes on her face. She's always filled with excitement and wants to learn about everything. When I was pregnant with Olivia, I remember Mike remarking that Hannah would go far in life and do great things. I would ask how he could be so sure, and he remarked that he just knew. I hope he's right because right now her life isn't too good. Then again, she's surrounded by love from so many people.

During dinner, Sam mentions they want to drive up and see Olivia tomorrow, and Hannah chimes in, saying that she wants to go as well. I feel so guilty, but driving back is the last thing I want to do. I just spent four days and nights at the hospital, and spending more time sitting in a car is at the bottom of my list.

Later in the evening, I speak to Kristin, and she encourages me to stay home if I'm not up for driving to the hospital with everyone else, but I feel so guilty.

The Feast
Mike, Evening

We head back to Olivia's room, and I decide it's time for Olivia to eat some real food. I'm exasperated by the diet they have her on.

I'm convinced it's keeping her from progressing at a higher rate.

So, feeling like we're involved in a stealth operation, at about 5 p.m. I push her stroller down the long hallways connecting to the Johns Hopkins cafeteria. Although I've been to the cafeteria before, I survey it in a different way and, strangely, look forward to having a meal here for the first time. Sure, it's a hospital cafeteria, and I'm not looking for a celebratory feast, but it ends up feeling that way to me! Olivia has orange juice by the spoonful, blueberry yogurt, some bread, and a little meat from my hamburger. I also give her some tiny pieces of potato chips since she has asked Kelly for them before. She does well, and we have a fun time. She seems happy and content even when I tell her that I think I'm going to get in trouble when we get back.

Sure enough, when we get back to the room, I find a note that says only nurses should feed her since I'm not trained! The note also says she should eat "semi-solids" only. Oh well. Olivia and I had a wonderful dinner at the "restaurant," as she calls it. What would be considered an ordinary meal by many was a feast for my daughter and me. My heart is filled with joy after what has been one of the happiest, most memorable days of my life. I read a few books to her, but by 7 p.m., she is fast asleep.

WEEK THREE, DAY FIVE

I'm convinced that the more she can feel like a typical three-year-old, the faster she will recover.

—Saturday, December 15, 2001

Apprehension and Joy

Kelly, Morning

We are up early. Hannah has always been an early riser, getting up at 5:30 a.m. even when she was a toddler. We eat breakfast and get in the car for the drive to Baltimore. I understand why they want to go; they haven't seen Olivia in six days and are looking forward to seeing how much progress she has made. Sam drives, and Hannah and I sit in the back seat.

I direct Sam to parking and see the look of fear on their faces. It is not a nice area, and they appear startled by the reality. I try not to dwell on it and don't want Hannah to sense their fear. Hannah seems excited to be here, bouncing up and down. She has always been a bundle of energy that others can't help but feed from.

We sign in at the security desk. Hannah is ecstatic about the huge aquarium in the lobby area. I have never stopped to look, always in such a rush to get from one appointment to another. It is a delight to see the joy in her eyes. Only a child can conjure this. We ride the elevator upstairs to Olivia's room. I feel Estelle and Sam's apprehension as we approach the room. Mike is sitting on the bed with Olivia, and they are playing with her beloved figurines on her tray table. Olivia looks thrilled as we enter the room. Hannah is still bouncing, and Olivia seems energized by this excitement.

The Desire for Progress
Mike, Morning

Kara, Olivia's roommate, is crying excessively in the early morning. I think it's about 5 a.m. when I first hear her. At 6 a.m., I wake up again to her crying, "Owwww!" repeatedly for more than a half hour. By 6:45 a.m., I decide to take my shower since I know I'm up for good.

Olivia wakes up at 8:15 a.m. very wet. Her diaper is soaked and so are her pjs and sheets. Now I know that with the feeding tube and her drinking on her own, I will need to change her diaper during the night. Olivia does a fantastic job at breakfast with her scrambled eggs.

Grandma, Grandpa, Hannah, and Kelly come to visit, and Olivia's face lights up. My parents keep commenting on how wonderful she looks. I'm pleased but also think about how she couldn't identify breakfast today, even after I repeated the items many times. Kelly and I decide to let her drink out of a cup since the spoon-feeding is laborious and takes too long. She does great.

I gave her a bath earlier, and she was fine but still very tentative and scared anytime I came near the feeding tube. It didn't help matters that I accidentally got the tube caught with the stroller. She cried so hard. I felt awful.

I feel the feeding tube is inhibiting her progress. I'm convinced that the more she can feel like a typical three-year-old, the faster she will recover. I am too impatient, but I'm looking at each step as a progression into her recovery.

A Quick Visit with Family
Kelly, Afternoon

Olivia's lunch is delivered a few minutes after we arrive. This is the first time I've witnessed a meal delivered for her. It's funny how such a simple act can be so welcomed. She has chopped ravioli, mashed potatoes, chopped carrots, and one ounce of juice. I sit and feed her slowly, and Hannah, luckily, isn't jealous of the food. Olivia eats a little but not as much as I would have thought. Then again, I don't really blame her. The mashed potatoes are not as good as Estelle's, and Olivia hasn't developed a taste for mushed-up food.

Once she is done, Hannah plays figurines with her and grabs a few pretzels. It breaks my heart, again, when Olivia asks for one and I must tell her she can't have one. How many times can a heart be broken and heal? I'm not sure at this point, but I must be reaching my quota.

A different physical therapist, Liz, comes to the room to work with Olivia. We can't expect Betty to work seven days a week, after all. The staff told us patients don't usually receive therapies on the weekends, that these are their days of rest, but Mike and I fought this directive, explaining that "rest" may hamper her progress. We want her to have as much therapy as possible so she can come home as soon as possible. We aren't going to discharge her before she's ready, but we want her recovery to proceed without delays.

Liz has Olivia walk up and down the hallway with her walker. Hannah is disappointed by the interruption of their play session, but she handles it well.

The hallways are so quiet compared to the normal activity during weekdays. Liz explains that many patients go home for a few hours on the weekends and the activity will pick up again at dinnertime. We are offered the opportunity to take Olivia outside the hospital for a few hours but decline. I'm still fearful she will pull out the feeding tube, and I don't want the responsibility of reinserting it. Besides, home is over an hour away, so most of our time would be spent traveling in a car.

Olivia practices walking with the walker while holding something small in her hands. I guess they're trying to build her balance but am not certain.

Mike, Estelle, and Sam come out of the room soon after and look proud and amazed as Olivia walks toward them with a beautiful grin. Their eyes light up like Christmas tree lights, for the first time since this ordeal began.

Back in the room, Liz strategically places items that Olivia must reach for and asks her to retrieve them, which she does. Once therapy is over, we see the exhaustion come over Olivia. She has always loved her naps but now needs them more than ever. Estelle calls Jeff and Aunt Mimi, her sister, to tell them how well Olivia is progressing.

Hannah has a *Nutcracker* performance this evening, so we soon say our goodbyes. During the show, while the parents wait in the stark school cafeteria for the dancers to return, Kristin comes by to visit me and share a few quiet moments. She brings me a coffee, which I appreciate. Sam and Estelle are watching the show in the theater. They plan to see every show Hannah dances this season and haven't missed one yet, though I think Sam has had enough of Tchaikovsky music for the year. I give Kristin a quick update on Olivia's progress, and per her usual style, she makes me laugh.

Dinner and a Movie
Mike, Evening

After everyone leaves to get ready for Hannah's *Nutcracker* performance (she was disappointed that I'm not coming today), Olivia has a nap. I try to read a magazine, but I keep glancing over the pages to see how Olivia is doing. I think I probably spend a half hour looking at the same page.

As usual, dinner needs something. The most appetizing part is the ground-up chicken with gravy, which isn't saying much. After she finishes, we go for ice cream in the cafeteria. Olivia loves the outing, of course, and I look forward to it now too.

Later, we go back to her room for pajama time. We watch *101 Dalmatians*, and then it's time for bed. I thought I would be bored by watching the same videos repeatedly, but just being close to Olivia makes it seem like a special time.

WEEK THREE, DAY SIX

Olivia would have loved to see her. I know she would have wanted to see Hannah dance and would love the chance to dance with her!

—Sunday, December 16, 2001

Making Progress
Mike, Morning

From 4: to 7:30 a.m., it is a bad night for me. Kara's alarm keeps going off. At times, it seems that I'm a caretaker of both our child and Kara since her parents aren't here. It is a night of constantly paging or finding the nurse since they don't always respond to the page.

Olivia is up after 8 a.m. She's in a good mood but only does fair with her breakfast. She is getting bored with the ground food diet.

She does well at physical therapy. She stands up, squats, and walks with her little walker quite a bit. She is still wobbly and has trouble staying on the straight line marked on the floor. Again, I notice that there are short-term memory problems.

Afterward, we go to the rec room where Olivia paints three wooden stars, looks at *The Lion King* book, and watches Barbie in *The Nutcracker*.

Then we play upstairs and have lunch; but again, Olivia is bored with the food. She drinks three ounces of grape juice. I suppose she enjoys the sweetness in her mouth. I hope that soon I won't have to measure how much juice she drinks.

Back at the Hospital
Kelly, Morning

Hannah and I have a relaxing morning at home following our busy Saturday. I think we both desperately need it.

I head back to Baltimore after lunch, feeling guilty leaving Hannah once again. I know she's in great hands, but it is still so hard to walk away. The drive is easy, which surprises me, but having lived in the Maryland/DC/Virginia area since college, I know traffic is always unpredictable. The sky is gray, and there is a chill in the air. I park and gather things I packed for Olivia and myself. The lobby area is busy with weekend visitors, so I quickly head to the elevator—a route I can accomplish blindfolded now.

When I enter her room, Mike is sitting in the chair, looking over some documents while Olivia sleeps in the bed beside him. We catch up for a bit. He is anxious to leave, so I get settled and relax in his spot. Olivia sleeps for quite a while, but when she wakes, her mood is very upbeat. I feed her two broken-up goldfish crackers along with two ounces of water. We have already increased the liquid by one ounce. Again, little steps in the right direction.

Feeling the Separation
Mike, Afternoon

I leave Kennedy Krieger at about 3 p.m., anxious to get home as Hannah has her next *Nutcracker* ballet performance tonight. After going through the radio stations, I settle and listen to Simon & Garfunkel's "Bridge Over Troubled Water." I feel my eyes well and struggle to catch my breath. That song is a promise to comfort and to always be there for the loved one in need. Although I have made that vow to my family, I wasn't able to comfort Olivia during those first terrible days when my family was being ripped apart by this tragedy. The feeling of helplessness will stay with me forever.

I go see Hannah in her evening performance. Strange to have only my mom, Hannah, and me together for an event like this. Anyway, Hannah is on cloud nine; she is so excited. Olivia would have loved to see her. I know she would want to see Hannah dance and would love the chance to dance with her!

First Visitors . . . Though Not Engaging
Kelly, Evening

We go to the lobby area for a change of scenery, and Olivia walks around with her walker. She really enjoys looking at the aquarium, and we stand there admiring all the colorful fish. I show her the decorated Christmas trees and the large inflatable Snoopy. She loves looking at all the lights and decorations. It is wonderful to see how just a little bit of change is impacting her in such a positive way. I make a note to change up our scenery any way I can.

We ride the elevator upstairs, and the nurses inform us that dinner has been delivered to the patient rooms. Olivia eats one bite of ground chicken, and it is a small bite at that. She doesn't have any issues swallowing but doesn't seem to enjoy the taste. She has a small bit of mashed peaches, and I'm surprised she doesn't want more. She has always enjoyed the canned or processed peaches. She also has three ounces of juice. She doesn't seem to have any issues drinking and consistently finishes the entire serving.

Once dinner is over, I get her ready for a bath. At home, baths have always been an opportunity to play. But here, as soon as she realizes we are getting ready for a bath, she starts sobbing and sits very rigid. I sense fear rising in her body. I try to engage her, but nothing I do calms her. We quickly make our way back to her room, and I apply lotion before getting her pajamas. She has stopped crying but is still very fussy. I don't understand why she's acting this way. I wonder if unconscious memories are sneaking into her mind.

Once she is dressed, I give her two Hanukkah gifts to open. The first is a pair of pajamas, and she comments that the pajamas are for a baby. The negative mood is increasing. Luckily, she seems pleased with a *Snow White* video and appears to recognize the character. She asks me to play it, which I do, but she is very distracted as it plays. In the middle of the story, she picks up some books and starts looking at them rather than watching the television. I turn it off and read books to her and then brush her teeth. Interestingly, she doesn't seem to mind brushing her teeth.

Olivia keeps telling me she wants "that," saying it over and over. Each time, she gets increasingly frustrated with me because I don't understand what she wants. I finally realize "that" means juice. This encounter again reminds me of the old Olivia. When she was learning to talk, she wouldn't try to say words. Instead, she would point and grunt. It was so difficult to understand, and the more we didn't understand her, the more frustrated she got.

I decide Olivia is frustrated due to fatigue, so we read some more and turn off the light directly above her bed to signal it is bedtime.

When she starts closing her eyes, I go to the other side of her bed and gather up the laundry, hoping the machines will not be occupied on a Sunday evening. I look over and she has rolled over and is staring at me. I explain what I'm doing, and she falls asleep.

WEEK THREE, DAY SEVEN

She goes to bed holding the two Play-Doh hearts she made earlier for a therapist. She holds on to them for hours in her sleep.
 —Monday, December 17, 2001

More Questions for the Doctors
Kelly, Morning

Another long and restless night. Olivia's sleep is very fidgety, due to all the alarms going off. As I wake up and get off the cot, I notice my head and neck are extremely stiff.

Olivia is sleeping soundly. The door opens and the technician says, "Good morning," in a singsong voice, leaving the door open and letting the noise and light from the hallway enter. Luckily, Olivia wakes in a good mood, excited to eat. She eats her waffle and drinks three ounces of juice before we must leave for occupational therapy.

The hallways seem brighter and bristling with energy this morning. Some of the patients also appear happier, and I wonder if this is due to Christmas only being eight days away. I have accepted that we'll still be here for the holidays, but I'm uncertain how we're going to handle all that is expected to go on this time of year.

During the occupational therapy session, Olivia plays with a farm set. I notice the therapist taking notes, but we don't go over any other skills. The time goes by quickly, and Olivia enjoys this session more than any other since she can direct the play.

Following this session, we head to our favorite therapy, physical therapy. Betty greets us enthusiastically, especially for a Monday morning. She shows Olivia a pull-along dog toy and asks her to walk him a bit. Olivia easily complies. The look of delight on her face is priceless. Betty has managed to tap into one of her loves, and it shows. She then asks Olivia to set up bowling pins and match the like colors before asking her to roll the ball and knock down as many pins as possible. Olivia rolls the ball and knocks over some pins, but when asked to go over and stand the pins up again, she can't follow the directions. Our time goes very quickly.

We leave just as Olivia's frustration is on the verge of a complete meltdown. We head to speech, and I am concerned how she will hold up. We rarely have three sessions back-to-back, and her stamina is decreasing quickly. Rachel greets us and directs us toward a round table. She takes out some pictures and asks Olivia to pick out body parts. She does well.

During the next activity, Rachel asks Olivia to repeat words after her. Again, Olivia does well, which surprises me. Finally, she asks Olivia to follow commands, such as "Hand me the blue block." After Olivia does this, Rachel then adds in a second command, such as "Pick up the blue block and put it on top of the red one." Adding the second command impacts Olivia's ability to succeed. At the end, Rachel brings out some Play-Doh, which helps ease Olivia's frustration.

We head up to the recreational therapy room. I know Olivia will relax once she's able to direct what she wants to play. Brenda asks her what she wants to do, and Olivia immediately mentions Play-Doh. She brings some out along with different-shaped cookie cutters. Olivia plays with the shapes but has a tough time pushing them through the dough. I've noticed her hand strength has decreased, and I'm seeing her ball her hands in a fist more often. I'm not sure what this means, but I remind myself to ask a doctor about its significance.

Our final session is neuropsychology with Dr. Nina. This session goes much better than the last. Olivia can't recall the doctor's name but is once again able to identify it when given choices. They move on to an animal guessing game, which goes well. While Dr. Nina continues different games, I notice that Olivia doesn't see things that are in her lower vision field. If an object is held down, she doesn't see it, nor does she move her head to try and see. The doctor starts noticing this as well and suggests we have her eyes checked.

Mike arrives just as lunch is delivered. This afternoon, we have our weekly steering committee meeting with the doctors and therapists to determine how she is progressing and how to proceed in her continued care. Mike and I chat a bit, catching up, and Olivia seems incredibly happy to see him. She falls asleep around 2 p.m., and I ask the nurse if we can move her recreational therapy appointment to later in the day, allowing her more rest time.

The Big Day
Mike, Afternoon

Today at 2:30 p.m. is the committee meeting with Olivia's doctors, therapists, social workers, etc., to review Olivia's progress and to make an estimate for her discharge.

Her right side is still weaker, and some manual dexterity is not there. Memory loss? One of the committee members says they have never seen a three-year-old change subjects or topics when they don't want to answer a question! Olivia seems to have mastered that.

Discussions include outpatient education, physical therapy,

occupational therapy, speech and language, neuropsychology, etc. Her head trauma will be part of her school records now so that her teachers will be aware of issues. Everyone finally agrees to change her diet. Little do they know she had an ice cream sandwich with me the night before.

Sooner than Expected
Kelly, Afternoon

Mike and I go to the meeting while Olivia sleeps, hoping she won't wake while we are gone. The family meetings are held in a conference room containing one long table and many chairs. The room seems much too small for the table and is stark compared to the rest of the hospital. There are some faces around the table that we do not recognize and friendly ones who smile when we enter.

We are asked to bring up any concerns we have, and we start discussing the feeding tube and her current diet. The nutrition staff member listens but insists we need to increase her caloric intake before the feeding tube can be removed. Our comments regarding the nursing staff are taken seriously, and the nursing supervisor listens intently. She offers a small refrigerator for Olivia's room that will be delivered tomorrow and gives us permission to use the shower in Olivia's room rather than using the one in the parents' lounge. She also brings a tape recorder to the room to record the alarms during the night and determine what is causing all the disruptions. These issues take up quite a bit of the time allotted to the meeting, and many of the doctors and therapists leave before we can hear their reports. We are disappointed.

The administrator at the meeting notes that the proposed discharge date is now December 28, 2001. We react with disbelief. Originally, we were told she would be an inpatient for six to nine months, then it was reduced to two months, and now two weeks from the date of admission. I mention that I would like her to be walking by the date of discharge since our house is not handicap accessible and all the bedrooms are on the upper level. The remaining staff feels this shouldn't be an issue since Olivia has been progressing so well.

Once the meeting is over, Mike and I stroll back to the room, pleasantly surprised and happy. We keep marveling at how quickly everything is progressing. When we return, Olivia is awake and happy to see both of us. I pack up a few things and say my goodbyes to Mike and Olivia before heading home to Leesburg.

It is always so hard to walk away and leave Olivia at the hospital, even though Mike is with her and will take excellent care of her. It feels as if I'm leaving part of myself in there with her. I don't feel whole, yet a part of me is so happy to go home and spend some time with Hannah.

My time will also involve looking for a car and going to the county school administration building to file the papers for special education services. All the things we need to take care of seem overwhelming and crushing. Mike and I usually complete big tasks together as a team, and it feels as if the team is falling to the sidelines, and it scares me. Will we all make it out of the dugout before the game is over, or will our whole team fall apart? These thoughts roll around in my mind as I drive home.

Play-Doh Hearts
Mike, Evening

After dinner, we head to the rec room. Olivia is uncomfortable as I read *101 Dalmatians* (what else!) to Jameeka and Sara. Jameeka has a very runny nose, and I must encourage her to get a tissue. Sara keeps reaching and touching my face. Her mother explains that she likes to touch men's facial hair. With the extra activity there, Olivia is not that into her book. I think she is jealous of the attention I'm getting from the two girls and having to share her time with me.

At about 9 p.m., Olivia is still awake and says she pooped in her diaper. She looks at me, genuinely concerned, and asks if I am mad. My heart sinks and tears well up in my eyes. I feel awful for her. I kiss her and tell her she makes me very happy, and I love her.

She goes to bed holding the two Play-Doh hearts she made earlier for a therapist. She holds them for hours in her sleep. When I check on her later, bits of dried Play-Doh are crumbled everywhere in her bed, with no way to salvage them.

WEEK FOUR, DAY ONE

Some of the employees had gone out to the intersection to see what happened. They thought the child taken out in the car seat was dead. This thought hits me like a ton of bricks.

    —Tuesday, December 18, 2001

Conquering the Stairs

Mike, Morning

At 6 a.m., Kara's alarm goes off. After a while, I page the nurse. No one comes in, and Olivia is now awake and sitting up. I complain to the staff about leaving the door wide open during the night, which floods the room with light, and about not answering the page, etc. Olivia, thankfully, goes back to sleep at about 6:40 a.m.

Later, a nurse delivers Olivia's breakfast, but it's the wrong order. I manage to get another but miss turning in the lunch menu because we are running late for a session. I rush to get Olivia awake and dressed and fed for 9 a.m. occupational therapy, but I'm informed by a nurse at 8:50 a.m. that Cindy can't make it. However, at 9:15 a.m., Cindy shows up at the room and says she never told anyone that she couldn't make the appointment. Oh well . . .

In physical therapy, Olivia walks up her first flight of stairs! She also shows improved trunk coordination and flexibility. She sits down, picks up blocks using her left hand, puts water on them from the right side, stands up, and then presses the blocks on a mirror.

In another occupational therapy session, Olivia picks up Cheerios in her right hand and "hides" them in her hand before eating, then repeats with her left hand.

I am more concerned during speech therapy because Olivia has trouble selecting certain pictures on a page when asked. One question is "What do you ride?" Olivia points to a comb, then a shoe, and finally a bike. Although I'm disappointed, I also think her fatigue might be keeping her from doing her best. I joke to myself, *Well, after all, she has never ridden a bike!*

The Dealership Merry-Go-Round
Kelly, Afternoon

I head to three different car dealerships—not my favorite activity. At each place, I calmly explain that I am not purchasing today but only looking at what the options are. I say matter-of-factly that we need to replace our minivan and are not looking for any other type of vehicle. This makes each visit quick and seamless. The first dealer mentions their minivan model won't be available until the beginning of the new calendar year and the parts may be difficult to find. That makes for any easy decision. My next stop is also quick and easy.

My final stop is at the Honda dealership at the corner where the accident occurred. I drive up to the intersection very tentatively. It's the first time I've driven through here since that fateful night. Unlike that night, the weather is very sunny and unseasonably warm for mid-December. A salesperson approaches as I exit the car, and I tell him I'm looking for a minivan. He remarks that a new model will take a few weeks to arrive, but he has a used one in mint condition with extremely low mileage. He asks if I want to test-drive it, and I freeze. I didn't expect the question, and there is no way I am going to drive through that intersection willingly. I decline.

As we're talking, I tell him what happened. He listens intently. His response is kind and empathetic. He witnessed our accident and goes on to say that they saw the first car get hit and do a full 360-degree turn. An employee immediately called 911. This was a car that the SUV hit before hitting our van. No one realized there was another car involved until the police arrived at the scene.

Some of the employees had gone out to the intersection to see what happened. They thought the child taken out in the car seat was dead. This thought hits me like a ton of bricks.

I explain that my daughter is alive and in an inpatient rehabilitation center, and we are hoping she will be home before the end of the year. He then tells me something that stays with me. Something that impacts my buying decision. He remarks that had we been in a minivan made by any company other than Honda or Toyota, my girls would not have survived. He goes on to explain that Hondas and Toyotas are made very differently from other minivans on the market.

I thank him for his time and quickly get into the car to drive home, finally. I can't get our conversation out of my mind. Of course, all the what-ifs rattle through my mind. At that moment, I decide we will only ever buy a Toyota or Honda minivan to keep our children protected.

More Doll Clothes
Mike, Evening

My older brother, Jeff, comes to visit, taking the train from New York to Baltimore. It is a surprise visit, and Jeff gives Olivia a Belle

Barbie doll from *Beauty and the Beast*. Olivia lights up, and I think there is a flicker of recognition directed at Jeff.

Jeff has been very affected by the incident and feels compelled to do whatever he can to try and improve the situation we're in. Olivia is very much a Disney type of girl, so Jeff also brings some framed posters of *Beauty and the Beast*. It is much appreciated . . . more so by me than Olivia!

Olivia has a great dinner. She has meatloaf with ketchup, a roll, chocolate milk, two pieces of cheese, and Italian ice. We'll see how she sleeps tonight, but I am exhausted!

I decide to do some laundry. After washing the clothes, I put them in the dryer. I find out the hard way that the dryer doesn't shut off automatically. Oh well, at least Olivia will now have more clothes for her dolls!

WEEK FOUR, DAY TWO

Betty asks us to try walking up the stairs. Olivia can walk up to the landing and back down again while we walk behind and in front of her in case she falls. I am so proud of her.

—Wednesday, December 19, 2001

Lucky
Mike, Morning

At 6:24 a.m., Kara's alarm goes off. I wait a minute and page the nurse. No one comes to the room. I go to the nurses' station two different times, but no one is there. Finally, a nurse comes into the room. Three minutes later, Olivia is awake. I thought part of rehab would be to get a good night's sleep. Olivia sure doesn't get that here.

After my shower, I ask Olivia what she dreamt about. She replies that she dreamt about our dog and cat, Gallagher and Liberty, at our house. When I say there is a big day planned for her today, she says, "I go to preschool soon. Mommy will take me." I don't say anything.

She loves preschool, and I can't break the news to her that she will have to wait until next September.

In physical therapy, Olivia walks up a full flight of stairs. The routine goes like this: She has a dog pull toy that she calls Lucky, from the *101 Dalmatians*, and takes him to the hallway of the first floor. We then go to the stairwell where I put Lucky halfway up the steps, and Olivia climbs to it, using the railing for support. After she reaches Lucky, I then put the pull toy at the top of the stairs. She is so proud of herself as she reaches the top. I must admit, I feel a bit guilty dangling the carrot.

After that, we head to her education class with Patty, the education consultant, who tells me that Olivia's test results show her to be at the age level of thirty-four months instead of the forty months comprising her physical age now. Although below average, it's considered within the normal range. Questions that no one can answer are 1) does her fatigue during the testing influence her test results, and, of course, 2) how would she have tested before the car crash?

Tired of Complaining
Mike, Afternoon

At 1:15 p.m., I put Olivia down for a nap. She is fast asleep within five minutes. Since Kelly has arrived to stay the night, I get ready to leave for Leesburg. While I'm in the hallway, Cindy, the occupational therapist, and Rachel, the speech therapist, come by. Cindy has a lunch for Olivia, but it's not what I ordered. I simply want a peanut butter and jelly sandwich since it is Olivia's favorite lunch item and she hasn't had it for about a month. Kelly and I talk with them quite a bit about all the mistakes with Olivia's schedule (she had four different therapy sessions scheduled for 10:30 a.m. today, for example), her meal and menu changes, complaints about some of the nurses, etc. I tell them that if they want to change her menu, they should tell us. If they want to see how she eats, then they can take the entire Kennedy Krieger staff to watch for all I care.

I really am getting tired of complaining. Everywhere I turn, there are too many missteps, complete lack of communication, and incompetence. I sometimes wonder if it's just me, but I know that Kelly has been experiencing this with me.

Olivia's roommate, Kara, has been moved to a different room. I hope that little girl gets attention soon and some type of family connection.

Finally, Some Good News
Kelly, Afternoon

A little while later, Olivia wakes up and immediately asks for some food. We have agreed to call Cindy and the nutritionist, as they want to observe Olivia eating a peanut butter and jelly sandwich. I guess they don't believe Olivia can swallow it properly. Dr. Nina enters the room at the same time, and Olivia's feeding tube starts coming loose. I quickly call the nurses, but they don't respond. So much for the assurance they will respond in a timely fashion. Cindy offers to find a nurse, and I gladly accept this offer.

When the nurses arrive and try to put the tube back, Olivia becomes inconsolable; in a way, I'm glad others get to see her reaction and know we aren't fabricating anything. Dr. Nina watches from the sidelines and when the excitement is over informs me that she will not need to do any more testing with Olivia until the following Wednesday or Thursday. I feel relieved, but there is so much happening in this small room that I can only focus on one thing at a time. More proof I am having difficulty multitasking.

We head to physical therapy with Betty, who greets her enthusiastically, as usual, and directs Olivia to kneel on a mat while they play a fishing game. The goal is to keep Olivia distracted while simultaneously working on her strength and trunk control.

They move on to stringing beads while standing and squatting. This proves to be much more difficult for Olivia. For the final activity, Olivia takes her walker and dog, and we head to the stairwell. Betty asks us to try walking up the stairs. Olivia can walk up to the landing and back down again while we walk behind and in front of her in case she falls. I am so proud of her. You can see the look of pride envelop her face. Interestingly, Olivia enjoys going into the dark, cold, and gray stairwell to practice. At first, it surprises me. Then I realize she likes the quiet. No one ever takes the stairs except for staff members. I think she relishes the quiet over all the other sounds she must process.

We say our goodbyes and head to the recreational therapy room. I read her *101 Dalmatians* and *The Lion King;* then Olivia goes to one of the bins and takes out Dr. Barbie and Kelly dolls. We start role-playing with them. I think it's interesting she picks these, given we are in a hospital setting. The director of therapeutic recreation approaches and asks if we would like to attend the field trip to the Baltimore Aquarium with other patients and caregivers tomorrow. I am thrilled—probably more than Olivia since she doesn't understand what we're doing. Brenda explains that the aquarium allows our group entrance after hours and opens some of the exhibits. A nurse attends as well in case there is a medical emergency.

Finally, we are going to have some fun.

The nutritionist comes in with more good news. She informs me that the staff has decided Olivia's feeding tube will be removed the following day. The nutritionist will need to continue looking over her calorie consumption to ensure she is getting enough calories, but this is cause for celebration.

Our next session is occupational therapy with Cindy. She shows Olivia how to walk on her hands like a crab, but Olivia refuses to cooperate. Cindy keeps trying to push her to do it, but I know we're beyond the cooperation stage. Parents know their children best. Olivia does not like this activity. She has always been stubborn, and that personality trait is starting to come back. Could this be a good sign? Cindy relents and then brings out a fishing game and has Olivia lie on her belly to play. Olivia is much happier doing this activity.

Joy in the Simple Things
Kelly, Evening

We've had a full day, and I have only been present for part of it, so I know she's tired. We go to her room, and she relaxes for a brief time before her dinner is delivered. The nurse comes in and removes her feeding tube. Total delight on Olivia's face. She doesn't seem to mind the tube coming out; the going in was the issue.

She eats a good dinner, and we decide to take a walk to the cafeteria in the Johns Hopkins building. I put her in the stroller, and we set off. Mike has taken her a few times and told me how much she enjoys it—the food as well as the change of scenery. The cafeteria is much easier to find than anything else has been. We walk through a long tunnel, though I wouldn't have known we were in one. It's decorated with large, happy pictures of people smiling and laughing, and the lights are bright.

I am surprised at the size of the cafeteria. As we walk in, it takes me a few moments to get my bearings and figure out how to manage a purchase and her stroller. I find the soft-serve ice cream machine and dispense a cup while trying to balance napkins and spoons and get my money out to pay. When we walk to a nearby table, I am proud of myself for not dropping anything. Olivia really enjoys her treat. She has always loved food, so it's such a delight to see her eating it with her old enthusiasm.

I consciously give her spoonsful at a slow pace because I don't want her to gag or get sick. She is so genuinely happy. We chat and laugh. I almost forget where we are. I clean her up as best I can, and we head back to Kennedy Krieger. We stop in the lobby so I can show her the large aquarium. The lobby area in the evenings is quiet, so

I know she won't be overwhelmed by noise or a lot of people. The fish tank is situated in the middle of the room, and there's a large Christmas tree behind it, all lit up. She admires the large blue-and-yellow fish. She's drawn to the larger, more colorful ones. I see her getting sleepy, so we say goodnight to the fish and tree and head upstairs.

A Call that Brings Back Memories
Kelly, Late Evening

My parents call soon after I get Olivia changed into her pajamas. They always sit at their kitchen table and place the phone on speaker. The calls get frustrating when one of them cannot hear me or they interrupt. I try to stay calm during this call since I'm in a public setting. They inform me of their plans to come for Christmas, and I remind them Olivia will still be in the hospital. They don't seem to understand the situation. This is not going to be the typical Christmas. I also explain Mike and I will continue taking turns staying at the hospital and home with Hannah since it is her winter break. They never offer to help, but I'm not surprised.

When I was pregnant with Olivia, they told me they were coming to help. I was very apprehensive because their idea of helping was not what I wanted or needed. I knew it would be harder juggling an active two-year-old and caring for a newborn, so I needed assistance with meals and playing with Hannah. They insisted they would provide that level of care.

I had a bleeding disorder, and the doctor decided it was safer to induce labor rather than let it evolve naturally. Mike and I left for the hospital at 6 a.m. the day my labor was induced. It was a long and difficult labor. Mike kept contact with my parents the entire day, and Kristin stopped by to take Hannah to a playground with her two young kids. We knew my parents were having a challenging time keeping up with our active Hannah. In the early evening, they asked

Kristin to take Hannah for the night so they could come visit at the hospital. I was furious at them for "unloading" Hannah but tried to take it in stride.

The first day Olivia and I were home from the hospital, we had a disagreement with my parents, and they packed up their things and left. I didn't know where they were for a few days until my father called and asked if they could stop by. It was a horrible time.

Feeling it won't be much different, I'm relieved they don't offer any assistance with Hannah while we're caring for Olivia. During the conversation, my mother asks how Mike's job is and comments how nice it is that they're giving him time off while we deal with the accident. I break the news he was laid off prior to the accident. Pure radio silence. They don't know how to react. I know there will be ramifications for this later, but I'm not worrying about that now.

WEEK FOUR, DAY THREE

Her nap lasts until we must leave for the aquarium field trip. She is so excited about the trip. She is even excited to put on her jacket and gloves.

—Thursday, December 20, 2001

Pulling in a Little Fun

Kelly, Morning

Both Olivia and I sleep well and wake up rested. I am surprised how quiet the room is now that she no longer has Kara as her roommate. Olivia is hungry when she wakes up, and luckily, her breakfast had already been delivered.

We head to occupational therapy first, and I hope we'll have a better session. Usually, if she is well rested and fresh, Olivia is very cooperative. Yet she tends to be very resistant to Cindy no matter what the activity entails. I don't think Olivia cares for her much, but I'm not quite sure how to handle the situation.

Once again, Olivia doesn't want to cooperate with any of the activities and reluctantly says she'll try finger painting. She ends up having a fun time with this activity, so maybe we crossed the threshold here.

Next, we move on to speech with Rachel. We're going from the least to most favored activity today. I try breaking this up with a little fun. We go to the recreational therapy room and read some books. This seems to help the fatigue, and we make it through physical and speech therapy without any issues. We head back for lunch and hopefully a nap. Her lunch arrives, and once again, the order is incorrect. Once she finishes eating, I try to get her to nap so I can attend the parent meeting.

The Aquarium Field Trip
Kelly, Afternoon

The meeting is held in the conference room on the patient floor to encourage all the parents to attend. I enter the room and see that pizza and drinks have been provided. There are more parents present than I expected, and after hearing all their stories, I am grateful that Mike and I are not alone.

During the meeting, the parents are relieved to have their voices heard, but I am not sure any significant changes will occur.

I walk into Olivia's room and am pleased to see she's still sleeping. Her nap lasts until we leave for the aquarium field trip. She is so excited. She is even excited to put on her jacket and gloves. We proceed downstairs to the loading area and wait while other patients are taken onto the bus. It takes a while since many of the patients are in wheelchairs or have other medical equipment. The bus is designed to accommodate the wheelchairs, leaving less seats overall but enough for their purposes. I take Olivia out of her stroller so we can sit together. Her eagerness is infectious.

She enjoys the aquarium but becomes very cranky and irritable at times. Unsurprisingly, her favorite event of the evening is the dolphin show. It is strange walking through the aquarium in the off hours. Kristin and I brought our kids here a year ago during spring break. We stayed at a local hotel, walked through the Inner Harbor, and took the kids to the aquarium. This trip is quite different. We are the only ones in the building, along with a limited staff. It is eerie.

During the return ride, the mood in the bus is more subdued. Everyone had fun, but the sense of exhaustion is evident. When we return to the hospital, everyone receives a dolphin toy and a package of chicken nuggets. I expect Olivia to fall asleep while riding the elevator, but she manages to stay awake. She's eager to eat her nuggets before we get ready for bed. Not surprisingly, she falls asleep quickly.

WEEK FOUR, DAY FOUR

Olivia really enjoys the bells and shakes them with a huge smile on her face. I can tell she is confused about the songs and doesn't know the words, but she sways and shakes her bells enthusiastically.

—Friday, December 21, 2001

A Different Therapist Means Different Challenges
Kelly, Morning

We have a good night, and Olivia sleeps well. She eats her breakfast while I take a shower and get dressed. Once we are both dressed, we get all our things together and head to a joint occupational and physical therapy session. She plays a game of catching butterflies with a net and throws the ball to Cindy. Afterward, Olivia draws pictures of me, Mike, and Hannah with markers. Cindy is impressed that Olivia includes eyes, eyebrows, noses, mouths, arms, and legs in each drawing.

We move on to speech and work with a different therapist,

Janine. As soon as we enter the cubicle, Olivia repeatedly asks for some Play-Doh. She is told they have other things to do first. Janine is not very accommodating. She seems upset every time she asks Olivia to perform a specific task and is met with even more resistance on Olivia's part. Finally, Play-Doh and cookie-cutter shapes are brought to the table, and Olivia wears a look of satisfaction.

When our session is over and it's time to put everything away, Olivia asks if she can take the shapes with her and tries to put them into her backpack hanging from the stroller. Janine tells her she can't take the shapes, but she will give Olivia a sticker instead. She rolls the Play-Doh along with three of the shapes into a large ball, and Olivia starts sobbing. I tell Janine that Rachel lets her take them after playing. She allows Olivia to make one more heart out of Play-Doh. Olivia grips the heart in her fist as if to say, "This is mine." She doesn't end up getting a sticker, but she looks victorious.

We get to the therapeutic recreation room for some needed downtime. As is our routine, we read books and play with paints. She then watches another girl play Don't Break the Ice, and she and I play when the others are done. She really enjoys the game, but I notice she doesn't have much control or strength to break the "ice." I help her a bit, and she seems okay with the help.

Still Noticing Missing Pieces
Kelly, Afternoon

When I notice Olivia's fatigue setting in, I suggest we go back and have lunch. As we enter her room, we're greeted by a huge surprise. A large bouquet of Dalmatian balloons is sitting on her bed. I read the attached card and tell her it's from Peyton, a friend from preschool. She seems bewildered and doesn't show much enthusiasm for the gift, which is surprising since she loves the Dalmatians and Peyton is a good friend. I am so touched that Peyton's family is thinking about Olivia and sent something she would truly adore.

When lunch arrives, Olivia eats everything on her tray. All the morning's work must have burned off more than she had in reserves. We read more before our 2 p.m. physical therapy session, and I notice she's getting extremely tired. I'm not too worried about her stamina because she really enjoys the time with Betty.

We get ready to go and take the familiar route to the physical therapy unit. It is now four days until Christmas, and I already feel the veiled excitement in the air. It seems there is less visible staff, and some of the kids are starting to get rambunctious. I'm still not sure what Olivia comprehends.

During physical therapy, Olivia walks while pushing the Barney car forward. She still hasn't figured out how to turn the car to walk back, so we help her navigate while also keeping her upright. We take the toy dog to the stairwell, walking up to the landing and back down again while Betty observes her balance and gait. We walk back to the room, and Betty sets up Silly 6 Pins—a child-sized bowling game made from plastic. Olivia enjoys rolling the ball to the pins but doesn't like having to walk over and stand the pins up; she would prefer that I do that task.

Finally, we kick a playground ball back and forth between us. Olivia can kick the ball but has a ridiculously hard time trying to stop it with her foot. Again, this requires a balancing move that she hasn't mastered quite yet. She becomes very frustrated when the ball rolls past her. She works on a lot of physical tasks during this session, so I know time in the recreational therapy room is next on our agenda.

Christmas Is Coming
Kelly, Late Afternoon

She sits in the stroller and seems content that her "work" is done for now. We walk the stark hallway and take the elevator to the next floor. She seems to recognize where we're going and looks happy. I take this as a positive sign that she is starting to remember what each door represents. This could be both good and bad. She wants to watch the Rudolph movie and is upset when I can't locate it. Olivia really enjoys the updated version of Rudolph where he and his girlfriend Clarice travel to the Island of Misfit Toys and transform the unwanted toys into new usable ones.

Soon after, one of the therapists passes around bells while leading the children and adults in singing Christmas carols. Olivia enjoys the bells and shakes them with a huge smile on her face. I can tell she is confused about the songs and doesn't know the words, but she sways and shakes her bells enthusiastically. This activity also briefly takes her mind off the movie she requested. Once the singing ends, she becomes agitated and very cranky, so we head back to the room for a bath, which might calm her a little. Now that she can sit upright in the tub, she enjoys the bath more. I grab a few toys to distract her. I'm accustomed to using toys as a motivator to allow her hair to be washed.

I'm quite surprised at how much fun she's having. In fact, she doesn't want to come out. Once the water cools and she starts getting goose bumps, I insist it's time to transition to pajamas.

She seems much more relaxed, so we watch a show on the local PBS channel. I end up falling asleep for a bit, and when I wake, she's asleep. I'm relieved. She really needed some rest. Her dinner has been delivered, so I reluctantly wake her. I promise her we can go for ice cream at the "restaurant" if she does a good job with her dinner. She refers to the Johns Hopkins cafeteria as a restaurant, so I've started using the same word. Like Mike has suggested, I think she enjoys the change in environment almost as much as the ice cream. It's so nice to feel like we are in a new place even though we haven't stepped outside the building since she arrived.

I get ice cream for her and an apple and coffee for myself. My meals have become very sporadic, eating when I can but also conscious that Mike isn't working, and our bills have to be paid.

Taking Steps to Set Boundaries

Kelly, Evening

Once we arrive back in our room, Mike calls, and we both speak to him briefly. He updates me on Hannah and mentions my parents have flown in and are going to stop by the house. They haven't seen our new house. I quickly remember that we moved six weeks ago, but it feels much longer since so much has happened.

My sister-in-law, Catherine, calls and asks whether I would rather they come on Christmas or wait until Olivia is discharged. I go back and forth, trying to decide how to say what I need to say. I decide it's better if they wait. I already feel the burden of trying to make Christmas fun for Hannah while we're in a hospital and entertaining my parents at the same time. I don't want the burden of worrying and entertaining them as well. I am so surprised that I'm able to say what I need at that moment. I know this is a great first step in building a skill I'll need in order to advocate for Olivia—as well as myself.

WEEK FOUR, DAY FIVE

We have often gone out for ice cream or to run errands or watch Hannah's soccer games. Of course, now we are in a hospital and must take elevators and walk through tunnels to arrive at our destination. But I would take this day over any other during the past few weeks.
—Saturday, December 22, 2001

A Break in the Routine
Kelly, Morning/Afternoon

We have another recreational therapy outing today.

The weekends here have quite a different energy compared to weekdays. Everything is much slower, quieter, and more subdued. Saturdays in the hospital mean less therapy, if any at all, and too much unstructured time. The techs are required to do hourly vital checks, and meals are delivered, but that's the extent of the structure. We still don't believe in taking time off. Some may think we're being unreasonable, but Mike and I feel the more therapy she can get, the quicker she can go home.

We're going to a bowling alley today. When I first learn we'll be bowling, I'm confused. How are these kids supposed to pick up bowling balls and roll them down the lane? The staff chuckle and explain we're going to a duckpin alley, which I've never heard of. Apparently duckpin bowling, popular in the Baltimore region, uses a smaller ball the size of a softball that weighs under four pounds. The bowler has three tries rather than the traditional two to knock down the pins, which are lighter and smaller than traditional pins.

We arrive on the lobby floor, and I put Olivia's coat, hat, and gloves on. She always fought putting these on prior to the accident, so I'm prepared for a struggle and surprised when it doesn't happen. Several patients are ready to go, and the energy is once again contagious. I wait while patients in wheelchairs are loaded into the bus before picking Olivia up, folding her stroller, and finding our seat. There are a few teenage boys sitting in front of us, and their mothers are there as well. We chat with them during the ride. It's wonderful to see Olivia interacting with them. She is smiling, and they enjoy making her laugh.

At the alley, I show Olivia how to hold the ball and roll it down the lane. At first, she seems tentative, but once she does it a few times, her confidence rises. She loves it. The boys cheer for her, and she eats it up. She shows off for them, and they howl with laughter.

The staff brings over pizzas and drinks for everyone, and Olivia eats two slices. I'm astonished. This is the biggest meal she's had since before November 27. This is a magnificent event for me, as well. I haven't talked to other adults in a relaxed setting in such a long time. I enjoy hearing their stories and realizing that others have tougher stories than us. As I listen, I glean hope and gratitude from other people's struggles.

When we board the bus for the ride back, Olivia looks exhausted. She got a good workout today. At the alley, she insisted on carrying the bowling ball each time, wanting her independence. Another glimmer of her stubborn streak.

Once we arrive back, we say goodbye to our new friends and go up to her room to relax for a bit.

Mike and Hannah come in the afternoon, and Olivia glows when they walk into the room. She recognizes them and keeps waving her arms up and down, unable to tame her excitement. It seems that the more excited she becomes, the more difficulty she has speaking—as if when she feels a strong emotion, the rest of her brain has a tough time doing anything else, treating those two functions as complicated multitasking.

Hannah and Olivia play a bit, eat some dinner, and then the four of us make our way to the restaurant for ice cream. It seems our family unit is finally coming back together. We have often gone out for ice cream or to run errands or watch Hannah's soccer games. Of course, now we are in a hospital and must take elevators and walk through tunnels to arrive at our destination. But I would take this day over any other during the past few weeks. A much lighter mood fills the hospital, and I assume it's the holiday bringing everyone to a more joyous place.

Once we go back to the room, the girls play a bit longer, but they are clearly fatigued. Olivia's eyes start drooping, and she becomes easily frustrated. Hannah's eyes lose their sparkle. I grab my things and say goodbye to Olivia and Mike as Hannah and I head out for our "special evening." Mike has arranged for us to stay at a local hotel in the Inner Harbor section of Baltimore. He figures this is better than driving home to Northern Virginia tonight and driving back in the morning. Most kids love staying at hotels, and ours are no exception. The excitement level usually reaches top velocity once we are safely inside the hotel room and the girls begin claiming their spots or trying to jump on beds or giggling endlessly.

The drive is no more than ten minutes, and we quickly park and ride an elevator to the lobby. Bright lights and Christmas music greet us as we exit into the large open area. The hotel is extravagantly decorated, and Hannah marvels at the lights and trees. The mood this evening is a bit subdued, but we are happy to have some mother–daughter bonding time. We quickly change and read some books, and we both fall asleep by 9:30.

WEEK FOUR, DAY SIX

I summon up my usual coping mechanism, which is to push all the negative feelings down and stifle them so I don't have to deal with them.

    —Sunday, December 23, 2001

Sound Sleep and a Swim
Kelly, Morning

I open my eyes and adjust to my surroundings, taking a moment to remember where I am. *Oh, yes, Hannah and I are at the hotel.* I roll over to check the time and am surprised that I slept soundly. It's now 6:30 a.m. Hannah is awake. She smiles and wishes me a genuine "Good morning." We both stretch a bit and start chatting. We eat breakfast, and I have my coffee. The pool doesn't open until 10 a.m., so we color and draw before getting ready for a swim.

The walk from the hotel room to the indoor pool seems so cold. We have coverups over our suits, but it seems counterintuitive to be going to a pool in winter. As I expected, the pool is deserted. She and I have a fun time swimming and playing before we head back to the room for showers. Hannah helps gather our things, which is a quick process since we only stayed one night, but I make sure to look under the beds and under sheets before departing. I'm always fearful that a beloved object will be left behind.

We drive back to see Olivia and Mike. Luckily, we arrive around lunchtime. Hannah is starving after swimming. Soon after lunch, we say our goodbyes, and Olivia looks like she is about to fall asleep. Hannah and I head to the car once again, but this time we have a longer ride in front of us. The traffic is light; we make it back to Leesburg in less than two hours. I realize I don't know what food is in the house, so we stop at the store to pick up a few things. Already, I'm feeling the enormity of all the things I must do over the next day.

Baby Steps of Progress
Mike, Morning

We have a good physical therapy session. Olivia walks up and down a flight of stairs. She even walks backward a bit with the dog toy. Later, she claps to pop bubbles. Playtime for her, but I scrutinize her actions with a smile. Love to see her with a burst of enthusiasm.

At occupational therapy, the sub, Bev, is ten minutes late. She asks and demonstrates to Olivia how to make a horizontal line by making a large dot on the left side of the paper, then on the right side, and slowly connecting the dots. Olivia follows and attempts to make a horizontal line, which I think is the first time, so this marks substantial progress. Later, it is question-and-answer testing, but Olivia is too tired to respond to the questions posed to her.

Visitors with Expectations

Kelly, Afternoon

Once home, we put away the food items and say hello to the pets, Gallagher and Liberty. I promise Hannah we'll decorate the Christmas tree tonight.

We are only home about thirty minutes before my parents ring our doorbell. I am frazzled when they walk into the house. Usually, whenever they're in town visiting, I am expected to sit down with them, make coffee or tea, and entertain. This evening, I'm not in the mood to make petty small talk when I have a tree to decorate and gifts to wrap. I'm also starting to feel the enormity of Olivia's condition and what it will mean for our family in the future.

I summon up my usual coping mechanism, which is to push all the negative feelings down and stifle them so I don't have to deal with them. I know expressing any feelings to my parents isn't going to help and, in fact, may hurt me even more.

We eat dinner, and I clean up the dishes while Hannah visits with my parents. She and I decorate the tree while they sit on the couch and talk, never offering assistance. When we finish decorating, Hannah gets ready for bed. It has been another long day, and she looks very worn out. Once she's in bed, I come back downstairs, and my parents are exactly as I left them. I tell them I need to wrap a few presents. Mike and I have only bought one or two gifts for the girls. My plan is to wrap them and leave them under the tree when Hannah gets in the car the next morning. When she comes home after spending Christmas in Baltimore, she will find the gifts Santa left for her and Olivia.

My parents comment that they should leave. They plan to come visit Olivia on Christmas, and I give my father directions. As they leave, I hurry to get the paper and gifts and suddenly realize we don't have any tape. In a panic, I dash outside and catch my father before he pulls out of the driveway. He offers to get tape at the local grocery store that has late hours. Major crisis averted!

He comes back about ten minutes later with enough tape to hold my house together. He is surprisingly sweet and asks if I need anything else. I wrap until my eyes start drooping. Once the task is complete, I realize it is past 1 a.m. Bleary eyed, I shut off all the lights, lock the doors, and head upstairs for bed. Once again, I don't have any trouble falling asleep.

WEEK FOUR, DAY SEVEN

When we step off the elevator, the mood is bright and cheery. Hannah is extremely excited to see Olivia and Mike. She almost runs down the hallway. Olivia has the same reaction to Hannah.

—Monday, December 24, 2001

A Monotonous Routine
Mike, Morning

As the morning begins, I tell Olivia that she has a busy day planned. She again asks me about preschool. After eating breakfast, she asks, "Can I go to Hannah's house on Sunday?" I say she'll go home to her house to see Gallagher and Liberty soon. She lights up when I mention Liberty.

She wants to play with her Dalmatian puppy figurines or Barbies and nothing else. It is monotonous for me. I play with her to appease her; other times, I change the subject or divert her attention. I am running out of ways to play with her! She naps, still holding one of her figurines in one hand; the other hand clutches an animal cracker box that I have been putting the puppies in.

Olivia does great in physical therapy with Betty. She loves going up and down a ramp with Betty and pulling Lucky, the toy dog. I ask, "Do all the kids love the ramp as much as Olivia does?" Betty replies that usually she doesn't get to this level here.

Olivia's attention span has been limited in her sessions. I know she is getting bored with the testing (books with pictures to identify).

A Christmas Eve Visit with Santa
Kelly, Morning

Hannah and I eat breakfast and gather everything we need to take back to Baltimore with us. I have already packed outfits for both Hannah and Olivia for Christmas Day and have chosen things for me as well. It's hard finding everything since a lot of our belongings are still in moving boxes. I shuffle a few things around in our closet and finally find something appropriate.

Hannah has not visited Santa, and today is the final opportunity. Kristin offers to meet us at the mall since she has some last-minute things to pick up. I have not seen her since Olivia was discharged from Fairfax Hospital, and I know Hannah will enjoy seeing Ian, Logan, Sophie, and Camryn. The line for Santa will be long. It is Christmas Eve, and friends will be a great distraction for Hannah.

She is excited on the short ride to the mall. We walk inside and at once feel the anticipation. We walk directly to the center atrium and get in line along with all the other people who have procrastinated for weeks. Well, at least we have an excuse for waiting, though I realize that is a nasty thought. I do not know their stories. Maybe they've also had a tragic event during the past few weeks and, like me, rushed here on the last possible day so their child can tell Santa what they want.

As expected, Hannah is thrilled to see Kristin and her kids.

They jump around singing and dancing (well, Hannah is singing and dancing). She's wearing her black boots with a little heel, making her tower over all of them. Her height makes her look older. Being around her friends is the perfect distraction. Kristin hands me an incredibly supportive card that melts my heart. Once again, she gives me hope when I really need it.

Hannah finally has her turn with Santa and asks him for the one thing she has been asking about for months: a *Wizard of Oz* toy she saw at a toy store. Luckily, Kristin picked it up for me and it is sitting at home, wrapped and under the tree. I was hoping Hannah would not say something we don't have.

As she finishes with Santa, we hear a loud noise. Suddenly, a piercing scream erupts from Hannah; she looks terrified. I glance around before consoling her to make sure we aren't standing in the middle of a falling building. I hold her in my arms as she cries. She can't say why the sound startled her so much, but she is able to calm down. As I hold her, I look around and realize some popping balloons caused the noise. She asks if we can leave because she doesn't want to hear the sound again. Of course, I oblige. On the drive back to Baltimore, I am surprised that Hannah sleeps most of the way. She was never a napper, even as an infant, so she must be either really wiped out or coming down with something. I hope it's the former.

We feel the exhilaration in the lobby of Kennedy Krieger as soon as we approach the door. The room is filled with visitors and patients extremely excited for the arrival of Santa. We quickly navigate our way to the elevator and ride it to Olivia's floor. When we step off the elevator, the mood is bright and cheery. Hannah is thrilled to see Olivia and Mike. She almost runs down the hallway.

Olivia has the same reaction to Hannah. Hannah quickly takes off her coat and sits on Olivia's bed, and they start playing with the Barbies.

Hannah has always had a vivid imagination, just like Mike. When she was less than two, he would play a game with a cloth dollhouse she had. He would pretend Papa Bear was making pizza and serving it to Baby Bear. The pizza would be too hot, and Papa would throw it across the room because he burned his paws. Hannah would laugh so hard and ask him to do it repeatedly.

The girls continue playing until dinner is served. Olivia has some of the dinner but not much, and Hannah eats what is left. Soon after, my parents arrive to visit. I can tell my mother is uncomfortable as she probably doesn't know what to expect. My father helps her to a nearby chair, and she starts talking. Her way of dealing with the anxiety is to talk. She talks mostly to me rather than trying to engage with Hannah or Olivia.

Hannah and I are staying overnight again in the hotel. We walk out with my parents after saying our goodbyes to Mike and Olivia. My parents are also staying at a hotel but not the same one, so I give my father directions and tell him we will see him tomorrow.

The hotel lobby is noticeably quiet, and I realize many people do not stay in hotels on Christmas Eve unless they are in a resort area. We get into our pajamas, and suddenly Hannah asks me if I am proud of her for not having her name "moved" at school. Her kindergarten teacher uses a behavior chart to encourage the students to behave and follow the rules. A name gets moved if a child misbehaves, and a folder comes home each week indicating whether your student wasn't listening or paying attention. Hannah is always pleased to show me the folder. Her comment makes me realize how anxious she is about this system. It has really affected her. She mentions that one of the girls at her table gets a bit too excited and has trouble controlling herself. Hannah is afraid she will get her name moved like her. I reassure her, and we read a bit before going to sleep.

I make a note to myself to reassure her more specifically now that her world has been turned upside down. She is going to need a lot more attention over the next few months to balance out some of her needs, which are vastly different from Olivia's.

Dancing with Rudolph

Mike, Evening

Hannah and Kelly come in the early evening. Olivia and Hannah start to get rambunctious, dancing and antagonizing each other just like old times. We put on *Rudolph the Red-Nosed Reindeer*, and Kelly's parents, Ann and Lenny, come in. Hannah gets annoyed with their talking; she just wants to watch the video. After the show, the girls start getting rowdy again. Olivia really is moving well! We go to the cafeteria amid concerns that Olivia is a little too playful and is stretching her limits.

Christmas Eve dinner is the hospital's chicken nuggets and french fries for the girls and me since I have their leftovers. Later, we go to the cafeteria where Kelly has lentil soup. Lenny has chicken and mashed potatoes, and Ann has a hamburger. Not what Kelly had in mind a month and a half ago when she envisioned Christmas Eve this year.

Olivia just doesn't like to go to sleep early. At about 10 p.m., I get into bed next to her. It strikes me (again) what a beautiful child she is—just as all the nurses and therapists say she is. She keeps talking and talking. One thing she says is "Mommy come to my house tomorrow?" I pause and say, "Sweetie, Mommy will come to visit you in the hospital tomorrow. This is the hospital. You don't live here. You will be home soon with Mommy, Daddy, Hannah, Gallagher, and Liberty." She doesn't say anything.

Words can't express how I feel—that my daughter thinks this place is her home and that Kelly and I take turns visiting her in her "house."

WEEK FIVE, DAY ONE

The morning was so much fun, and it was such a surprise to witness all the awe and wonder. . . . I would love to bottle up those feelings. The day then took a turn once my parents arrived and my father's nasty behavior cast a cloud over everything.

—Tuesday, December 25, 2001

A Christmas Surprise
Kelly, Morning

When I wake up, I'm surprised we've both slept until 7:30. We have both been extremely tired. Hannah can't wait to head over to see Olivia. There's a party in the recreation room, and she doesn't want to miss it. She dresses in one of the white-and-purple dresses my mother sent to the girls. She looks beautiful. We get our things together and head out.

Not surprisingly, the traffic is light at this time of day. The sky is gray, and the temperature seems colder. We park and enter the building, which is more subdued than yesterday. When we walk into Olivia's room, she is awake and in her pajamas but thrilled to see us. She loves Hannah's dress. She is so excited when I tell her she has a matching one to wear. Once she is dressed, the four of us head out of her room to go to the gathering.

As we step off the elevator, we hear laughing and giggling down the hall. We walk into the room, and everyone is sitting in a large circle. There are so many unfamiliar faces. Some patients have one parent present during daytime hours, but now there are two, along with siblings and grandparents. The mood is very festive and upbeat. I note the number of wheelchairs and walkers and wonder if others will be curious about why we are there. Olivia's injuries are mostly invisible to the untrained eye.

Some therapists are there, and they ask for our attention. The room gets extremely quiet. They explain that Santa has stopped by and left several presents. A universal "AHHH" is heard. The therapists get to work passing out gifts. Olivia opens her first gift, and her eyes light up. We are surprised to see there are presents for all the siblings as well. The gifts were selected to coincide with each child's interests. Hannah receives a Barbie, some books, and arts and crafts. Olivia gets a robot dog, some Dalmatian toys, books, Play-Doh, and coloring books. We later ask how they can purchase all these things. They tell us they make a list corresponding to the patients' needs and the likes of their siblings, and a donor provides everything. We are amazed.

Learning More about the Kids at Krieger
Mike, Morning

A restaurant in the Fells Point area of Baltimore conducts a pizza party each month for the kids. They stop by Kennedy Krieger with a carload of toys. Other companies have toy drives just for the Kennedy Krieger kids. With the money that Kennedy Krieger receives, they go out and buy gifts that they know the kids will want. One of the therapists remarks, "For Olivia it was easy to figure out what gifts she would enjoy."

Kelly and I take time to speak to some of the parents and learn about the kids there. Jonathan, a teenager, has a neurological disease. He was an active kid in many sports, but after a leg break, he has had several operations on his leg. Olivia loves him and vice versa. Scott is a big ten-year-old who was walking to school when a Mustang hit him. As Scott was trying to move away from the road, another car hit him, putting him in a wheelchair with nerve damage that causes him quite a bit of pain. Luke, who is about twenty years old, was hit by two trucks. The kid comes up to anyone and everyone, shakes his or her hand, and says hello. Once, he offered me a Chex bit from a bag he had. The nurse says he adores his dad, who is single, so he approaches every woman to see if she has a wedding ring. He even asks Kelly if he can see her hand!

A Heartwarming Gesture
Kelly, Afternoon

When we notice Olivia getting fatigued, we gather up our stuff, which is a lot, and head back to her room. Hannah is eager to open the gifts we brought for her. Olivia rests a bit while Hannah plays, and we head back downstairs for a lunch the hospital is holding for all the families. Again, we are so impressed. All the tables are adorned with white tablecloths, and the tables are set formally. There are beautiful centerpieces on all the tables. The food is good and plentiful. We've had a few problems during our time here, but witnessing how well they treat the patients and families is heartwarming. They don't leave out a single detail. December 25 in a children's hospital can be a sad event, but they have gone the extra mile to ensure it's a special day for everyone.

A few days prior, Lisa, a friend from college, called me after hearing what happened to us. We had lived in the same dorm and become close friends. She is one of the kindest people I know and has an incredible sense of humor.

At first, she asked us to celebrate Christmas with her and her family since they live close by, but I declined and told her I did not want to take Olivia out of the facility, even for a short time. She insisted on bringing dinner for us and my parents on Christmas Day. I reluctantly accepted. It is still hard for me to accept help from anyone. I mention it to my parents so they know dinner is handled.

Looking Normal but Knowing We're Not
Mike, Afternoon

We go downstairs for the holiday lunch. In a crowded ballroom, turkey, ham, potatoes, desserts, and more are being served buffet style to patients and their families, and the staff and their families. Each table has a gingerbread house (there are more for all the families). I see Jameeka, who is about five years old, sitting with her mother and a man. Jameeka always gives me a big hello or a hug. Now she is completely satisfied with her big plate. Her table is quiet, though. The man never looks up; his eyes never leave his plate as he devours the food. The mother takes a bite here and there, but she keeps looking around the room, not necessarily looking for someone or something. She just seems to want to be elsewhere.

Our kids are having a wonderful time and eat well. Everyone comments on how beautiful they look in their matching purple-and-white dresses.

I feel a bit awkward at the holiday lunch. The other patients have a wide variety of physical injuries and impairments. How normal must our family look, including Olivia? I question whether we belong here, even though I know how serious Olivia's condition is. The "problem" is that Olivia looks like a "normal" three-year-old.

A Sad Game of Chutes and Ladders

Kelly, Afternoon

We've already had a very eventful day, and both girls seem very tired. We head back upstairs, planning to put both girls down for a nap. Just as we're doing this, my parents arrive. They are carrying some gifts, but the girls are too tired to look. Mike stays with the girls while I go with my parents to get some coffee. The cafeteria is not as busy, which I take to be a good thing. Hopefully, some patients have been discharged so they can spend the holiday at home.

A few minutes after sitting down, I notice Mike walking toward us with Hannah and a board game. He mentions she couldn't fall asleep and quickly heads back to stay with Olivia. We play Chutes and Ladders, which Hannah received as a gift from my father. My mother observes while drinking her coffee. Hannah is a bit irritable and cries toward the end of the game when she realizes she isn't going to win. Suddenly, my father starts putting all the game pieces in the box and folds the board before we can finish. His temper is getting the best of him again. I suddenly feel sick to my stomach as memories of my own childhood rush back to me.

There were so many moments when my father got angry or didn't feel a child (me) was acting in the manner he thought was appropriate. He would become frustrated, and instead of trying to talk things through, he would make a negative statement and storm out of the room. I recall a time he threw away some of my Barbie doll clothes because I didn't put them away as I was instructed. Another time, both he and my mother punished me very sharply for sticking my tongue out at him when he told me to go home and I didn't want to. I was subjected to sitting in one chair for the entire day. I would watch my mother descend the stairs to do laundry and go back, each time glaring at me.

Like No Other

Mike, Evening

Now it's time for Christmas Day dinner. Nothing like heating up plate after plate in the small microwave in the parents' lounge, but that's what we do. Everyone squeezes into Olivia's room with a paper plate. I go back and forth, preparing plates of pasta, salad, and garlic bread.

Lenny is in one of his moods where he just glares a lot and doesn't say much. He won't touch his food. I think he feels this is no way to have a holiday meal, so he sort of takes it out on Kelly and me. It is a quiet dinner as no one really speaks. The tension is thick, as we expect Lenny to erupt at any time.

I never could figure him out. The most extreme example was when Olivia was born.

It was a difficult delivery, and Kelly was in the hospital for several days. My schedule was rather hectic, visiting with Kelly and the baby, stopping by the office, and heading home to take care of our "visitors." Ann and Lenny were staying with us to "help out" Kelly, but I wasn't sure what that meant. I came home early one evening with a plan to go home and make a quick pit stop before visiting Kelly. Well, Ann and Lenny were in our living room having coffee and tea when I opened the front door. They asked about dinner, so I managed a quick meal, and we talked a bit. Then I cleaned up the dishes and said that I was going to the hospital.

Lenny looked at me without saying anything for a bit and then said, "So, you are just going to leave us here?" I said that they could join me. He followed up, saying how dare I come home and just leave them like that. I said very calmly that since Kelly had a difficult time with the delivery and was still in the hospital, I wanted to go and visit her and said again that they could come with me.

The "Lenny glare" increased in intensity. Ann said nothing, which may have been wise at that moment. "Well, just 'f' off then!"

I was stunned. "Lenny, I don't know why you are so upset as I just want to see Kelly. After a busy day, I came home, made dinner, cleaned up, and now I want to spend some time with your daughter who . . . is . . . still . . . in . . . the . . . hospital." (I emphasized that last part!) "You and Ann are more than welcome to come with me, or you can stay here, and I'll be back in a bit."

Steam was coming out of his ears. "I just told you to 'f ' off. Are you going to just take that?"

Astonished, I could only ask, "What do you mean?"

Lenny exploded, "This is your house and I told you to 'f ' off. This is your house! What type of man are you to have someone in your house telling you to 'f' off? Are you just going to take that and leave?" Ann just bent her head and looked at her lap. I wasn't going to get any help from her.

"Yes," I said, my body shaking, battling the rage as I told myself, *These are Kelly's parents. Don't say anything that you could possibly regret or that might make her more upset later.*

"Yes," I said, again. "I am going to take that and visit your daughter and granddaughter in the hospital." I opened the front door and thought, *Okay, that is something I won't share with Kelly right now.*

Even with memories such as this, Christmas 2001 is like no other. I can't help wondering how the person who caused this crash is celebrating the holiday. Is he with family and friends, laughing and drinking away? Does he realize that his victims are miles away from their home, balancing paper plates on their knees in a hospital room? Too many issues are filling my mind, but I'm diverted a bit as Hannah and I get ready to head back home.

Nothing Like a Grumpy Christmas
Kelly, Evening

After Mike and Hannah leave, I witness my mother staring into space and see my father's scowl. My mother has asked the same questions all day long, and it doesn't stop after Mike and Hannah leave. She wants to know Olivia's prognosis, her discharge date, and how Hannah is doing. Each time she asks, I get more irritated than the last. I try my best to hide my irritation, but I am not sure how well I'm doing. I have been holding it together for everyone else over the past four weeks, and I'm exhausted.

They stay for a while longer, not sensing Olivia is exhausted and needs rest. Finally, my father indicates they should go and says he's hungry. I offer him some food once again, but he turns it down. They depart in a huff and say they will stop by tomorrow before driving back to Virginia. They are staying in a hotel near our home for one more night. I walk them to the elevator after getting Olivia ready for bed.

When I return to the room, Olivia is still awake. We read a few more books, but my fatigue is setting in. As I lie on my cot, the events of the day keep going through my mind. The morning was so much fun, and it was such a surprise to witness all the awe and wonder in a room filled with families and their children who are battling several different diagnoses. I would love to bottle up those feelings.

The day then took a turn once my parents arrived and my father's nasty behavior cast a cloud over everything. I feel so horrible for Hannah. He was so mean and horrid. He showered Olivia with a ton of attention but could not give Hannah a moment of praise or encouragement. He didn't understand or try to understand what she is going through. Why I am surprised by this, I don't know. I'm always hopeful things will be different, hoping my parents will be more empathetic, loving, accepting, and encouraging. Each time this doesn't happen, the disappointment feels worse than before.

I go to sleep before 11 p.m. and am amazed Olivia is still awake, chatting quietly to herself and her figurines.

WEEK FIVE, DAY TWO

I stop the stroller in the hallway, kneeling so we are at eye level, and explain that Daddy, Hannah, Olivia, and I all live together in a home. I go on to tell her we will be going there in two days—Friday—and will stay there from then on. She likes this and calms down a bit but still doesn't smile.

—Wednesday, December 26, 2001

Substitute Therapists Bring a New Set of Problems
Kelly, Morning

I wake up feeling a bit refreshed and happy we only have two more days before discharge. Woohoo! We are in the homestretch. I don't think Olivia comprehends we are going home. She is often asked where she lives, and she stares with a lost look. I do hope she remembers once we arrive, but she may not.

She is quite irritable this morning after having a restless night. I wonder if maybe we shouldn't have given her cake last night. Perhaps the sugar altered her sleep rhythm. It doesn't help that we have occupational therapy first thing this morning.

Olivia is not very cooperative with the substitute occupational therapist, who is covering for our usual therapist today. She brightens up once little bears are brought out to play with. Olivia has always loved animals and enjoys free play with them.

Next, we head to Patty. Olivia really shows her irritability by refusing to get out of her stroller. After many attempts, we finally get her out and seated at a table. Patty tries to do some testing for a discharge report showing the progress Olivia has made over the last two weeks and recommendations for the future. Olivia, again, is not very amenable, so we try alternating a testing section with free play. The only thing Olivia wants to do is play with the preschool school bus.

Once we finish the bulk of the testing, Patty remarks her scores are average in some areas and below average in others. I ask her how we should explain she will not be going back to preschool once we are home. I know she won't ask immediately but assume she will once winter break is over and Hannah returns to school. Patty does not have a suggestion. This surprises me since she is the "educational person," and I'd think this question would have arisen before with other patients. Her only piece of advice is that if Olivia asks, we should just say she isn't going today. I am skeptical of this but don't pursue it any further. She does encourage me to put pressure on the public-school system to move Olivia's special education eligibility meeting to an earlier date. I don't think that will be necessary since the coordinator explained the law gives them ninety business days to look over her files and conduct their own testing before the eligibility meeting.

Our next session is physical therapy with a substitute therapist, John. The session is a complete disaster. He tells her he wants to see her ride a tricycle, and the moment he shows her the helmet, she starts grabbing the sides of her head and screaming. My heart breaks! I'm not sure whether a repressed memory returns when she sees the helmet or she fears the helmet won't come off. He keeps trying to coerce her into cooperation, and after a while, I make the decision to end the session. We obviously are not going to move past this. What is the point?

I gather our things and help her into the stroller while she continues to sob. As we walk away, she says, "I want to go to Hannah's house!" I stop the stroller in the hallway, kneeling so we are at eye level, and explain that Daddy, Hannah, Olivia, and I all live together in the same house. I go on to tell her we will be going there in two days—Friday—and will stay there from then on. She likes this and calms down a bit but still doesn't smile.

Rushing to Prepare
Mike, Afternoon

The rush is on to finish Olivia's room! I drop Hannah at Mary's house and put two coats of paint on the walls and one coat on the baseboards. I feel driven to get this done, so I really appreciate Mary watching Hannah.

My day starts, and I'm completely focused. "Get it done, get it done," repeats in my head. There is so much I must get done that I can't be distracted by other influences, including what is happening with Olivia at this exact moment. Everything must go exactly as planned . . . except it doesn't.

Earlier this morning, I called the Toyota dealership to tell them that I would be there between 12 and 2 p.m. to pick up the new minivan that we were buying. At 12:20 p.m., the sales rep calls me to say that they sold the car I placed my deposit on! He says they will drive to Bowie, Maryland, to pick up another one of the same color and model. Upset by the news, I make a few calls to other dealers to find one that has the minivan I want. I end up going with another dealership and am glad to tell the Toyota dealership they no longer have my business.

A Good Session—Finally

Kelly, Afternoon

We approach the elevator, and I tell Olivia we will go back to the room and rest a bit. As we exit the elevator, we run into Jonathan's mom, who suggests we go by his room to say hello. I'm not sure if she sees the look of exhaustion and despair on my face or Olivia's, or if Jonathan needs some cheering up. He has been having a challenging time accepting his diagnosis, including the prospect of not being able to return to sports as he hoped. We walk down, and as soon as Olivia sees him, she smiles. The first one all day. Of course, it helps that he offers her a lollipop!

We visit with him and his roommate a bit before heading back to the room for lunch, which is waiting for us. Olivia eats a lot. I wonder if hunger has been the issue all morning. She doesn't know how to tell me she's hungry, or maybe she doesn't connect the feeling in her stomach to hunger.

Dr. Nina comes to check on Olivia and see how her Christmas Day went. I mention how irritable she has been all morning and tell her about our experience with Patty and physical therapy. She agrees we need to explain to Olivia she won't return to preschool until September because we will be busy doing other things. She believes Olivia was upset during physical therapy because it was a change in her routine and the substitute therapist didn't help. Dr. Nina also suggests when Olivia is irritable, we should give her choices and indicate she must choose one. She goes on to explain the irritability will continue for some time.

Dr. Nina stays for quite a while, playing with Olivia. I suspect she is attempting to test her in the process of playing without Olivia realizing what is happening. It is a great tactic to use, and I should remember it.

Soon after Dr. Nina exits the room, my parents come in. Olivia is happy to see them, and I am pleased she recognizes them. A good sign. She asks them to play puppies with her, and they agree. When I tell everyone it is time for physical therapy, she asks them to accompany us. I am amazed when they again agree. Luckily, Betty is ready when we arrive. Betty has her walk the stairs, and my dad follows to observe while my mom stays in the physical therapy room.

Finally! I am so glad we have a positive session under our belt. We proceed to Dr. Nina's office for more testing, and my parents opt to wait outside the office, which is a good decision.

WEEK FIVE, DAY THREE

Words can never adequately describe how much we appreciate his help. It is a special and rewarding time, one I know I'll never forget.
　—Thursday, December 27, 2001

The Gift of a Helping Hand
Mike, Afternoon

Have I really lost fifteen pounds? How strange to see the scale indicating that I now weigh 147! There are only two pairs of jeans that I have been wearing much. The other pants are cinched too much from the belts that I've had to wear.

I take Hannah to Kristin's house (seems that I'm doing that a lot).

Our former next-door neighbor, Steve Garnier, calls and asks what he can do to help us out. Everyone knows that Steve has a big heart. Never has this been demonstrated more than today. Many other kind people have asked the same question, but we never can think of anything specific (other than getting me a job!). So I thank

Steve, about to say there really isn't anything that he can do to assist us when one thought suddenly comes to mind.

Being that we just moved into a new house, Olivia never had the chance to spend much time in her new home, and her bedroom has not been decorated yet. I ask Steve if he will help me apply her wallpaper border in her room, which I just painted. We think it will be a great surprise for Olivia to come home to her newly decorated bedroom. Steve is so accommodating that he stops by after a party he and his wife, Sue, attended. Steve arrives at our house at about 10 p.m. and works with me until late into the night—well, early into the next morning. Not only is Steve meticulous in his work, but he also provides great company. Words can never adequately describe how much we appreciate his help. It is a special and rewarding time, and one I know I'll never forget.

We finish at about 12:30 a.m. Then I take care of some miscellaneous tasks in the house and go to bed at 2 a.m. During the day, I had the plumber come over to adjust the water temperature in the shower, and Leah from the attorney's office stopped by in the early evening to pick up some papers.

Although I should feel exhausted, lying in bed, I keep thinking that there are other things I should be doing. My mind is racing, but I manage to fall asleep.

Invisible
Kelly, Early Evening

Following our time with Dr. Nina, I decide Olivia needs a little relaxation. I tell my parents I'm going to take her to the recreation room. They accompany us. We sit down at the long table where the staff has placed Play-Doh, cookie cutters, and mini rolling pins for patients to do hand-strength play. My mother sits and keeps watching a little girl, Jameeka. She cannot take her eyes off her, though I try my hardest to keep her interested in Olivia. I get very uncomfortable watching this scenario. My mother turns to me and whispers, "Oh, look at that little girl. Don't you feel so sorry for her?" The anger boils over. My father, meanwhile, is walking all over the room, looking at toys, peering out at the Baltimore skyline, doing anything he can not to interact with us.

He comes back to the table and asks if we want to walk to the cafeteria and get some coffee. I agree. I'm afraid that if we stay any longer, I may blow up.

As we sit drinking coffee and Olivia has a little snack, my father keeps looking at his watch. He says, "Well, I think we need to head out and get some dinner before we drive to our next hotel in Virginia." I look at him expectantly. He doesn't offer to go get dinner for me, and once again, it is all about him. I realize at that moment it is better they leave. The less time I must spend with them, the better I will be overall.

I pack Olivia's stuff up, she gets in her stroller, and we walk back through the tunnel. As we arrive in the lobby, I bid them goodbye. We exchange very quick pleasantries, and Olivia and I head to the elevator. As I get in, I let out a long breath I didn't realize I've been holding in. I can finally breathe fully again.

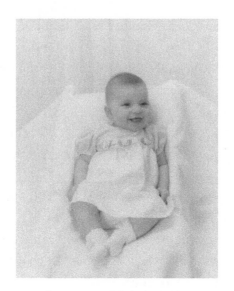

Presenting Olivia in 1998.

With sister Hannah in 2001, Olivia loved her Halloween costume of Belle,
one month before our lives changed.

Olivia enjoying preschool on November 27, 2001,
the morning of the crash.

"Was there anyone in the back seat?" asked the worried EMTs, since it
was completely compressed.

Another view of the vehicle.

Visiting airline pilots bring gifts and smiles to Olivia and the other kids.

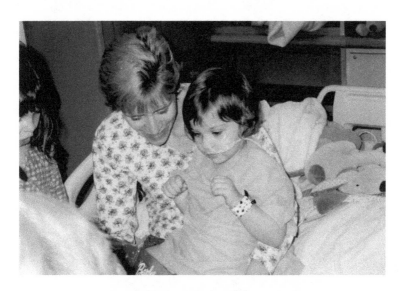

Olivia with Kelly.

Santa pays a visit with Olivia and Mike.

Dressed up for the holiday dinner with Hannah at Kennedy Krieger.

Homecoming as Hannah and Logan wait for Olivia.

Loving her 5th birthday.

Olivia in 2003.

Fairy tale dreams in 2005.

Hannah, Olivia, and Anya in 2008.

William, one of the guide dogs Olivia helped raise in 2011.

Olivia at 13.

In 2014, the sisters with Grandpa Sam and Grandma Estelle.

Brain Injury Awareness Day in 2017, before her speech at a congressional panel discussion.

High school graduate in 2017!

Olivia in *A Place to Be* production in 2018.

Kristin Campbell congratulating Anya and Olivia after a show.

Kelly and Anne McDonnell, Executive Director,
Brain Injury Association of Virginia.

The Langs. (Photo by Sharon Hallman)

Olivia, our Miracle Child. (Photo by Sharon Hallman)

We finally meet two of the EMTs, Daniel Neal (left) and Sean Scott (right) who saved Olivia's life almost 20 years ago. (Photo courtesy of the Loudoun Times-Mirror)

PART 3
A STRANGE PLACE IN OUR NEW LIFE

HOME, DAY ONE

We take the girls and head inside. Mike and I are cautious with Olivia on every step. Getting into our house requires two steps up to the front door and one step into the house. That part is easy.

—Friday, December 28, 2001

Olivia's Return!
Mike, Morning

I set the alarm for 4:45 a.m. Less than three hours of sleep, but there is so much to do! I vacuum the entire house, take out the garbage, clean up, and paint a *Welcome Home* sign for Olivia.

At 9:30 a.m., I leave for Kennedy Krieger. Traffic is awful on the Beltway, nothing new there. I get off in Bethesda, go through Bethesda and Silver Spring to get back on the Beltway, and make it to Kennedy Krieger at 11:30 a.m. To say that I am a bit impatient would certainly be an understatement.

As I walk into the room, I see Olivia is in a great mood. I think she finally realizes that she is coming home.

All the Preparations

Kelly, Morning

I wake up knowing today is departure day. Olivia and I both sleep until 7:50, and I'm surprised to see her breakfast sitting on the tray table. I wonder how I missed hearing the delivery. Usually, the cart containing all the meals noisily goes down the hallway, and I hear food service employees announcing their arrival. Today, I slept blissfully through it.

We have a very packed schedule today, which is surprising to me since we are scheduled to leave and finally go home. While eating breakfast, Olivia keeps asking when Daddy will be here to take us home. Is she excited or anxious? Only time will tell.

I wonder how she will react to our home. She had only spent three weeks there before the accident and hasn't been there since Tuesday, November 27 at 5:45 p.m. Will she remember it?

Mike has been busy setting up her room. One of the first things Mike and I decided to do when we moved was set up Hannah and Olivia's rooms. We painted and decorated Hannah's first and were about to move on to Olivia's when our life blew up. A few days before that fateful evening, Olivia mentioned she would like to switch rooms and take the larger one between Hannah's bedroom and ours. We had been surprised when she originally chose the smaller room but thought she preferred having two windows.

Now, with her coming home, we want her to return to her newly decorated bedroom. We've been planning it out and got most of the supplies over the past weeks.

Here at the hospital, most of our things are packed up and ready to go home with us. The room looks so bare since I took down all the pictures and cards decorating the beige, cinder block walls. All the balloons are tied together, and the stuffed animals are bursting out of bags. I've left out a few books and other small toys to keep Olivia amused during any downtime we have today. She seems unfazed by all of it.

Tipping the Tower of Frustration
Mike, Morning

We find out that Olivia is not having an MRI scan, even though she was supposed to have one yesterday. There was some confusion regarding whether she should be sedated and, if she could, whether it would be by an IV. The doctors decided no sedation was necessary. The MRI never happened because Olivia would not lie down on the table. Anyway, one of the doctors explains that she is doing so well that it isn't necessary.

Kelly and I hit the roof. I request a meeting with the guest relations director and go over all my complaints, from the poor scheduling of therapy sessions to the changing of Olivia's schedules without notice, to the nursing problems, and just poor overall communications. Kelly and I thought and were told before that having an MRI at this stage would be helpful in establishing another metric about Olivia's injury and seeing some type of improvement from before. A formal complaint will be issued, but there is not much we can do on this last day.

A Day Filled with Appointments
Kelly

Our first appointment is physical therapy with Betty, which is one of Olivia's favorites and always a good way to start our day. She immediately gravitates to the pull dog and brings him over to the play kitchen while she pretends to make something with the play food. She prepares us tea and carries it over to where we're sitting.

Olivia has always loved to play dolls, house, or role-play with the hundreds of figurines we have at home. This simple action gives me the sense that things are starting to return to our "before" activities.

We have a short break before the next session, so we head to the therapeutic recreation room and play for a short bit before she is distracted by the movie playing for some other patients. Disney's *Bambi* has just begun. I'm not sure I want her to see what happens. To be truthful, I have never seen the movie, so I'm not sure how subtle the killing of the mother is or whether Olivia will comprehend it. Luckily, she doesn't recognize what's happening and leaves with a smile on her face. These breaks between her sessions always help to ease the transitions.

We enter the speech therapy office, and Rachel is still out, so we work with Janine in her absence. They play a game of Go Fish, and I am surprised at how well Olivia does. During the game, she works on various skills but mostly memory and hand-eye coordination. Both have proven to be deficits. Once again, she really amazes me.

She has been carrying her four Dalmatian puppies with her for the past few days. They have gone everywhere with us. Mike brought them a few days ago, and she was so excited. The set includes Pongo, Perdy, and two puppies. The four figurines fit perfectly in her hand so she can clutch them close to her when she needs some comfort. Some kids use a stuffed animal or blanket, but she has chosen the puppies as her security. For those not familiar with Disney's *101 Dalmatians*, two Dalmatians meet and fall in love, and their owners also fall in love. The dogs, Pongo and Perdy, have a litter of puppies.

Olivia insists they sit on the table and watch the game with her. This either helps her confidence during the game or gives her a sense of security. Janine uses the puppies to her advantage. She tells Olivia they will be reading a book together, and afterward, they will have time to play with the puppies. Janine asks Olivia to tell her certain colors in the book, but Olivia is either having trouble or doesn't want to cooperate. Sometimes it's hard to tell the difference. Once we're done with the book, Janine tells Olivia the session is over, and it's time for her to work with her next patient. As expected, Olivia falls apart at this news, having been promised she would have time to play with her treasured puppies. She is inconsolable, and I am left to pick up the broken pieces.

It takes me quite a while to calm her down so we can leave and move on to our next appointment. I finally get her back into the stroller as she sobs and sobs. While walking down the hallway, I stop several times to try and console her. My heart breaks for her. She is only three years old, and her life consists of one medical appointment after another. This is not the life we envisioned for her. We should be home playing with Hannah or friends and doing the things we enjoy. We aren't supposed to be going to specialist after specialist, making her do "work" and, when it takes longer than necessary, removing the reward from her grasp.

Dr. Nina meets us in the hallway as we approach her office. I'm not sure whether she heard us coming or she was looking for us. I don't expect this session to go very well given what just happened. Olivia's mood is deteriorating quickly.

Dr. Nina tells us she wants to try to complete Olivia's final evaluation prior to discharge. She has attempted it numerous times over the past few days, but each time, Olivia has answered a few things, if we were lucky, and then refused to cooperate. I'm not sure whether she doesn't like Dr. Nina, she is tired after all the testing, or if she's bored or frustrated. Of course, it could be a mixture of all these things.

The session goes better than I expect but not well enough to get all the "required" testing complete. The session is scheduled for one hour, but Olivia is only able to complete thirty minutes before erupting into a temper tantrum and refusing to cooperate. We decide not to push it, so I tell Olivia I have to step outside in the hallway and speak to Dr. Nina.

Walking out of the room, so many questions fill my head: What happens next? What is her recovery trajectory? I need answers.

I ask her what this means for her final report, as well as how to proceed into the next phase of recovery. Dr. Nina states we will need to return in six months for a reevaluation. She hopes Olivia will be more cooperative at that time with the extra time to recover. She feels we aren't going to progress at this point. Olivia has decided not to cooperate, and without that, we won't be able to successfully evaluate her cognitive deficits.

She wishes us luck and proceeds down the hallway. I stand there a few minutes, trying to collect my thoughts and reduce my thumping heart rate. What is going to happen once we arrive home? How are we going to handle all of this? I think about my hopes of having another child and realize how unrealistic it is to bring a new life into our family. We have a lot on our plate right now. Mike doesn't have a job; we don't know how we are going to pay our bills; Olivia is going to need a lot of therapies and other unknown interventions; and we have to help Hannah with her thoughts and feelings as well. There isn't enough time or energy for anything else. The plan to have another baby is off. It's a conversation I need to have with Mike later today.

Olivia and I return to her room for some needed rest. A few minutes after I get her settled, a nurse enters the room and hands me the discharge paperwork. As I look over the few pieces of paper, I notice Olivia's follow-up appointment is scheduled for January 31 at 8:30 a.m. I ask her to schedule us for a later time since we are coming from Northern Virginia.

She checks with the doctor on duty, and he indicates that if I want to change it, I need to call his office. I also ask to speak with him prior to leaving since the papers don't include much information and I have some questions. She assures me that she relayed the information as she looks at me with a scowl.

Mike arrives a little while later, looking exasperated. I see it as soon as he enters the room, and I notice the tired look in his eyes. As I suspected, he has been busting himself to get things done before we come home. He relays his frustrating experience getting our new minivan and his guilt for reaching out to Kristin to watch Hannah so he could pick up the car and come up to Baltimore to get us. Of course, Kristin reiterated she was more than happy to help. I feel terrible as well, knowing she is planning Camryn's baptism, just two days away. One of the things I admire most about her is her ability to handle multiple demands so competently and never let anyone see her frustrations, though I know she must have them.

Olivia is ecstatic as soon as she sees Mike walk in. She keeps asking when we will go home, and we keep trying to reassure her. Mike relays that he spoke with our insurance agent, who will be coming to our home on the thirty-first to sign paperwork to change our car insurance policy as well as other documents. About a year ago, we decided to change our auto insurance to save a bit of money on premiums. We should have realized that lowering our premium also meant we would be reducing our coverage liability. With all that has happened, we want to make sure our coverage is the best it can be, given the new circumstances. It won't help us with the current accident or the lack of coverage, but we want to ensure we have the best available safety net in case something like this happens again.

We wait a bit for the doctor to come, then Mike goes into the hallway to track him down. We ask a bunch of questions regarding the follow-up visit, which we were originally told would occur in three months, not the one month indicated on the paperwork I received. He denies saying the follow-up would be in three months. We then question why her MRI was not completed the day before, and he informs us it isn't medically necessary, denying saying the opposite at our last family meeting.

When I proceed to question why Olivia was not given IV sedation prior to the MRI, he responds very belligerently that the technicians were wrong and should have realized a three-year-old cannot lie still during an MRI and refuses to discuss it further. He also indicates that he was opposed to the MRI and that Dr. King had ordered it while he was out. He tells us that if we have any questions, we should direct them elsewhere. I don't understand why we cannot get an MRI to determine the extent of the damage. This is medical facility number two that has refused this test. Is it the money?

Mike asks the nurse to page Dr. King and tell him we are hoping to speak with him prior to leaving. During the intervening time, Dr. Nina comes to our room and proceeds to continue testing to get as much information as possible for her final report. Surprisingly, Olivia does well. I don't know whether the bit of downtime helped, Mike's presence soothed her and confirmed she was really going home, or a combination of both.

As Olivia answers questions, I'm not sure whether she is making up her answers to be done or understands what is being asked. I figure Dr. Nina can determine this, and I will learn the answer eventually.

After Dr. Nina is done, I ask her if it is unusual that Olivia hasn't asked why she is in the hospital or questioned what happened. I have wondered about this since we arrived. Why hasn't she asked why she's here and why she has to do all this work? Dr. Nina tells us it isn't unusual for a three-year-old to not question the hospitalization. She notes they most often ask for their parents if no one is present, then commends us for ensuring one of us has always been present.

We also ask her what she understands about the follow-up appointment, and she confirms one of the doctors suggested a three-month follow-up following discharge. This information helps Mike and I confirm the details we previously received. Given all we have been through in the past two months, we know it's possible we have confused all the details. It's nice to know we haven't misinterpreted this piece of information.

Someone Willing to Listen
Kelly, Afternoon

Dr. King arrives a little after 1 p.m., and we discuss our concerns. He listens empathetically as we speak. He indicates that the file was reviewed by another doctor who didn't think the MRI was necessary because Olivia's recovery progressed so quickly. He admits he feels differently. Though he agrees he doesn't think it is critical, it will provide information we most likely need. If we feel strongly about having the test done, we can schedule one, but given the previous day's experience, an IV sedation will be necessary. The only way to make sure she gets the tests completed is to have Olivia stay longer. Of course, we aren't going to go that route, so we indicate how disappointed we are with all the misinformation we've received during this experience. He is very professional and never blames anyone or denies previous statements. Instead, he comments they will strive to do better in the future.

Dr. King continues to listen to our concerns and answers our questions about what to expect in the future. We ask if there are specialists we need to schedule before our next follow-up with Kennedy Krieger. His manner is the exact opposite of another respected doctor. We greatly appreciate him and thank him for all the time he has spent with us. As soon as he leaves, Olivia asks when we will get to go home.

Coming Down on the Drive Home
Kelly, Late Afternoon

One of the nurses comes to the room soon after Mike leaves to pull our new van up to the front door. The nursing staff helps carry some of our things, and we start our walk down the hallway to the elevators. My emotions are more overwhelming than I imagined they would be. We are finally going home. We can finally resume our life as a family of four with our two pets. On the flip side, if there is a medical emergency or other issue that crops up, there won't be anyone around to assist us.

The nurses and technicians come to say goodbye, and Jonathan is waiting to wish us farewell as well. It is such an emotional scene.

A kind and sensitive teenager giving the three-year-old a beaming smile and high-five. As the elevator opens on the lobby level, Olivia immediately asks where Daddy is. I explain he went to get the car, and once he pulls up, we will put everything, including her, in the car and go home. She keeps looking around, hoping to see him. I explain that we no longer have a burgundy van, and our new car is blue. This information doesn't faze her, and she never asks why, so I assume she doesn't remember the other car.

Finally, a blue van pulls up and Mike gets out. Once we get everything into the car and strap Olivia into her car seat, I sense he is waiting for me to ooh and aah over the new car. I can't ooh and aah. Our other van was nicer. This one is very basic and doesn't have the bells and whistles the other one had.

Everything begins to hit me now that we are finally on our way home. Immediately, my mood starts to go down. I think about all we have been through over the past two months and all we are now forced to give up as a result. My disappointment with the car probably is more about the events of the past four weeks. We lost so much, and the losses keep mounting. Having Olivia in the car also makes me more anxious. What if we are involved in another accident? How difficult would it be for us to get her back to where she is now?

We are surprised when we suddenly hear her trying to sing along to the Disney CD playing in the car. We didn't think she would remember any of these songs, especially not the words. We both look at each other in disbelief. About twenty minutes into the drive, I notice she is very quiet and turn to see her clutching her baby blanket and sleeping soundly. I can't blame her, given the whirlwind of a day we've experienced.

I finally break the silence and tell Mike how I feel about us trying to have another baby. I wasn't sure how the conversation would go, but apparently, he has given it a lot of thought as well. He agrees with my assessment, and that ends our talk. I'm not sure whether this is why I'm feeling down or whether it's a combination of things. We drive in silence for most of the ride.

Celebrating Home
Mike, Evening

When we arrive home, Kristin is outside, along with her four kids and Hannah, who is bouncing around excitedly. Olivia is happy to see Hannah. The kids made a welcome-home banner for Olivia, in addition to the one I made, and placed it across our front door. It is a wonderful way to arrive home. Kelly and I know Kristin must leave quickly so she can finish getting ready for Camryn's baptism. We also want to take time to regroup as a family. We thank her for everything once again. I know that Kelly in particular feels that there is no way to possibly thank someone who has done so much for us, not just over the past month but throughout the time we've known her.

When Olivia sees our home, she is excited to be outside with the kids, but she is a little maxed out!

We take the girls and head inside. Kelly and I are cautious with Olivia on every step. Getting into our house requires two steps up to the front door and one step into the house. That part is easy. Unfortunately, we don't have a handrail on these steps, but Olivia is still small enough that we can pick her up when needed.

Hannah immediately orchestrates a play session with Olivia and me. Olivia is bound to tire much quicker, and Hannah may not pick up on the signs or may be expecting the same Olivia. We eat the dinner Kristin made and enjoy being back together in our family home.

A bit later, as Olivia calms down, we make a big production of showing Olivia her new room. She is a little confused when she opens the door, as it used to be the guest room. She likes it at first. A while later, she says she's scared, but by the time we have our typical bedtime routine, she is fine. We brush the girls' teeth and then go to Olivia's room for stories. She lies down to go to sleep. We leave the room quietly. She must be exhausted because the room is quiet soon afterward.

Kelly and I head downstairs and just sit in the kitchen. We don't say much, afraid of not hearing Olivia if she calls for us.

It is a quiet evening. Tonight, silence is truly golden. Kelly and I have so much to talk about, but we are both so tired, and it's hard to express how thankful we are that all four of us are finally under the same roof.

HOME, DAY TWO

How will we get back to our "normal"? Will there ever be a normal?
　—Saturday, December 29, 2001

Old Routines and New Ones
Kelly, Morning

I awake in the morning, surprised that I slept as well as I did but feeling so very groggy and confused. I slowly get out of bed, and I'm not surprised to see Mike and Hannah downstairs already. Both have always been early risers. Hannah went through a stage where she would wake up at 5:30 in the morning. Of course, she has never been the type of kid to snuggle in bed before starting the day. She must have her breakfast immediately. This doesn't always work for me, but I go along with it for her sake.

Olivia, like me, is not a great morning person. It takes her a bit before she is ready to eat anything. Hannah always greets her enthusiastically and entertains Olivia while I take a shower or clean up. I enjoy seeing them play together.

I make my way downstairs and greet our dog, Gallagher, and cat, Liberty, and find Hannah and Mike playing in the family room. I have a strong cup of black coffee, which starts the juices running through my body. I'm happy to see the paper waiting for me on the kitchen table. I really missed this routine. I usually have my morning coffee and read some of the paper each morning. I never finish the entire paper, but at least I get a piece of the news.

As I sit reading, I struggle to comprehend anything I'm reading. I must be either very tired or distracted by all the activity surrounding me this morning.

Suddenly, we hear Olivia exclaim, "I am awake!" and we proceed upstairs to assist her on the stairs. This is one of the things that concerns us about living in a multilevel home with a child who now has severe balance and gait issues. We know the diligence on our part will increase immensely.

The in-home physical therapist left a message for us yesterday. I need to return the call and set up Olivia's appointments. The doctors at both Fairfax Hospital and Kennedy Krieger stressed the advantage of having a brain injury as a child, early in life. They explained our brains are very repairable, especially a child's brain. The neural pathways can be rerouted very quickly, which makes recovery easier. The doctors have also stressed that the first two years post-accident are the most imperative. I have taken their words very seriously and thus want to start her therapies as quickly as possible.

Once Olivia comes down, she plays with Hannah for ten minutes before starting to cry out of frustration, so Mike and I intervene and suggest she may need breakfast now. Hannah looks defeated but quickly recovers. This back-and-forth keeps up all day. When Olivia isn't getting frustrated or angry, both are vying for either my attention or Mike's. It is difficult. How will we get back to our "normal"? Will there ever be a normal? The realities of our new life with traumatic brain injury feel strained and uncertain. Nothing like we imagined.

HOME, DAY THREE

Everyone marvels at how well Olivia looks, not having any scars or obvious delays. I've styled her hair so the patch missing on the left side is not as noticeable. . . . I am quite exhausted by the time we leave, having to shuttle between caring for my parents who are not very social and checking on Olivia.
    —Sunday, December 30, 2001

A Special Day
Kelly, Morning/Afternoon

We wake up to our new routine this morning. Hannah is excited, as usual, but especially because we are attending Camryn Campbell's baptism. Camryn is the newborn who sat with her mom in the waiting room on the night of our accident, waiting for news about Olivia and me. The Campbells have a large family and are planning a celebration at their home following the ceremony. Kristin insisted my parents come since they are still visiting from Arizona.

We get the girls dressed and ready to go, then head out to the hotel to meet up with my parents. My father has always been very good about navigating his way in a new area, but he feels more comfortable if we lead him to the church and afterward Kristin's home.

When we arrive, we find my mother sitting in the hotel lobby in a chair all by herself. Apparently, my father went upstairs to get something, and she stayed. When I walk in, I see confusion—or is it fatigue?—in her eyes. She brightens up when she sees us and, of course, comments on the girls' outfits. She has always been about the clothes and appearances.

The ceremony is beautiful. Kristin and David have a close friend from college, a priest, conduct the ceremony. It is very personal and includes some nice antidotes. I wasn't sure how Olivia would do during the ceremony, but she handles it very well. She sits still and is quiet, which has always been her nature. I am thankful that has remained after all this.

Afterward, we head to their house, and I get my mother situated in the kitchen. My parents do not move from their spots. I continually check up on them throughout the party. I chat with a lot of Kristin and David's family, who all know what happened and are so gracious and very happy to see Olivia at the celebration. Mike and I try to keep a close eye on her while also allowing her some space to play. She clings to us, not sure what to do. She is still picky about what she eats, and many of her previous favorite foods no longer elicit the same effect. I make note of that in the back of my mind.

Overall, our first large social event is quite successful. Everyone marvels at how well Olivia looks, not having any scars or obvious delays. I've styled her hair so the patch missing on the left side is not as noticeable. Her hair grows quickly, so I know it will be back to its previous state in no time at all. I am quite exhausted by the time we leave, having to shuttle between caring for my parents who are not very social and checking on Olivia. I am most embarrassed by my parents' behavior but don't have any recourse. We lead them back to their hotel and head home. Everyone is exhausted.

HOME, DAY FOUR

What a year this has been. My first thought is *We made it!* It can only get better at this point, I hope.

—Monday, December 31, 2001

Looking Back

Kelly, Morning

It's finally New Year's Eve 2001. What a year this has been. My first thought is, *We made it!* It can only get better at this point, I hope. Thinking back, I'm not sure how we're still alive and sane.

We dealt with a miscarriage in August. How horrific that was, but nothing compared to the accident to come. Next, Olivia was diagnosed with strabismus, a misalignment of the eyes, which was upsetting to me but, again, not as bad. The same day she was diagnosed, Mike was laid off from his job. A job he really enjoyed. The news came as a total surprise. He had been laid off in the past, but he was usually prepared for the worst—not this time. Once we got over the initial shock and confusion, the car accident happened, and Olivia suffered a severe traumatic brain injury. This was the worst in a series of events.

I keep thinking how bad each event has been, but when compared to the events of November 27, 2001, they all seem so trivial. We are hopeful the coming year will prove much better. Mike is still earnestly looking for a job. I plan to contact the store where I was hired to work prior to the accident. My hope is to determine whether I can get some hours now that we are home and trying to figure out how to get some extra money. We still haven't figured out our schedule; Olivia's therapies will take adjustment as well.

Therapy and New Year's Eve
Mike, Midmorning/Evening

The physical therapist has come by. She tells us we can have the in-home therapy, which is a great relief since our insurance will cover it. She will come by on Mondays, Wednesdays, and Fridays. She says that Olivia is still weak in some areas, but overall, she looks good. We're also told that if Olivia catches the flu, it could be quite dangerous for her since her system is weak. So, *if* we are thinking of preschool this year, she recommends that we wait until flu season is over in March. If we wait until then, we might as well skip the semester since she will only have two months left and we will need to reserve her spot and pay for the whole semester.

Hannah and I go food shopping and take care of a couple of errands. At 1 p.m., we have a meeting at our house with the State Farm agent. We want to drop the other company after all the problems we've had.

We decide to stay home for New Year's Eve. I don't feel comfortable on the road with the other partygoers, especially this year. I think it is the right decision since Olivia seems very irritable. We think she overextended herself yesterday and needs to rest.

Anyway, we set the clocks several hours early to celebrate the New Year. I think that they're having a good time, especially Hannah. She chooses to watch *The Swan Princess* with us, and I prepare a few snacks before our New Year's toast. When I ask everyone what they want 2002 to be like, Olivia says, "I WANT TO PLAY WITH MY PUPPIES!" enthusiastically. We all laugh.

Thinking Back, Hoping Forward
Kelly, Evening

A few years prior, Mike had a brilliant idea. Now on New Year's we always set the clocks ahead so Hannah and Olivia will think it's midnight around 8 p.m. They have a fun time celebrating, and we put them to bed so we can have a quiet celebration on our own.

Tonight, we know Olivia will fall asleep before, so we plan to put her to bed at her normal time. Once she is asleep, we play games and watch a movie with Hannah. She is so disappointed when she falls asleep after eleven but before the magical hour of midnight. We carry her upstairs and wish her a happy New Year, hoping 2002 will bring all of us some needed happiness, tranquility, and stability.

Mike and I clean up as best we can. We head upstairs exhausted but hopeful. It has been a whirlwind these past six months. We need real joy. If I can be honest, I feel our family deserves happiness. We have struggled so much and yet we have managed to grow stronger through this arduous year. I can only imagine how joy will glue our bond even more.

JANUARY 2002

Kelly

January is usually a time of renewal amid the cold and dreary weather. This year we are hoping for more happiness and healing. Hannah is excited to return to school, and she needs some stability and structure. Her days at school are short, but she loves it.

Our home physical therapy is set to begin, and the therapist will be visiting us at home three times a week until Olivia is able to safely support herself and regain her walking skills. Our most pressing need is to have her safe on the stairs. Living in a three-level home will be challenging until she navigates them safely.

Another priority is Mike's job search. Now that the holidays are over, most companies begin filling vacancies at a steady pace. With his type A personality, Mike jumps into the task quickly.

The physical therapist comes the first day Hannah goes back to school, so it allows me to be fully present while she works with Olivia, trying to build her strength and stamina. The therapist is surprised to see how well Olivia is doing on her first visit. She asks to observe Olivia in play, as it becomes apparent she is not going to follow directions. We go to the basement where a lot of toys are set up, allowing Olivia free space. The therapist feels it's better to watch how Olivia navigates her surroundings in a less stressful environment. The tactic is successful. As we talk, she shares that the reports received from Kennedy Krieger gave a much different impression of Olivia's progress.

She gives us a bit of information that was not originally shared with us. Since Olivia is receiving home therapy, she can only leave home for doctors' appointments; otherwise, the therapy will be discontinued. This is a severe blow. How am I going to get Hannah to her activities, run errands, and allow my children to "be kids"? This is going to be a challenge.

We were instructed at discharge that she would also need occupational and speech therapy. Those were not set up prior to discharge, and the task has been left to us. I start making calls, trying to arrange those services, but am quickly discouraged. There are not many pediatric therapists in the area. I find a few who work with adults but are not versed in the intricacies of the pediatric population. We are placed on many waitlists and told not to expect a call for at least four months at the earliest. This is the most difficult information to grasp. According to the doctors, Olivia needs as much therapy as possible the first two years post-injury to heal. Progress after the two-year anniversary will be minimal. A few practices refer me to others, but they are all located a good distance from our home. Coordinating between Hannah's schedule and driving time is overwhelming. I feel boulders keep blocking our way forward.

Mike

What will 2002 bring? On one hand, I don't see how it could be a worse year than last year. On the other hand, I'm not sure what to look forward to. No job, no income coming in, expenses mounting, an abundance of work we need to do for Olivia, needing to make Hannah feel part of a united family and home, and more. I don't think we need to add the pressure of any New Year's resolutions this year.

I am thankful to have in-home therapy for Olivia. This is huge, so Olivia truly feels this is her home; having that one-on-one attention helps, too. I'm trying to have the therapists work with Olivia without my looking over their shoulders. Olivia certainly doesn't need me as a distraction. She needs to focus totally on the therapist.

Kelly and I decide that we need to figure out how to make things work financially, so we both are looking at the job market. Kelly will try for a part-time job while I focus on a full-time position. Neither one of us are looking forward to spending the time away from home and our kids, but since there is no alternative, we try not to dwell on it.

I also have to keep in mind that I still have a wife and another daughter to support. The harsh reality is that whatever happens with Olivia, I am faced with the responsibility of providing for my family, in addition to the medical bills.

So as for my job search, I am not sure what to look for. Here is what I want: a steady paycheck. Oh yes, great healthcare coverage, no travel, a job close to home, a job with flexible hours, and one that will allow me to be home early in the evening. Aside from that, the type of job isn't nearly as important.

I devour the want ads in the *Washington Post* and try to connect with as many people as I know to see about any open positions. It's difficult to search for a full-time job while feeling that I need to check on and be with Olivia at the same time.

Kelly

I haven't held a job since Hannah was born five years ago, and it proves a bit more daunting than I anticipated. My first day consists of training. I walk to the back of the store and meet with the store manager. I watch a series of videos explaining policies and procedures. My mind keeps wandering, thinking about what the girls are doing, how Mike is holding up, will he get a job that provides good medical benefits because it is vital, especially now. Each time I notice my wandering mind, I am brought back to the here and now. I am suddenly fatigued just sitting here. Having worked in human resources, I know this is not the ideal way to train, but that is no longer my concern.

Following the training videos, I am assigned to the bath and housewares department and spend most of my shift folding towels, unpacking inventory, or helping on the registers when the customer lines are long. Though it's nice getting out and talking with other adults, a large part of me does not enjoy it. I cannot help feeling I am missing out on something at home.

Folding towels is monotonous and allows me more time to think than I need. The feeling of loneliness hangs over me wherever I go. I keep thinking, *When will it all be normal again?* Unpacking inventory consists of going to the back storeroom and getting boxes from the conveyor belt. It is cold and the lighting is poor. I unload boxes and boxes of towels, comforters, blankets, etc., put them in a bin, and transfer them to the appropriate place on the floor. One thing I learn is the towel section can be messier than the women's shoe department. Customers pull out towels, feel them, and shove them back. The folding never ends. I come home exhausted and try not to complain, as we need the extra money to help cover our COBRA insurance payments, mortgage, and other obligations.

Mike

It is great that Kelly landed a part-time job at a local retail store. We try to balance the family life as much as possible, but it means Kelly works mostly on weeknights and weekends. Although it isn't nearly the same as the last couple of months, once again, our family is divided.

The girls are a handful. Hannah needs her own time, but so does Olivia. Of course, they also want to play with each other. Sometimes those moods do not sync with each other or with the time I need for my job search. So, when Kelly is running errands or taking time with phone calls, making and updating appointments, I find myself alternating between playing with Barbies, other dolls, toy figurines, and more to balance the playing needs with the girls individually and together.

On a mild day for mid-January, I take the girls to a local playground to let them burn off some energy. Olivia and I are spectators as Hannah bounces from the swings to the slides to the climbing walls. Olivia laughs at me tossing some leaves at Hannah while she goes back and forth on the swings. I pick Olivia up and hold her while she glides down the yellow slide a few feet from the bottom. I get a workout, picking her up and moving her feet up the climbing wall a bit. We have an enjoyable time, and I suppose Olivia doesn't feel that she is being held back from participating more in the playground.

There are tears and times of frustration, but also, thankfully, some quiet and pleasant times with each other that we truly cherish.

Kelly

After only two full weeks of physical therapy, we are informed Olivia no longer qualifies for in-home care. The therapist tells us Olivia has achieved the goal, ambulating safely in the home. We need to watch her on the stairs, but home care cannot be justified. I meet this news with both trepidation and happiness. Yes, I am glad Olivia can safely navigate our home, but what are we going to do now? In addition to reaching out to occupational and speech therapists, I am also looking into physical therapy. It is a daunting task.

I feel myself sliding down a slippery slope. Something heavy is pushing me down. So much to do, and yet I'm not sure where to begin. We need resources, but I don't know where to get these.

While we were still at Kennedy Krieger, Mike obtained an attorney to represent us in our case against the driver who caused so much damage. We learned due to state law he would not be able to represent me. He could only "work" for the girls. He made a few referrals, and I have an appointment on my birthday. This is not going to be a celebratory year anyway, so I took the appointment.

I come downstairs after showering, and Mike has the unfortunate job of telling me the attorney's office called and canceled the appointment. They are not interested in representing me. Another disappointment. Luckily, I have two other prospects.

Finally, I receive a call from a speech therapy center that has an opening for a consultation.

Finally, we can start the healing.

Mike

Finally, a celebration—of sorts: Kelly's birthday. When a couple starts a family, birthdays no longer belong to the adults. Kids own them, as kids love to see the expression on their parents' faces as the adults overexaggerate their excitement at the homemade cards.

Charles Fleet, a great friend of mine, arranges for me to interview with his brother, Phillip Fleet, who works in the customer service arena of a technology giant headquartered in our area.

Charles and I first met back when I joined as a volunteer at the Downtown Jaycees more than ten years ago. In fact, I asked him to introduce me to a pretty volunteer I spotted from the other side of the room at the Midtown Youth Academy in Washington, DC. The Midtown Youth Academy was a safe place in a rough part of the city where kids could come to play, read, and just talk and be around volunteers like the Jaycees. Anyway, on that day in March, which happened to be my birthday, Charles introduced me to Kelly. That introduction was the best birthday gift I would ever have. It must have been fate, as I found out later that Charles and Kelly share the same birthdate in January! So, Charles helps once again with connecting me to his brother Phillip.

Although Phillip prefaces in the meeting that there are no openings in his division, I think it will be good for me to begin the interview process, hone my interview skills, and see what doors could open for me with this meeting.

I think I interview well and arrive prepared. I am not nervous since there is no pressure on me. I dress professionally, although my clothes hang on me a bit as I am still under my normal weight, and I bring my briefcase full of work samples, letters of reference, and extra copies of my resume. Phillip greets me warmly and expresses his regrets over what happened to my family. He asks me what type of work I am looking for, questions me about my background, asks what skills I bring to a future employer, and more. I am comfortable with our meeting and believe I answer his questions fully and with confidence. I thank Phillip for his time, and as I leave the office, I feel that it has been a good start in my interview process.

Later at home, I tell Kelly how things went. As I recap the meeting, I put myself in Phillip's position and it strikes me what an awful interview that must have been. What now stands out in my mind is that when Phillip asked me about samples of my work experience, I pulled out of my briefcase various papers, some in plastic protective sleeves, thin binders, and loose hard copies. Looking at this mess from his point of view, I realize he probably thought that I was not the most organized worker around!

Then I think about my interview style and how relatively passive it seemed. I think back to when Phillip asked me about my project management experience. My simple response was that I enjoyed seeing a project from its inception to completion or a final deliverable. That was the best response I could provide. I didn't mention anything about collaboration with others, staying within budget, steps of execution, performance monitoring, or anything more. I can only wonder what he thought of the interview, but knowing the circumstances, I am sure he would downplay the meeting and my lack of preparedness. Now, however, I am embarrassed about how I presented myself.

Kelly

Now that Olivia is no longer confined to our home due to therapy, I make plans to meet Kristin and her kids at a local mall. There is an inside play area the kids always enjoy, with space to run and objects to climb. I feel it will be good for both girls to get a change of scenery and see some friends. As we wait for them to arrive, I watch the girls play. Olivia has a challenging time keeping up with Hannah. This is not a surprise, but watching her thoughts process and some of her movements, I am startled. Will she always be "different" now? Others will not know her story or the "why." Is she destined for kids to make fun of her and torment her? We will have to be vigilant to make sure she is protected not only physically but emotionally. These thoughts swirl in my head.

Luckily, Kristin and her kids show up, and I am taken out of my own head. Everyone is genuinely happy to see each other, and we marvel at how much they have all grown. Her baby is now four months old and resembles all her siblings, and yet she is unique.

Olivia tires very quickly during the playtime, and we give the children snacks before going to our respective homes for nap times before dinner. It has been a great reprieve, and I note how important these will be in our future.

As we drive home, Olivia comments, "There's my preschool. When am I going back?"

Girding myself, I respond, "I don't know. Daddy and I can talk about this later if you want to try and return."

Her response is "Yes."

FEBRUARY 2002

Kelly

After Olivia's comment about going back to preschool, Mike and I speak about the feasibility of her returning. We are excited she remembers but not sure how she will navigate all the sensory issues. I'm also adding speech therapy into the schedule.

While Olivia was in the hospital, Mike contacted the preschool and informed them Olivia would not return. At the time, we did not see any chance of her returning. I decide to pursue whether this is now a possibility. I speak to the preschool director, and she is delighted Olivia wants to come back. She informs me a spot remains open for her. I explain her stamina will prohibit her from staying the entire three hours, but we can try two hours and reevaluate if needed. One caveat we do not mention is her toilet training. We have not completed the toilet training since her discharge from Kennedy Krieger in December. We tried, but Olivia was not very cooperative. Mike and I decide not to mention this to the school and see how it goes.

One factor that plays into our decision is the level of trust we have with the school. Hannah attended their program for two years, and we know both the teacher and the director very well. In fact, we have become friends with her teacher. Olivia adores both of them and beams whenever the director makes a fuss over her dress or a piece of jewelry she wears. During the few weeks she spent there before the accident, Olivia went out of her way every morning to be sure she put a different piece of jewelry or hair accessory on. Her biggest thrill was when she wore a tiara to school.

Mike continues to look for a job. In fact, that itself becomes his job. I give him as much space as he needs so he can focus. I still have a difficult time keeping up with all the scheduling of school, therapies, and my part-time job. I pray he will get a job soon so a chunk of stress will be removed.

I sometimes find myself wondering why I am filled with an underlying anger. I do not like this feeling and do not want to express it outwardly, but it's always simmering right below the surface. I equate it to a pot of water boiling. It takes a while to boil the water, especially when we are impatient; but once the heat increases, the bubbles start forming, and if we are not careful, it will spill over the top. This is how I find myself many days. I attribute some of these feelings to the stress we all feel. It is palpable. We are navigating the effects of Olivia's TBI and the aftershocks to our family. I feel increasingly tired and worn out. I am not sure why. It could be stress, being more vigilant about Olivia's safety, working, financial concerns, or random parental stress. I have a mantra for myself whenever I feel ready to blow: "Take a deep breath."

Mike

I can't imagine Olivia going back to preschool this early after the incident. There are so many developmental issues that we need her to work through and learn again, and I don't want to rush things.

Admittingly, I am under quite a bit of stress. I try not to think about how much time we have spent living on our savings, worrying when the tap will run dry. I need to figure things out, and that starts with a job. I can't spend time thinking about anything else except for bringing money into the family.

I am churning out resumes and making calls. Not a very targeted approach, and I know I should be tailoring my cover letters around specific job openings, but I am operating a one-man assembly line of sorts. I must keep the machine going. I realize I need to broaden my search based on geography, scope, travel, work type, and more. I am looking at various sources and applying for positions not just in the Washington, DC, area, but also, throughout Maryland, Virginia, and West Virginia. Hoping something will turn up soon.

Kelly

Olivia's return date for preschool is scheduled, and it happens to coincide with an interview Mike has scheduled. He follows us in the other car so he can head out afterward. On our drive, Olivia chats excitedly while we listen to a Disney CD. I arrive at an intersection not far from our house and notice a few flashing lights. My heart rate soars as I approach and discover I'm coming upon an accident scene. I feel frozen in time. My breathing is short and labored, so I consciously take in several deep breaths, hoping I can calm down prior to continuing on our way. "I need to be strong for Olivia" is my mantra, and I say it over and over to myself. I know I'll encounter scenes such as this over and over, but when it does happen, it's still a shock.

Once we arrive at the preschool, Olivia becomes extremely excited as I help her get out of the car. She bounces into the building. Her class is eagerly awaiting her arrival, and the tears well up in my eyes. We are finally returning to some "normalcy," aren't we?

Mike

Following Kelly and Olivia is difficult; I want to be in the same car. Even though the preschool is less than ten miles away, the ride seems excruciatingly long.

As I park next to Kelly, I can tell that Olivia is shaking with excitement. Walking into the building to return to school is an event I wasn't planning and couldn't even imagine just a short time ago.

Maybe today truly is a new beginning. After seeing Olivia getting settled in her classroom, Kelly and I walk out, and she wishes me good luck with a kiss. Strange that I am heading into the Tysons Corner area of Virginia, about fifteen miles away, for a job interview! I responded to a small ad in the newspaper for a marketing position just the week before. It is a company I had never heard of. When I received the call for the interview, I hope I didn't seem too eager; I wanted to yell, "Yes!" into the phone. I researched the company, but the website was a bit vague. All I know is that the company is a small government contractor for the DC area, and I am heading to their headquarters.

I meet with the president of the company for a brief interview, fielding questions and comments like "How do you manage projects? Are you a good writer? Describe your multitasking skills. Can you supervise people? How many people have you supervised before?" along with other questions. Well, I answer every open-ended question with appropriate information, and the answer to every close-ended question is yes. Had he asked me if I was ever an astrophysicist, I would have said yes.

Anyway, he only answers a few of my questions before he says that they will be in touch. I walk away thinking that I really don't know anything about the job he interviewed me for, nor can I figure out whether he thinks I'm a good candidate.

Time to head home and hear about Olivia's day and process the day's events.

Kelly

Our eligibility meeting for special education services has arrived. Mike and I arrive at the meeting with many questions but also a lot of trepidation. I've spent the past thirty days taking Olivia to various appointments with the school occupation, physical, and speech therapists who evaluated her current condition. I also had a lengthy phone interview with the school social worker, who had to provide a report as well. The social worker observed Olivia at preschool. Her report is difficult to read. She indicates Olivia sits at the table with her classmates but does not partake in the Play-Doh without encouragement from the classroom teacher. She sits and looks at her classmates but does not initiate any interaction. She also notes Olivia prefers to play on her own rather than with a classmate. She seems to eventually play alongside, but if the other child's voice becomes animated and loud or they enter Olivia's personal space, she immediately backs away.

As I read her observations, my heart breaks for Olivia. She seems so lost in her own little world. This is so different from her previous self. Another testament to how much has been stolen from her.

An enormous amount of anxiety wells up in my body. Along with the anger, I have noticed this happening more and more recently and am still not sure why.

Mike and I are brought to a large conference room. There are five other people in the room who introduce themselves before we start. The school psychologist and occupational, physical, and speech therapy reports are read aloud. It is obvious she qualifies for services, but we still don't fully understand what it means or what types of services she will receive. Each of us at the table are entitled to one vote, including Mike and me. The consensus is Olivia qualifies for special education services. Such a relief! We have made it over another hurdle.

We assume she will receive speech, physical, and occupational therapy through the school system, and we will not be charged for these services since she qualifies under the state special education laws. However, it also means Olivia will be in a special education preschool program for up to four hours a day, up to five days a week for her to get all these services. She will also receive assistance with socialization and potty training if we wish. I am completely overwhelmed by all of this. We set up another meeting date which, by law, must be within thirty days.

During this time, I realize something is truly not right with me. I am extremely tired, cannot comprehend anything that I read, and my neck is extremely stiff and sore. I schedule an appointment with my family doctor to discuss my symptoms. I arrive at my appointment and have the usual vital checks of weight, blood pressure, and temperature. Today, I am seeing the nurse practitioner, who enters the examination room smiling. She is older than me but not by much, tall and blond, and has a friendly demeanor. I feel comfortable talking to her. She is very attentive and asks a lot of questions. At the conclusion, she tells me she wants me to see a neuropsychologist and suggests one who is local and respected. She also encourages me to take care of myself, get plenty of rest, eat nutritious foods, exercise, drink lots of water. I nod in agreement and know not all of those things will happen.

I am not sure what a neuropsychologist will do for me, but I figure it's worth a try. I find the office easily. It is in an old house in downtown Leesburg. Many of these homes have been converted into offices, and I enjoy looking at the old architecture and imagining what it must have looked like when a family was living here.

The office does not appear to be a doctor's office, but it is not a therapist-type office, either. The walls are white, and there is a harsh fluorescent light overhead that makes the room appear even more drab. The doctor and I talk for a long time as he takes my medical history and suggests we start some cognitive testing. It takes two days to complete. Some of the tests involve building towers, computerized games, memory recall, reading comprehension, and number recalls. I am exhausted afterward.

I arrive at my follow-up appointment not knowing what to expect. The winter has been especially gray and cold without much snow. This day is no different. The computer and table where the testing was held is in the corner, looking lonely. We sit facing each other. I am on a red, fake-leather couch, and he sits opposite me, appearing higher in a tall chair. I feel as though I am in the principal's office at school. A coffee table is strategically placed between us. He goes over my results, and most of the words sound like a foreign language. I do not understand what he is trying to convey. I keep waiting for this agony to end. Finally, he says I have some "cognitive impairments." I sit there in shock, trying to hide it. He hands me the paperwork, which indicates a diagnosis of "post-concussive syndrome." He recommends I make an appointment with a neurologist and consider cognitive rehabilitation as well.

I walk out of his office feeling dizzy and not sure when I will find my equilibrium. I drive home in a daze, which seems to happen more frequently. The house is quiet. Mike is calm and suggests I find a neurologist and research the diagnosis beforehand. I hoped for a more empathetic response but am aware of all the stress he is currently experiencing trying to find a job. I look up the diagnosis as he suggested and learn post-concussion syndrome is a mild TBI. I am astonished! Not only do I have one daughter with a severe TBI and another dealing with the trauma, now I also have a brain injury.

As I look over the paperwork again, I notice the doctor has recommended physical therapy for my neck stiffness in addition to the neurologist and cognitive rehabilitation. Upon reading this, I immediately feel overwhelmed. How am I going to fit all this into my already packed schedule of trying to get help for my daughter? I decide my appointments will wait until I have a clearer vision of our "new normal."

Mike receives a job offer from a consultant group he interviewed with. The job is a good fit for him, and it provides good benefits, including health insurance, which we desperately need in order to rid ourselves of the COBRA payments. The only negative aspect of the job is the location. He must travel into Washington, DC, every day. He has never worked in DC, so he takes on the task of researching public transportation options so he will not need to drive in and park daily. He negotiates his hours to arrive early and leave before 5 p.m. so he is home for dinner. We enjoy family dinners together and feel it is imperative now in our family rebuild. He is willing to trade the early wakeup to be home in the evening.

I resign at the retail store. We are still not sure everything will work itself out, but there is no way I can continue working and be available for the girls. I am more than happy to do this, and I feel a sense of relief once it is done.

Mike

When I receive the phone call from the government contractor's human resources director and she offers me the job, I am ecstatic, but I calm myself down since I don't really know much about the position, pay, or, well, anything. I will be working under their Department of Transportation contract in Washington, DC. I accept the job and start the next day.

Kelly and I are thrilled . . . even though I can't explain what I will be doing in my job. I decide that I should keep my job search active and continue to send resumes as I am not convinced that this job is going to work out.

MARCH 2002

Kelly

The past two months have proven to be a whirlwind. I wonder when this flurry of activity will cease. I wake each morning with a racing heart, feeling as if it will beat right out of my body. So much to do and so little time to do it. Mike's job seems to be going well, though his early hours are a bit of an adjustment for all of us. We were used to seeing him every morning, and now he is not there to wish everyone a good day. He leaves before any of us are awake. Hannah's school bus arrives at 7:25 a.m. every morning; therefore, we also have an early start. Olivia usually sleeps through the chaos of getting Hannah off to school; she is only woken on preschool days.

She attends ninety minutes each day, and we are hopeful the time will increase as her stamina does. Slow and steady always wins the race, right?

The traffic court case comes to the docket, coinciding with Mike's first weeks at work. Since he cannot provide testimony, we decide he should not take the day off his new job. I will testify about what I remember from that night three months ago. It seems so long ago and yet as if it had just happened yesterday.

I arrange for a friend to host the girls for a playdate while I attend the hearing. Both the attorney representing Olivia and Hannah and the attorney representing me are in attendance. The court is an eight-minute drive from our home, but I plan to arrive early. I easily find the parking lot and get out of our new minivan. It is a sunny and unseasonably warm day.

I approach a house bearing a sign that indicates it is the traffic court building. The location seems odd since a beautiful brick building sits across the street and houses courtrooms as well. Others are walking to the building, and I wonder why they have to come to court. What is their story?

My stomach is a ball of knots and my heart thumps heavily. I have to take a few deep breaths to calm my mind and thoughts. It is odd to walk across a front porch to enter the court. A small desk with a sign-in sheet sits in the dark hallway, and I ensure the hearing is still scheduled. I immediately spot both of our attorneys, and they greet me warmly. They speak to me in a very calm manner, which soothes my nerves a bit.

We walk into the courtroom and sit in the first row of seats closest to the door. Several people sit in rows behind us, and I am surprised the front row is vacant. I assumed our hearing would be just us, but apparently that is not how it works.

This is my first time in a courtroom. I studied criminal justice in college, but ironically, I have never been inside a courtroom. As we wait for our case to be called, we hear other cases of speeding, running red lights, disobeying traffic signs, etc. One case involves an individual speeding past the police station; when pulled over, the gentleman was discovered to be driving without a valid driver's license. I have a hard time understanding why someone would speed past a police station. My naivete is coming out. I focus on the other cases to take my mind off my situation.

As we sit, the door to my left opens, and a dark-haired man enters the room. I immediately recognize him as the man who walked out of the hospital before me on the night of November 27. It is the driver of the car who careened into two other cars prior to hitting us. The man who caused all this misery for my family and especially Olivia.

I quickly utilize my deep breathing to calm myself, then look away because I'm afraid of losing my composure. Where does he decide to sit? Right next to me! I cannot believe it. No one else knows who he is. I can no longer focus on the other cases. I want to turn and tell him all the misery he caused, yell in his face, spit at him. But of course, I cannot do any of those things. I must sit calmly until our case is called.

Finally, it is our turn. The judge asks the attorneys to approach the bench, but only my two approach. Where is the attorney representing the driver? The judge calls his attorney's name again. The defendant is called, but since his advocate is not present, he is not required to answer any questions. The case is postponed for another few weeks. The judge asks us to return on April 1, 2002. April Fool's Day—how appropriate.

The defendant gets up and leaves the room, and my attorneys escort me outside. As soon as we are a few feet away, I tell them who was sitting beside me in court. They are flabbergasted. They ask me to point him out, and suddenly he comes walking out the front door as I turn around to avoid eye contact. They are surprised he had the nerve to sit next to us since he knows who we are. We walk to our cars and say goodbye. I sit in the car for a few minutes and calm myself before driving away. As much as I do not want to postpone this process, I am so glad to get out of his orbit.

Mike

Not being there for the court case has me dragging through the day at work. However, Kelly and I decided that I couldn't do anything to jeopardize my job, and I haven't told my employer the issues we're dealing with, especially since I just started. Somehow, I manage to get through the day.

My days start with me leaving the house very early in the morning to get to the bus stop. After a few stops along the way, I get to my office before 7 a.m. The trade-off is that I leave the office by 4 p.m. and take the bus home.

At the Department of Transportation office, I am a project manager in the research and technology division, primarily managing research publications and abstracts, and I have another contractor reporting to me. Proofreading and editing the studies is not exactly the marketing job that I had accepted. On the other hand, I am extremely grateful to have a job, healthcare benefits, and the opportunity to contribute again to my family. Plus, I return home at a decent hour and don't have to drive—so, though it is a long bus commute from home to the office, no complaints!

Although the work isn't difficult, working with and indirectly working for the federal government is challenging at times. I am not used to the bureaucracy and the red tape. Some of the federal employees are brilliant, but it seems that their efforts are stymied by "the process." Of course, there are others who simply feel entitled as a federal employee to have job security, whether they are literally sleeping at their desk, applying nail polish, or studying for advanced degrees, all paid for by our taxes.

Kelly

Since Hannah's reaction during our mall outing in December, we try to keep loud noises to a minimum. I also notice Olivia is startled very easily whenever an unexpected noise occurs.

Lately, the vigilance with the environment has grown. We always keep an extra eye on Olivia, fearful that she may fall easily. The doctors warned us she is susceptible to more damage if she falls on her head. Her skull has been fractured, and it will take a minimum of six months to fully heal.

We meet with the public-school special education team where Olivia is to begin preschool the first week of April. The school is in its first year of operation and located about fifteen minutes from our home. As we walk inside, everything seems so new and bright. The layout is a carbon copy of our elementary school but includes more windows and light. We meet the lead teacher of the class, the assistant principal who is tasked with administering Olivia's individualized education program (IEP), an administrator from the district office, the director of her private preschool, along with a school speech therapist, occupational therapist, and physical therapist. We discuss Olivia's goals and how the team will work with her to achieve these goals.

Once again, I feel as if I am listening to a bunch of people speak a foreign language. I do not know how to specify the goals and do not understand how to help her meet these. They inform us she is entitled to the public-school system's bus transportation to bring her to and from school. The school day at all elementary schools began at 7:50 a.m. This is the exact time Hannah must be at school. I quickly calculate what time Hannah's bus arrives and how much time that will allow me to get Olivia to school. I inform the team she will most likely be late in the morning because I am not comfortable putting her on a school bus. The team agrees, but I know this is going to be a grueling task. She will have to be up, fed, and dressed before Hannah leaves for the bus.

We discuss how many times per week she will meet with the

therapists and the routines of the class. We are surprised lunch time is included in their day. Kindergarten meets for three hours, but the preschool class meets for four.

The class consists of eight children, all with varying degrees of learning challenges. They range in age from two and a half to five years old, so Olivia is right in the middle, which we are thankful for. The staff take us on a quick tour to view the preschool room and explain the drop-off and pick-up procedures. As we leave the meeting, Mike and I shrug and comment we are not completely sure how this will all turn out, but we have to at least try.

It is amazing to think that a short time ago, we were not sure whether Olivia would even open her eyes again, and now she is in preschool. I am hopeful that she will begin relationships with others outside our family and make friends. I so deeply want her to feel like a kid. Playing and laughing with other boys and girls will be great therapy for her, as well as for Mike and me.

APRIL 2002

Kelly

I arrange another playdate for the girls. This one is with a family from our previous neighborhood. They moved further west to an older home. I drive the girls once Hannah arrives home after school and head to court to meet Mike. He decides to work a half day after hearing how difficult the previous session was for me.

I told Mike the building looked like a house, and he is waiting for me when I arrive. The day is sunny, and I feel the air getting warmer. Flowers are beginning to bud, and some daffodils have already sprung up from the earth. Our attorneys are also there, and we chat a few minutes before going into the courtroom. I keep an eye open for the other driver, and when he enters, he nods in acknowledgment to a man sitting on the other side of the room. I realize the other man is his attorney. The attorney appears disheveled and unkempt. His hair needs to be cut, and his suit does not seem to fit properly. He is not what I expect from an attorney.

We sit on the same bench as last time, but I am more comfortable here knowing the defendant is on the other side of the room. Our case is called, and the other attorney asks for all the witnesses to leave the courtroom while others are testifying. The judge agrees.

There are five of us in attendance, and another is on his way. A clerk escorts us to a room adjacent to the courtroom. We can talk quietly but are instructed to not share what we witnessed on the evening of November 27. One gentleman explains he works at an insurance company across the street from the court. He was on his way home when he witnessed the accident. It made quite an impression on him since he also has children. The following day he bought a Chevrolet Suburban because he felt they were built as strong as a tank and the only vehicle able to withstand the type of impact we endured.

Everyone asks how Olivia is. It's hard to answer. We are thankful she's doing so well, but we do not know what her future looks like. I am the last witness called to testify. Our attorney interviews me first, followed by the defendant's attorney. It is difficult, but I'm satisfied at the end. I am dismissed and sit down next to Mike. The judge asks some additional questions, including the sentence our attorneys feel is justified.

In the end, the judge decides he is guilty of reckless driving. The verdict is hard to accept even though we were told it's the harshest we could expect. He is issued a $600 fine with $300 forgiven and three months of a driver's license suspension, but he can drive to and from work. I am incredulous. The monetary fine doesn't mean anything to me, but allowing him to drive to and from work is hard to accept. He was returning home from work when he plowed into two cars before hitting us and dragging us sixty feet into a guardrail. How can this be happening? Where is the justice?

The attorneys try to ease my pain by reminding me this is the traffic portion. We are pursuing civil charges against him, and it is the best avenue to get retribution. I understand this, of course, but it doesn't make it better.

Mike

I can't believe that I'm sitting so close to the man who caused all of this. My entire body is as rigid as a rock. Sitting in the courtroom, I control every urge to avoid becoming a problem. I can't bear to look at him since I don't know how I will react. Oh, but I want to. I want to get a long look at the man who caused my family's lives to be altered forever. On the other hand, I don't want his face seared into my memory, to recall it every day. I don't want to see his face every morning when I kiss my girls and wish them a good day at school. I don't want to see his face whenever I see Olivia stumble or at a loss for words. I don't want that image in front of every financial compromise that we have to make to take care of our family. I am afraid to see that face every night in my dreams.

The first thing I would say to him is "Do you know how much pain you caused us?" Then a flurry would follow: "What happened that night? Where you drinking or high? [The police never tested him.] Were you reaching for something in the car and lost your focus? Did you fall asleep at the wheel? Did you ever ask about what happened to the family that your car smashed? What happened to the little girl that fell into a coma? How do you live each day? Do you sleep contently each night? Do you ever think about how our family is? Do you regret what happened?"

Kelly is remarkably composed on the stand as she speaks about that night. Is this man even listening? Does he look remorseful? Kelly comes off the stand and sits to my right. There is not much of a buffer between her and the person who turned our world upside down. Walking out of the courthouse, I am livid. A small financial penalty and limitations on driving for a few months. A slap on the wrist even though our attorney explained what the limitations were on the possible penalties. Yes, we will pursue civil charges against him, but I want him to feel more than writing a check. That's too easy.

Kelly

Olivia starts the county preschool program in addition to the private preschool two days a week.

Mike and I are running ragged. We're throwing as much therapy at her as we can, but we struggle with the fact that she is only three years old and needs to have time to play. How are we going to fit it all in?

My heart continually aches for both my girls. Hannah is only in school three hours each day, which allows us time to do some "fun" things. Next year, she will be in school all day, and I will miss that time with her. I worry she will resent attending all these therapy sessions. She does not complain, and I always bring things for us to do while we wait for Olivia. Sometimes we work on crafts such as making pot holders, or coloring, or reading. She is easily entertained, which makes it so much better. Hannah really enjoys the Junie B. Jones series by Barbara Park, and we recently went to the library and borrowed *Junie B. Jones Is a Beauty Shop Guy.* During one of Olivia's speech therapy sessions, as I read it aloud to her, we break out into uncontrollable laughter. We can barely talk. A mom comes in with her children and delights in our laughter. It is a great moment of joy during this cloudy time.

I cannot stop thinking, *Olivia is being shuttled to school, therapies, and back again. When will she be able to be a kid again?* I keep my eye on the prize at the end of this—a healed girl who will go on and have a wonderful life.

PART 4
THE PRESCHOOL/ELEMENTARY/
MIDDLE SCHOOL YEARS

Kelly

At the end of the school year, we have an IEP meeting with Olivia's team of preschool teachers, and they inform us that Olivia is eligible to receive extended school year (ESY) services. ESY provides a child with a disability the services necessary to retain the educational growth made during the regular school year.

Olivia will attend for two or three days per week for the month of July, the only month the program is offered. Private occupational therapy services have been hard to find, and she is in desperate need of this therapy.

The summer preschool classroom is in a different elementary school with unique teachers and students. The only constants in this experience are transportation and that the occupational therapist is the same one she had during the school year.

The first day, we struggle to get out of the house in a timely manner. Olivia has never been a morning person, and she is even less cooperative now. We all need extra sleep, but for the next thirty days, our mornings will start early. The school is a bit closer to our home, but the commute is still a fifteen-minute drive.

We arrive to a traffic jam in the drop-off line and encounter difficulty finding a parking spot. I finally find a space and assist Olivia out of the car; Hannah dutifully follows along to get her to class. Olivia immediately tightens her grip on me, and I sense her feelings of overwhelm and fear. I'm learning that any time her routine changes, she experiences a week of withdrawals. I keep thinking, *I hope this experience proves worthwhile.*

We reach the front doors of the school when staff members stop us in our tracks. They immediately inform me in a brusque manner I'm not permitted inside the building to escort her to the classroom. I don't turn around and run us all back home at that point, though I do consider it for a split second. Instead, I protest and explain she is three years old, has a traumatic brain injury, and needs me to escort her to the classroom. They quickly relent. I have a strong feeling there will be countless lessons in advocating and protesting when I feel the need, and they will come rapidly. I have never been this assertive or angry.

The school is one year old and is the school my girls would have attended if we had not moved last fall. As we approach her class, I hear a commotion. We enter the room; I notice the teachers are not very attentive to the nine students in the room, ranging from two and a half to five years old and varying in level of disabilities. Immediately, I question this decision but reaffirm to myself what we were told by doctors. Olivia needs as much therapy as possible because the clock is ticking on the two-year recovery window. We are already past six months and need to take advantage of all therapies that are offered.

Every morning, she cries before leaving the house, and the tactics get more elaborate. As fatigued as I am, it's hard dealing with this. I keep hoping the adjustment will happen, but today, now into the second week, Olivia screams and cries the entire ride. As we walk to the classroom, I hold her hand and try to stay strong as she keeps sniffling and crying. It breaks my heart. I feel guilty leaving her; it feels as though she is getting punished for something she has no control over. I can't stay this morning to insure she calms downs since Hannah has her summer reading camp. After driving Hannah to her camp, another twenty minutes away, I drive back to check on Olivia to make sure she's okay before turning around to pick up Hannah and then once again pick up Olivia at dismissal time. It is exhausting, and I don't know how I can sustain this schedule.

The culminating incident happens the last day of class. The teacher planned Pet Day as a celebratory last day of summer school. She brings her pets and their respective crates to "educate" the students about animal care. I'm not sure how she received permission to bring animals into an elementary school. At dismissal, I walk into the classroom and see Olivia is in one of the dog kennels, locked in like a caged animal. She cannot get out, and both teachers are outside. The classroom has a back door that leads to a grassy area where the children can play for recess and outdoor games. I unlock the kennel to let her out. I walk down a small hill, shaking with anger, and question the teacher about why Olivia was in the crate while both she and her assistant are not in the classroom and how she got in there. She shrugs and tells me Olivia wanted to be in there. I vow at that moment that NO ONE will ever treat my daughter like that again.

EARLY SUMMER 2002

Kelly

Mike and I continue our never-ending advocacy for Olivia. I call the county public school offices to determine who oversees the ESY program. We write letters and copy them to the director of special education. The responses do not apologize for the teacher's actions or assure us that Olivia will not be placed under these teacher's care again, and this does not satisfy us. We now know we will have to scrutinize everything Olivia is exposed to, follow up on everything, and become our daughter's advocate.

We also decide that rather than send Olivia to both the special education program and private preschool, we will take her out of private and increase her time at the special education school. I am heartbroken when I must make this call. I love the preschool, and they were so supportive before, during, and after the accident. The teacher is upset and disappointed with me and lets me know that she's not happy with our decision. Of course, I feel terrible.

Mike

On a sweltering summer day, Olivia is outside with a few neighborhood kids. The adults are standing at the end of a cul-de-sac, chatting. The homes on this street have recently been completed, and it is our first opportunity to meet some of them. Our neighbor attaches a red Radio Flyer wagon to his bike and gives kids a turn riding in the wagon behind him. When it is Olivia's turn, her excitement doesn't last long. As they round a corner, she falls out of the wagon. I rush over, and she is hysterical and bleeding profusely from a gash in her chin. Kelly consoles her, and I rush to get towels and the keys to the van. Hannah is visibly upset and scared and chooses to stay with one of the families while we are gone. Our neighbor understandably feels horrible, but I am mad at myself for allowing this to happen.

Upon arrival, the triage nurse sees us and rushes us to the back. She must have heard Olivia's cries and seen the blood seeping into the towel. The nurses try to calm her while we await the doctor, but how do you calm a four-year-old who has already experienced trauma?

The doctor arrives and immediately assesses stitches are in order. He suggests using dissolvable ones so there will be less chance of scarring and no need to remove them and further upset her. I insist on staying in the room. Kelly stands behind Olivia, trying to hold her head still while I stand next to her, rubbing her leg and talking to her to console her. I am not sure how to effectively calm her. I start feeling nauseous and try to fight it. One of the nurses looks at me and asks if I am feeling all right. I am not but have a hard time admitting it. A few seconds later, I rush out the door into the hallway. I am embarrassed. The sight of blood normally doesn't affect me. However, seeing Olivia's discomfort and the blood feels like a wave engulfing and suffocating me. How I wish it were me getting the stitches instead of her.

Kelly

It is a few days before the 2002–2003 school year begins, and Olivia's teacher holds a parent orientation for the class. I am thrilled to learn that there will be more girls in the class this year and they are closer to her age. Unfortunately, the parents of these girls are not present, but I look forward to making some connections.

Being thrust into this environment, I can't help but look for some companionship, as I'm sure many do—someone who will understand what we're going through. It is so lonely to have a child with special needs, and I think it is especially so when the first three years of Olivia's life have not been spent involved in this community. I have so many questions and concerns that I would love to share with fellow parents.

The school day begins at 7:50 a.m., but I choose to have Olivia start school at 9 since it has been so difficult to motivate her in the mornings. I thought the drop-off during the summer was bad, but it was a piece of cake compared to this. I am driving her, and since the school day has already begun, I must go through the office, get a pass, and walk her to the classroom. As we walk the long hallway and turn the corner, Olivia begins crying. It takes me about least ten to fifteen minutes to depart. I talk to the teacher at dismissal, and she suggests Olivia may be upset because she is missing circle time—an activity that gets the kids ready for the day. Apparently, Olivia loves the time they spend going over the calendar, talking about the weather, and sometimes even singing a welcome song.

I agree to bring her to school by the 7:50 start time, and surprisingly the tears end. I feel bad, but I didn't know this mattered to her so much. She doesn't realize it, either. Another difference in her morning routine is that the teacher meets us outside and walks the children into the classroom as a group, making it a much quicker transition as well.

LATE SUMMER 2002

Kelly

Now that school has been in session for a few weeks, I ask when the therapies will begin. Her IEP states a daily sheet indicating what therapies she's had and how she is progressing will accompany her home. She is to have physical, occupational, and speech therapy three times per week. These progress notes are imperative since I cannot always rely on Olivia accurately relaying information. I notice that she is not receiving speech. In fact, she hasn't had any speech sessions since the beginning of the school year.

Once we get home and she has a snack, I begin my telephone calls to determine which speech therapist is assigned to her and why the therapy has not begun.

This process is proving to be quite difficult. I leave a message.

It's been a week without a return phone call. I leave more messages and start going up the chain of administrators. Two weeks after these messages, I receive a return phone call from one of the therapists, who informs me she has been working with Olivia. I ask which days she works with Olivia, and she responds Mondays, Wednesdays, and Fridays. I laugh, though I am seething inside. Olivia goes to school Tuesdays, Thursdays, and Fridays, and it's impossible for her to receive all her speech on Fridays, the one day they are both in the building.

The next week after numerous phone calls and messages are left to the assistant principal, I walk into the school and ask to speak to the principal. She listens to my concerns and informs me that she needs to look into it and will get back to me. *Great!* More lost time. I finally speak with the assistant principal and principal two days later via conference call, and it is determined that, somehow, Olivia was never assigned a speech therapist, and this will be rectified as soon as possible. They are unable to explain why the therapist I spoke to told me Olivia was on her caseload when she, in fact, was not.

Olivia will begin speech therapy two months after the school year has started. So much time lost.

FALL 2002

Kelly

Hannah is now in school all day, and Olivia is attending more regularly, so I decide to focus on some of my needs. My neck has never been the same after the accident. I am constantly in pain. In October, my doctor orders an MRI to determine if there is a disc issue.

I meet with my doctor a week after the recent MRI. It's now October. He informs me I have two herniated discs in my neck, which is why I am experiencing pain. He orders physical therapy and some anti-inflammatory medicine.

I find an office that takes our insurance and start sessions two days a week while both girls are in school. The woman who is assigned to me is lovely. She is young and newly married, and we have easy conversation. One morning, I get the girls off to their respective schools and come home to use the treadmill after cleaning up the kitchen. After a shower and getting dressed, I take advantage of the extra time and decide to clean the closet. During the process of sorting, my phone rings. I am surprised it is the physical therapist asking why I have not shown up for my appointment. I gasp and immediately realize why I've had so much extra time. I am embarrassed and confused. These little things keep happening. Forgetting appointments, inability to multitask or balance the checkbook, and fatigue.

After a few weeks of physical therapy, I notice my fingers going numb; I drop things, or when driving, my hand starts tingling. I ask the therapist if she thinks it's related to our sessions. She doesn't but suggests a few things I can do. It is odd since it is in my non-dominant hand. I try her suggestions, but the tingling gets worse and happens more frequently. I am not sure what is happening.

At my neurologist appointment the first week of November, I describe the tingling in my hand. The doctor suggests I discontinue physical therapy. Her reasoning is sometimes physical therapy exacerbates a problem. She refers me to a different type of neurologist who specializes in nerve issues and orders an electromyography.

Just what I need—another appointment.

When Olivia was discharged in December, Kennedy Krieger scheduled follow-ups and ordered a neuropsychological test in November or December to determine the progress made over the past year. Mike can take the day off, so he, Olivia, and I drive up early in the morning. As luck would have it, it is a dreary, rainy day, matching the mood in the car.

The Neuropsychology Department is a bustling place. There is a large waiting area filled with adults and children waiting for siblings or their own appointments. The three of us are escorted to Dr. Smith's office so she can explain the process and what to expect. She speaks to both Mike and I and directly to Olivia, rather than over Olivia, allowing her to be a part of the conversation. She explains some of the tests or games she will use to complete her assessment and remarks that Olivia's inpatient rehabilitation discharge does not include a completed neuropsychological report for comparison. I confirm there isn't one and explain the doctor tried numerous times but was unable to perform the required tests.

She tells Olivia they will play for a bit in her office, and she shows her some building blocks. Olivia looks anxious and confused as Mike and I leave the room, and I turn to him and say, "I am not sure how long she will last before crying and demanding one of us accompany her." He nods in agreement.

We try to relax in the waiting area, which proves impossible. How do you calm yourself, knowing your daughter is being evaluated by a stranger in one of the rooms? My mind jumps all over the place, thinking, *Does she remember anything? Is she afraid we have left her here all by herself? Does she feel abandoned?*

Less than an hour later, we see Olivia walking toward us along with the doctor. I quietly say, "Uh-oh," to Mike. The doctor explains Olivia refuses to do any of the tasks unless we accompany her. Mike and I glance at each other and stand to accompany them back to the office. It is a small, windowless room painted in a drab beige color. There is nothing to give it a cheery appeal to an adult, much less a child. The doctor tries to get Olivia to complete tasks building blocks, drawing pictures, counting, recalling words, and following directions. She will do the task the first or second time but loses focus and turns to a toy or some other item. I am unsure whether it is a focus issue or an avoidance.

The doctor attempts different tactics for the next forty minutes before stating we need to end the testing. We gather up our things, and Olivia appears triumphant as we pack up to go home. Everyone is tired. It has been an exhausting day. During the drive home in the rain, there is once again an overwhelming sadness in the car.

My appointment with the neurologist for the electromyography is the following week. It is a sunny but very chilly day. The office is adjacent to the hospital we were transported to following the accident. I am thankful I do not have to enter that building.

Surprisingly, I am escorted to the examination room immediately following the paperwork. This is a pleasant change from my other neurologist's office where the waiting room is full, and the wait is a minimum of forty-five minutes.

He listens to my issues and concerns and nods occasionally as I explain the history of events. He agrees with the other doctor that physical therapy may have exacerbated an issue that was brewing but also explains it didn't cause it. He explains even though it is my left hand that brought me in, he is going to test both since these issues usually occur in both hands and wrists.

I lie on the examination table as he wheels in a large machine. I see a paper with lines attached, almost like an electrocardiograph that doctors use to record heart rhythms. The doctor explains he will conduct two different tests. He cleans my arm and inserts a small needle, which doesn't hurt much as it is inserted into the muscle in a few different areas. Each time, he asks me to flex my fingers. Following this, he conducts a nerve conduction study. It will determine if nerve damage is present in my arm, wrist, or hand, causing the symptoms.

This test is the most painful. An electrode is attached to my wrist over the nerve, and a stimulating electrode is placed away from the recording electrode but still on the forearm. The nerve is stimulated by an electrical shock. The most excruciating pain shoots up my arm. It feels as if my entire body is being zapped. The only analogy I can use to describe it is when a cartoon character puts his finger in an electrical outlet and his whole body lights up, his hair stands straight up, and a look of both fear and pain radiates from the face. The electrode is moved around the arm, testing other nerves, and the pain intensifies. It is one of the most painful experiences. He apologizes but explains he needs to do this in order to make a diagnosis.

The right arm is also tested. The pain is not the same. There is some discomfort but not to the same degree. As I regain my composure, he explains that I have severe carpal tunnel. I am stunned. I ask how this crept up out of nowhere. He asks further questions and theorizes when we were hit in the accident, I gripped the steering wheel too tight and damaged the nerves. The pain caused by nerve damage does not always present itself immediately. He refers me to an orthopedist and recommends I get a wrist brace to stabilize my hand and wrist, especially at night. The pain in my arm has been worst at night, often waking me.

I leave the office stunned. Walking outside into the bright sunshine blinds me at first, but the cold air in my face wakes me up. I get to the car and call Mike with the news. He is as surprised as I am. I immediately start worrying about more doctor appointments, but pragmatic Mike reminds me to take it one step at a time. He is right. I need to pick up Olivia, meet Hannah at the bus, make some calls, and get dinner on the table.

A week before Thanksgiving, I return to Baltimore to meet with the neuropsychologist and get the results of Olivia's most recent testing. I embrace the meeting with a mixture of excitement and dread. We are finally getting some quality information on the areas Olivia where has progressed and where she still needs help. I do not wait long in the busy waiting area. She greets me warmly and escorts me to the same office we were in a few weeks ago. She doesn't hand me a report but directly reiterates the history. I realize this is protocol, but it is still annoying. I know all this. I was there. I endured all this right alongside her.

She reminds me since there was not a full neuropsychological exam at the time of discharge, this report cannot fully compare progress between the discharge date and her testing. I am aware of all this information, but she must have gained some insight. She narrates some of the tests to me, and it is hard to process and understand how the information is related to Olivia's cognitive impairment as well as social growth. Much of this is a foreign language to me. All I really want to know is how she is recovering and what additional steps we need to take. There is a clock ticking in my head. The doctors told us the first year is the most important in a brain injury recovery. The second year is also important but less so. I think, *Please hurry. I need to get home so I can make sure she continues to recover.*

As she continues explaining things, I start comprehending this is not good news. She is not recovering as expected. All the therapies over the past eleven months have not proven successful. These words stood out.

Her scores on this evaluation were slightly lower than on her previous evaluation, suggesting failure to make appropriate developmental progress skills over the past year. It is likely that her distractibility and frustration behaviors interfere with her ability to learn new information and therefore to make age-appropriate gains in skills. This combination of language difficulties combined with behavioral changes and attentional difficulties is often demonstrated by individuals with disruption in the functioning of left hemisphere frontal-striatal circuits and is very consistent with Olivia's documented left frontal lobe finding shown on CT scans.

At the end of the meeting, she hands me my copy of the report and encourages me to reach out if I have any questions, and to continue with Olivia's follow-up appointments at the clinic. I walk out of the office dazed. This is not what I expected. I know she is not fully recovered, but I did expect some progress. Is all the work we have been doing worthless? Why isn't she improving?

Mike and I talk about the report once the girls have gone to bed.

It is sobering. The following day, I call a local agency that provides case management to brain injury and stroke survivors. Olivia was approved for the pediatric program but is awaiting placement. I need advice on where we go from here. I keep thinking we are missing something. The executive director takes my call and informs me a new pediatric case manager was hired but will not contact us until the beginning of the year. She asks me a lot of questions, and I tell her about the recent report. She seems surprised after we review all the therapies Olivia has been doing over the past eleven months. Her response reassures me: "WOW, you have done a lot for her. I really don't know anything more you could have done."

Though reassuring, those words do not tell me where to go from here. I feel as if we are climbing endlessly uphill.

WINTER 2003

Kelly

It is a new year, and therefore I am hopeful things will continue to improve, not only for Olivia but for all of us. I bring Olivia to my first appointment with the orthopedist to treat my carpal tunnel syndrome. We walk into a busy waiting area. There are babies, children, parents, adults, and older adults patiently sitting and waiting for appointments with their doctors or for family members. It is a bit loud, and I notice the concern on Olivia's face. She stands closer to me and furrows her brow as if she is worried about something.

We find two seats and sit down. I always come prepared with books, coloring supplies, and small toys to keep her entertained. She sits nicely and just looks around at all the people, a little unsure. I remind her we are here for me; she does not need to meet with any doctors, and no one is going to touch her. She has developed "white-coat syndrome." She is fearful of anyone in a white coat such as those worn by doctors. I notice her begin to relax once we start playing.

We are escorted back to the examination room, and the fatigue shows on Olivia's face. The doctor enters and greets us. He is very charming and can meet Olivia at her level. I see her relax. He looks over my paperwork and agrees with the neurologist that I have carpal tunnel in my left arm, and since I don't have any prior symptoms, it was most likely caused by the automobile accident. He surmises I gripped the steering wheel so tightly that it caused inflammation.

He suggests alleviating the pain with a cortisone shot in my wrist and seeing how long it subdues the symptoms. He chats with us as he prepares the shot, which is the largest needle I have ever seen. He quickly and painlessly inserts it in my wrist. I look over at Olivia as she sits watching in horror. He jokes with her that it's good Mommy is getting the shot rather than her, and she nods enthusiastically. As we wrap up the appointment, he explains that if the shot works, we can continue the regimen, but if it doesn't ease the pain and discomfort, surgery is another option.

As we leave the office, I see a huge weight lift off my little girl. I wonder what goes on in her mind. What does she remember—if anything?

I hope the shot will take care of the issue, allowing me to return to my life. I'm not sure what type of life I am hoping to return to, but I don't want another procedure after all this.

The last weekend of January, I accompany Hannah to a birthday party for one of her classmates. While the kids are playing, the adults congregate and catch up. All those in attendance live in our neighborhood, and many are aware of what happened. During a casual conversation, another mom approaches and remarks how happy she is that everything worked out for Olivia. I stand there speechless. How am I supposed to respond? There isn't any etiquette for these types of conversations. Lacking anything profound, I simply respond with a polite "Thank you."

How do I convey she isn't fine? We are not lucky. Although there aren't any visible scars, she is still injured. I am constantly faced with these questions: How do I explain things are not how they seem? Do I want people to know that I have a brain injury, too? I feel the need to keep it to myself. I wonder why I don't want to share this piece.

My life's routine has shifted from finding moments of rest and time to get errands done to a life of rushing to appointments, picking up kids on time, hurrying to get meals made, and the list goes on. I never feel I'm doing enough or getting anything done well. While rushing through the grocery store, I notice my hands are tingling again. My first thought is *Darn, this keeps happening and the frequency has increased.*

One day as I am walking down the dairy aisle under the bright lights, Olivia lying in the cart exhausted as usual, I am perplexed as I look down at my feet. A second ago, I was looking at the array of yogurts, trying to decide which one to buy, when I dropped my bag. I have no chance to try and catch it or stop the free fall. I stop and pick everything up, hoping the feeling in my hands will return. I cannot figure out why this keeps happening. What if I'm driving or carrying Olivia, which has become increasingly difficult as she has grown, and lose sensation?

I make a mental note to call the orthopedist tomorrow. Hopefully, all I need is another cortisone shot.

SPRING 2003

Kelly

Hard to believe Mike and I will be celebrating our ten-year wedding anniversary in April. We have been through a lot during these very short years, with job losses, deaths of family members, health issues of our parents, miscarriage and, of course, the near fatal injury of our daughter; we have heard from many that the last one has ruined many marriages. We both agree our marriage is stronger because of all we have faced together. We, as all couples do, also have our moments.

We decide to take a weekend away, and Mike's parents agree to come and stay with the girls. The last time we did this, I was five months pregnant with Olivia as we celebrated our fifth wedding anniversary.

We go to Berkeley Springs, West Virginia, for a relaxing weekend. My preference would be relax, read, take a nap, get pampered, but Mike usually needs to be on the go. So we compromise. Isn't that what marriage is all about?

Berkeley Springs is a ninety-minute drive consisting of small highways winding through the West Virginia country. April is usually a very beautiful time of year, when the trees are filling in and flowers are beginning to bud. The heat and humidity have not set in, making walks and runs more bearable.

I am reminded of our wedding day. We were married at a resort where the ceremony and reception were held in the same venue. When I learned there was an option to conduct an outdoor ceremony, I jumped at the opportunity. It was nice to have an alternative in the case of rain. The day of our wedding was beautiful and sunny. Later in the day, a fierce wind settled in, and the sky became cloudier. I was asked numerous times if I still wanted to have the ceremony outside, and of course I replied yes. My only reason for relocating would be in the case of rain.

As we stood on the dais, reciting our vows, a huge burst of wind swept over us, causing my veil to swoop over my face. My dear sister-in-law rushed up to fix my train numerous times. It was beautiful day, and I do not have any regrets.

Berkeley Springs State Park, one of the country's smallest state parks, is referred to as the first spa. The spring water flows at a constant 74°F from the base of Warm Springs Ridge. There are stone pools. Berkeley Springs itself is also a noted art town and friendly haven surrounded by West Virginia's splendid outdoors.

After a leisurely breakfast, we walk around the shops and galleries. Of course, we pick up a trinket for each of the girls. We head back to the spa for our treatments, including massages, which is a first for Mike. I can tell he is a bit nervous.

When I meet up with him following the massages, I notice he doesn't look as relaxed as I was hoping. At dinner later in the evening, he relays all the things his masseuse told him about the area. I remark how much conversation they engaged in, and he retorts that he kept talking to feel more comfortable. I laugh hard. He finds it so hard to relax.

The weekend allows us time away from the girls to reconnect and discuss our plans for Olivia. She seems to be doing well, and even though she is eligible to attend kindergarten in September, we decide to give her another year of preschool. She won't be the youngest in her class, but an extra year will help her catch up to her peers. We also decide to reenroll her in private preschool three mornings a week and discontinue the special needs preschool program at the public school. She will still be eligible to receive speech and occupational therapies both privately and at school.

Mike and I leave Berkeley Springs feeling renewed and more committed and now have a plan for the coming year for Olivia.

Mike

Kelly and I go furniture shopping with the girls. Olivia and I buy a child's rocking chair for a friend. Olivia spots a fly buzzing near us. She is so scared that she is trembling. I pick her up and hold her, which only alleviates the situation a little bit. A man tries to step on the fly but keeps missing. The other people in line think the whole scene is comical. Of course, they don't have to hold a fifty-plus-pound child shaking with fear.

During Olivia's last week of preschool in May, the class goes to a farm. Kelly is there, and Olivia spots a peacock. The peacock simply struts along probably fifty yards away. Suddenly it screeches, "Caw, caw, caw." For whatever reason, Olivia's knees buckle, and she becomes hysterical. Kelly can't calm her down until they leave the farm. When Olivia tells me later about this, I see the fright in her face. Throughout the day, she keeps asking me if there are peacocks in her room, the kitchen, and even the bathroom. I keep her company while she takes a bath.

How do I respond when people ask how Olivia is doing? I am grateful that people are concerned, but if you look at her, she looks great. Overall, she is a happy little girl who finds so much joy in just being with family. On the other hand, her rehab continues with occupational therapy, speech and language therapy, and special education.

We tell her that she will be returning to A Child's Place Preschool, the private preschool that she attended before the incident and a couple of months in the spring afterward. She seems excited that she will have the same preschool teacher. She also shows enthusiasm about getting to see the director and founder of the school. While I am priming Olivia for her return to A Child's Place, I show her and Hannah some DVD home movies of Olivia at the school. She asks if the director will be the Easter Bunny again as she was before. Overall, it goes well, but I don't think it really sinks in.

Every child (and adult) has fears. Hopefully, through the patience of parents and others, children can overcome some of these. Dealing with Olivia's is more challenging. Humorous to some—because the fears she now faces can seem unbelievable—but nothing short of a nightmare for us. Since the incident, Olivia's fears include trees, leaves, flags, the wind, moon bounces, dogs, peacocks, frogs, flies, and every other bug that flies, crawls, slithers, etc. In short, everything that flies, crawls, and everything above her head causes her great fear. She is always afraid that something will fall on her head. She goes into hysterics when she sees leaves blowing near her. She wants constant assurances that no leaves will land on her head. Other people can't fathom the depth of these issues. I know that being calm and slowly getting Olivia acclimated to her fears should help. It is just difficult to have your child shriek and go into a form of hysteria when she gets near something like a moon bounce. Everyone looks at you in disbelief or simply laughs and shakes their head.

In the last two months, suddenly, Olivia has demonstrated a great interest in arts and crafts. She is enjoying coloring, painting, cutting, and using her hands with other projects. It is so gratifying to see her with this newfound interest as she draws a picture of me with purple hair and stick legs that are about five times the proportion they should be. I love it.

Kelly

Mike and I inform the special education preschool in June that Olivia will not be returning the following school year. The staff is disappointed, especially since they enjoy having her and seeing some growth. She has two close friends in the class, and one will be going to kindergarten and the other will continue in this program. We are confident the decision we've made on Olivia's behalf is the right one for her. All parents try to choose the best option based on the individual child. Sometimes it is the right one and other times it is not.

At the conclusion of the school year, most classes have a final party. The preschool is not an exception. Her teachers decide to hold a pool party. Some kiddie pools are collected and filled with water as the kids splash around and play. There are bubbles, a ring-toss game, and of course a lot of food. Olivia has a fun time. She loves splashing in the water but does not enjoy swimming. The parents in attendance supervise their children and chat about summer plans. It is an enjoyable way to top off the school year.

Olivia and I leave after drying her off and changing into dry clothes. As I drive home, I reflect on the progress she has made in the last year. She still has a long way to go, but we must celebrate these small victories.

SUMMER 2003

Kelly

The carpal tunnel in my left wrist is getting worse. Each night, I wake to throbbing pain and am unable to get comfortable. At my last appointment, the doctor stated if this does not work, I will need to consider surgery. He also wrote a prescription for a brace to wear at night. His explanation for the nighttime pain is the pain radiates when the arm is still and increases as time passes. The brace helps a bit, but I am not getting restful sleep.

In July, I call to schedule surgery, but the unwelcome news is I must stop taking any anti-inflammatory medicines two weeks prior to surgery. I am unsure how I will handle day-to-day tasks. I do not envision any other options, so I resign myself to grin and bear it. My surgery date is in early August.

Our summer is more relaxed without school, but Olivia continues her therapies. I take her to two different locations twice a week. Hannah comes along and dutifully entertains herself with her summer workbooks. She looks forward to doing these and enjoys the sense of completion at the end.

Our days are also filled with trips to our community pool to cool off and get the girls some exercise and socialization. Olivia has a tough time connecting with some of her peers, and the difference in maturity and cognitive ability becomes more apparent. She has always enjoyed playing with children a little younger than herself, and this has become a more commonplace activity.

In August, Mike's parents offer to come and watch the girls while he takes me to my surgery appointment. They arrive the night before and will spend the night so Mike and I can leave to get to the surgical center by 6 a.m. I have a rough day. The pain in my left wrist is excruciating. Every few minutes, I feel as if electrical jolts are shooting up my arm. I try to quell the pain by either staying still or moving the arm, but neither tactic works.

After dinner we sit playing games with the girls in our family room before they go to bed. On the couch, I wince in uncontrollable pain. I notice the concern on Estelle's face. I try to hide the reaction, but it has become increasingly difficult.

Early the next morning, Mike and I awake, and it is easy to get out the door quickly. As we drive to the hospital, we remark how it's like a date. We cannot remember the last time we were in a car without the girls. It is eye-opening to think how little time we have shared alone. Our trip in the spring is a distant memory.

I am nervous prior to the surgery but also looking forward to not being in pain. I am reminded that the procedure is not guaranteed, so I remain cautiously optimistic. Mike meets the surgeon for the first time, who shares my optimism. He is an upbeat, charismatic man without the arrogance sometimes observed in surgeons. I mention to the doctor prior to sedation that my right hand has started tingling, and he agrees to give me a cortisone shot while I am under anesthesia.

I awake to the doctor telling jokes to others in the room. We are still in the operating room, so I immediately panic that I am not supposed to be awake so early. He chuckles and reassures me he is done. He and the anesthesiologist explain they prefer a lighter sedation so the recovery is quicker and less taxing to the body. He gives me my post-surgical instructions and cautions I cannot put any pressure on the palm of my hand. I cannot lift anything, vacuum, or push a mop for at least two weeks. I have already set up the appointment to remove my stitches, and he will assess my progress. The stitches are placed on the palm, aligned with a crease. I am a bit confused, but he shows me he went in through one of the lines on my palm. I had expected the incision to be on my inner wrist. He explains this method is less invasive, and the risk of scarring is much less.

We stop at a local diner for breakfast and, again, enjoy some uninterrupted time together. The girls are busily playing and doing arts and crafts when we arrive home. They shower me with love and affection. They are both careful not to touch my bandaged hand, and Sam and Estelle are surprised to see how much better I look.

The summers always seem to go by quickly. It's hard to believe Hannah is now in second grade. She's looking forward to this year. The second week of September, Olivia returns to preschool. We are delighted to see a few familiar faces. Some of the children who were in her class before are still enrolled since they have missed the kindergarten cut-off.

Olivia is excited to be back and walks in confidently. She immediately places her backpack on the hook under her name tag and looks around the classroom. She is a bit overwhelmed, so I gently steer her toward some toys I think she will enjoy before saying goodbye. As I give her a kiss and tell her I will pick her up soon, she grows a bit panic-stricken. I hesitate. Her teacher comes over and reassures her and distracts her while I leave. Phew! I was a little worried.

When I pick her up three hours later, she bounces to the car, smiling. She gets in, and immediately her face falls and she starts crying. I remind her to get into her car seat before I can pull over to talk to her. She is inconsolable. I try to understand what happened. She is upset because she couldn't play for a longer amount of time. As the story comes tumbling out, I realize there are a few things going on. She is exhausted. Three hours of being at school, stimulated, and listening to directions has taken a toll. There are a lot of transitions built into the day, and she has not mastered all of them yet. This is an area she has much difficulty accepting both at home and at school. She will be receiving some of her services at the preschool this year, so I'm hopeful these will help ease her transitioning issues.

FALL 2003

Mike

Two years have passed since our lives were turned upside down. Yet, through it all, our family has never wavered in its commitment to each other. I reflect on many trying days, yet I have a profound . . . appreciation for Kelly. Not just because of the love she has for our family but also for her dedication to Olivia and our family as a unit. Words such as "appreciation" or "unit" may seem cold or limited in scope, but there is so much truth behind them. Kelly and I may not have agreed with every step we've taken concerning our kids over the last couple of years, and there have certainly been compromises; with every decision, we are field generals of sorts, using the best intel we can gather and leading our forces into battle, not afraid to run over those who stand in our way. We fight for our family. Okay, sounds cold again!

Anyway, the relationship that Kelly and I have has strengthened through it all. I can't imagine life without any of our kids. Without

Kelly, I don't think I could function. Our love for each other flourishes, but I don't really think of it in those ways. Maybe "appreciation" doesn't go far enough to convey how much Kelly means to me. I simply revere her.

SPRING 2004

Kelly

May is always a busy month. So many changes are happening, so many decisions awaiting resolution. Mike and I are blindsided when we receive a letter from the school system informing us Olivia is recommended for a pilot all-day kindergarten class. I am aware there is a class at our elementary school for all-day kindergarten, but that is the extent of my knowledge. We are one of the few school systems in Virginia that still has half-day programs. One class meets in the morning, and the other arrives soon after. Each class has three hours to learn all the kindergarten-level curriculum. It is a fast-paced environment, and the teachers are under a lot of pressure to fit it all in.

I schedule a meeting with the principal to understand why Olivia is invited to the program and learn more about it. The principal and I have a good relationship, and she is happy to assist in our decision. I learn Olivia was chosen based on the number of services she is receiving through the special education program. There is a formula they utilize in determining who should be invited. Most of the other students will be from other elementary schools, and many have either never experienced preschool or are enrolled in a county Head Start program. Head Start is a federal program that promotes school readiness for infants, toddlers, and preschool-aged children from low-income families. Some of these children are also from homes where English is not the primary language, and they need additional services.

The main takeaway is an analogy the principal uses in comparing traditional half-day kindergarten to full day. She states, "Half-day kindergarten is like running on a treadmill. The teacher must keep the pace, and everyone is required to fall in place. The full-day program has a lot of extra time built into the day, allowing for repetitive lessons during a school day. If Olivia needs repetition, this is where she belongs." I leave the meeting with much more understanding but still conflicted.

The following day when arriving at preschool, her teacher asks someone to watch the classroom, and she walks me to a conference room. She tells me she knows how conflicted I am about choosing all-day versus half-day. She reminds me Mike and I have been advocating for Olivia for the past two and a half years, trying to get all the services she needs. This is an opportunity for her to get more instruction and allow her to transition to first grade in a stronger position. She encourages us to take advantage of this opportunity. More importantly, she addresses the issue that is really bothering me. Her experience will be different. It will not be same as Hannah or any of their friends. She has a rougher road ahead of her, and maybe this will help her navigate it.

I leave the building feeling much better and call Mike. We chat and decide the all-day program is the best solution for our girl. I need to learn to handle my feelings of her being different and not fitting in with the other children.

The week before Memorial Day, her preschool holds their annual graduation for the four- and five-year-old class. My family always comments on how emotional I get during television commercials, movies, and of course preschool graduations. The tears I shed today are more tears of joy. Olivia has come so far. She stands at the front, towering over some of her classmates; I remind myself she is a year older than some. She is singing or pretending because she doesn't always remember the words. She is so proud when her name is called and she walks up to receive her "diploma." I am a mess. I observe the misty eyes of both her teacher and the director. They have traveled this journey right beside us and are deeply moved by this event.

We do not know how kindergarten will go for her, but we did not know how well she would do this year, either. Mike and I are elated to see her walking, talking, laughing, running, and being a kid. These are things we will never take for granted.

SUMMER 2004

Kelly

One scorching summer day, we plan a pool date with friends who have children similar in age to Hannah and Olivia. We met the family when Olivia and their daughter Laura were enrolled in the special education preschool. Hannah is one year younger than their older daughter, and Olivia and Laura are the same age, but Laura started kindergarten a year before. It gives Dianne and me a chance to catch up while the girls play. As we sit in the pool area, I keep an eye on Olivia, always watchful of her. She climbs out of the pool and looks stunned. Her motion freezes, and she looks lost.

I motion to her, and she squints at me and waves. This happens a few more times during the day. I make a mental note to ask her doctor about it when we have her next appointment.

Olivia's birthday falls the week before school starts. Mike and I make a big deal over their birthdays. A party with friends is usually held at our home. Olivia prefers a smaller number of guests, but we plan arts and crafts activities, games, lunch, and of course cake. While everyone is finishing their lunch and chatting away at the kitchen table, I notice Olivia isn't talking. She looks straight ahead as if in a trance. I approach her and lightly tap her shoulder to make sure she is okay. I don't want to bring any unwanted attention to her. She looks at me, still a little dazed, and nods. I start to wonder if she is having a seizure.

The girls talk about how excited they are for school to start. Olivia is thrilled to finally go to the same school as her sister.

The week before school begins, I meet with her classroom teachers, physical education teacher, and assistant principal to go over her IEP. We sit at a round table in the school library, and I give a description of her needs. The teacher looks concerned, but she quickly recovers. I decide to check in with her on a regular basis. Olivia will ride the bus to school with Hannah in the mornings and at dismissal will ride the bus that takes all the children from her class home. She is thrilled about the bus ride. She has watched Hannah ride the bus for so many years and is looking forward to having her turn.

The day before school begins, the girls are always nervous, and they usually do not sleep very well. A light breakfast is all they can handle. Mike takes the day off from work to accompany them to school. We drove Hannah her first day, and we are doing the same with Olivia. I think he is also concerned about how I will handle this transition. It's bittersweet for me. I'm excited for her and yet sad she is growing up, but that's what parenting is all about.

We await her arrival outside our house, and the bus stops in front. She comes skipping out with a huge smile on her face and runs to us with a big hug. Her first day has been a tremendous success.

It's interesting what changes come and go as time moves forward. Olivia has been terrified of balloons. Whenever she sees one, all her muscles tense and she'll stand still, refusing to get close. Suddenly, today, she picks a couple of uninflated balloons out of the kitchen "junk drawer." We placed them there because a while ago we tried to slowly introduce them to her . . . but failed. Anyway, she puts them in her mouth and blows into them. She enjoys inflating and letting the air out. Before we know it, she and Hannah are blowing balloons and letting the air out. Hannah ties some with knots, and they play with them.

Olivia says she wants a balloon party. The girls inflate some, and Olivia tapes a balloon to each kitchen chair. This is a rare occurrence.

November marks three years since the accident. I finally decide to focus on my recovery now that Olivia is in school all day. My follow-up neuropsychology appointment indicates I have recovered from most of my cognitive deficiencies. The doctors tell me I need to address my depression, anxiety, and grief. I've been having heart palpitations, which I didn't realize were unrelated to my heart. They are anxiety attacks.

I start looking for a therapist but have difficulty finding a good fit. I have issues with time management, organization, short-term memory, and fatigue. A benefit of all this is I can understand some of the issues Olivia has. I recognize her need to have things broken down into tiny steps because that strategy also helps me. I am unable to accept that I am impaired. It's ironic because I don't have an issue accepting her injury. I pretend I'm okay when I'm not. It has taken me a long time to accept the fact that my memory is not the same and I must write things down to remember them. This is one of the hardest things for me to accept.

Together with Olivia, we continue to improve, and we are advocating for those with brain injuries. We educate others about the devastating effects to both adults and children. I have joined a speaker's bureau and talk about our accident. I also speak at refresher training classes for emergency medical technicians and assure them their work matters to us, the victims. The audience is always very appreciative of our stories. We have all been through a traumatic event and hope to impart some knowledge to those risking their lives.

We know Olivia will always have to work extra hard. Her life is heavily scheduled with therapy and tutoring that takes time away from her ability to just be a kid. She experiences headaches, and it is harder for her to keep up with other kids her age, both academically and physically.

During a typical school day, she requires supervision to get started; initiation is difficult for her, and she gets easily distracted. It is best for her to follow a daily routine as she can get apprehensive when there are changes.

SPRING 2005

Kelly

The school year is quickly ending. Why does it always seem slow in the beginning, but once the New Year comes, the year seems to fly? I continue to volunteer in both girls' classrooms. I love seeing them during the day and having a chance to give back.

As I walk down the back hallway of the school, Olivia's case manager approaches me. She is responsible for coordinating Olivia's services within the school day and works one-on-one with her during the school day, assisting her as needed in meeting the goals the IEP team develops. She comments how well Olivia has adapted this school year. It is a big jump to go from a three- to a six-hour day and deal with constant stimulation. She continues telling me Olivia has blossomed and is a leader among her classmates, outpacing many of them in skills both academically and socially.

I immediately tense up. I know she's taking this conversation somewhere I do not want to go. She suggests I authorize discontinuation of services. I am incredulous. She notices my reaction and counters with the suggestion that we can let Olivia shine next year in first grade and not be encumbered with services. I stare at her for a moment and tell her an emphatic no. I am not going to authorize discontinuation of services. She needs these services and is entitled to them by law. Yes, she is doing remarkably well right now, but quite frankly, she is not among her peers. First grade will bring a new set of challenges. Her class size will be larger, most of her classmates will not be attending this school since they are required to return to their neighborhood school for the remainder of elementary school, and most importantly, she needs the assistance.

As the conversation ends, I walk away with anger brewing. How dare she think I will sign off on Olivia's services? I cannot help thinking she has been instructed to reduce services and chose my daughter. I am on high alert.

2006

Mike

Kelly and I are thrilled to find out that she is pregnant. We have two beautiful girls, and we're excited to have a third child on the way. Just like the previous pregnancies, we decide not to find out the gender during her pregnancy.

As we near the end of the first trimester in September, we decide to announce the wonderful news to the girls. We have Hannah and Olivia sit on our couch in the family room. Hannah, no surprise, is so excited. Our smiles turned into confused frowns as Olivia starts to cry. When she is composed, I ask her why she is crying. She wails, "I don't want to be a middle child!" I blame myself, as I always joke about the trials and tribulations of being a middle child.

When school starts and Hannah begins her first days in fifth grade, she tells her teacher and class that she is going to be a big sister again. It has taken a while, but now it is wonderful to see how happy she is.

I'm sitting in my office just two days later when Kelly calls me and says she's had a miscarriage. We thought we were safe, so we had been public with the news of her pregnancy. The miscarriage is a difficult time for all of us. It really feels that part of us has died. Olivia's earlier feelings faded, and she too was looking forward to being a big sister herself.

Kelly

As the school year progresses, Olivia has a harder time. She wants to be like everyone else. She doesn't like being pulled out of the classroom to work with the speech therapist or work in small groups along with a special education teacher. Leaving the classroom with a few other students singles her out. She is beginning to resent it more and more. One of the issues seems trivial to the rest of us, but for her it is huge. The teacher distributes white binders to all the students for reading logs, worksheets, and notes on the books they are reading. Olivia's group consists of herself and two other students. They leave the classroom during "reading time" and do not receive binders. Olivia really likes her teacher, as all the kids do, and feels she is missing out by not having the binder. A few of her classmates ask her where her binder is. I don't know if they're genuinely curious or being mean. She explains she doesn't have one because she works with the other teacher; the conversation about why leaves her feeling different.

She comes home and complains about this issue. Mike and I suggest she ask the teacher if her group can receive binders to hold their things. We do not want to intervene and think this is a good opportunity for her to speak up for herself. The special education teacher promises her one, but they are never distributed. Olivia's disappointment grows each day. All she wants is to be just like everyone else.

She cannot get past this slight, and I witness a girl in her class making comments to her because she doesn't have her binder. I decide it's time to speak up for her. I mention to the teacher Olivia is disappointed she doesn't have an opportunity to work with her individually as the other students do. The teacher's response is she doesn't have time to work with three additional students. I am at a loss for words.

Mike and I know we cannot make a teacher work with our daughter, but we can provide the binders. We purchase identical binders, and Mike prints out pictures correlating to interests of the two other students to individualize them as the rest of the class has. Olivia takes them to school the following day. She is thrilled. I see how much joy this little binder brings her and kick myself for not doing it sooner.

2007

Kelly

In January, Olivia starts noticing things in the classroom that single her out or areas where she can't keep up with the development of the other students. It's heartbreaking to witness alongside her.

I schedule a meeting with the principal to discuss my concerns. As soon as she hears me request placing Olivia in a classroom consisting of only students with learning disabilities, she vehemently says no. We discuss the issues Olivia is experiencing in the classroom, and she responds appropriately. The tipping point for me is when she informs me most of the students in these classrooms have not only learning issues but also serious behavior issues. She believes this placement would only push Olivia further back. I leave agreeing with her assessment, and yet I am still unsure how to help my daughter.

After this meeting, I start thinking and praying about what alternatives we have at our disposal to show the school Olivia needs more help. They still don't believe us when we tell them she has a really hard time with processing information, memory, reading, and math. The school talks about what a wonderful, happy child she is. Mike and I try to find a way to prove she is really struggling.

Mike

The wait is excruciating in the summer. This time, Kelly and I wait the full time to officially tell anyone that she is pregnant again. I'll never forget how difficult it was to tell our girls that Kelly had a miscarriage last year. At forty-two, we are a bit older than typical parents in our circles having another baby, and we want to make sure that all indications are favorable that the baby is healthy. So at three months, we gather Hannah and Olivia in our family room to give them the news. Both are ecstatic and cry tears of joy. Kelly and I proudly soak in the moment, feeling the love and warmth of our family.

2008

Mike

About two years ago, the Brain Injury Association of America (BIAA) approached Kelly about a media kit they were putting together to help educate others about traumatic brain injury (TBI), coinciding with Brain Injury Awareness Month. The kit includes a large poster of the United States with five photos of people with brain injuries and a short bio of their story. Olivia is the only child on the poster. Each bio is represented with a fact sheet in the kit. Olivia's fact sheet contains more information about the crash and her interests.

Olivia is very anxious to see the poster. I suppose she thinks this is her way of being famous. She does not focus on why she is profiled, which I suppose is a good thing! Anyway, on a few occasions she asks to see it. Finally, we relent.

We show her the poster and read the fact sheet (well, most of it) to her. We watch her face, but she doesn't seem to react much at all. Hannah is much more focused. I guess Olivia's curiosity is taken care of . . . A few days later, though, she asks if she can take the poster to school. Kelly says she will check with her teacher, but we have reservations about doing so. Olivia, thankfully, sees the poster as simply her photo for all to see. We feel strongly about the intended message but are concerned how other children might react if they learn more about Olivia and note her deficiencies.

April 10 is another big day for our family as we expand from four to five members. Kelly and I can't wait for my parents to arrive with Hannah, age eleven, and Olivia, age nine, to meet their new sister, Anya. We tell my parents not to tell the girls the gender of the baby.

When Hannah steps in the room and sees Anya, she grows flush with excitement and cries again the joyous tears that she shed last fall, but it is more controlled. She's thrilled to welcome her baby sister to the family.

And Olivia? I think it is quite a bit to soak in. Even though she sees how Hannah reacts, which is usually how Olivia gets her cues on how to act, she doesn't cry and instead smiles broadly. Although Hannah asks to hold Anya, Olivia is simply content to be close to her sisters as I take photos to mark the momentous occasion.

In the years to come, many people ask Kelly and me, with a knowing smile, "Oh, she wasn't planned, was she?" or "I guess she was an oops baby!"

That makes us so upset. Yes, having a baby ten years after our second child wasn't exactly the plan. Of course, our "plan" didn't include Olivia's incident and the years of medical appointments, tests, therapy sessions, and the frustrations along the way. And should our response also include that we had two miscarriages?

So, they are right. No, we didn't plan our life to be this way.

Kelly

Anya's birth brings a lot of joy back into our home. The girls are thrilled when meeting their new sister. Olivia adjusts to being referred to as "the middle one," and she likes it. She aligns with Mike now. Our lives are hectic, but that isn't anything new.

One evening, the older girls are upstairs doing homework and Mike holds Anya while I make dinner. He is standing on the other side of our kitchen island, admiring Anya as she sleeps contently in his arms. We catch up on the day's events, and he comments, "I realize I haven't felt any joy since the incident. Olivia's injury took all the joy out of my life, but now looking at this beautiful baby, I can feel joy again." I glow, watching the two of them as tears roll down my cheeks. I did not realize the gravity of his emotions until this moment. How is it possible? At this moment I feel both heartbreak and expansive love. Is it possible to feel both emotions simultaneously?

Mike

One day in November, we are in the family room, and Olivia becomes distraught after arguing with Kelly. Kelly asks her to clean up, and Olivia does not want to do it. She disappears upstairs to her room. She returns to the family room a bit later with her backpack and says she is running away. She leaves through the door that opens to our garage. We are stunned, but I say let's wait a bit. Hannah is upset and yells that we can't let her run away, but we don't believe Olivia will go very far. After a few minutes and glancing at the door, I walk into the garage. She is sitting on the back bumper of our van, head drooping.

I ask her, "What are you planning to do?" She says she wants to run away because she doesn't fit in with our family and everything else. I pause and ask if I can walk with her. She hesitates and says okay, so we start up our street without saying a word. I'm not quite sure what to say.

As we turn onto another street, I ask her where we're going. She says she doesn't know.

"Well, where are you going to live?" She says again that she doesn't know. "Who are you going to live with? What are you going to eat? Who are you going to play with?" Silence. I turn to her as we continue our walk and show her my outstretched hand and say, "Do you see my hand?" She nods and looks up at me quizzically. "How many fingers do I have?"

She says, "Five."

I stop walking and look at her closely. "You're right, I have five. How many members do we have in our family?"

She says, "Five."

"Yes, we have five members in our family just like five fingers on my hand." I point to each digit. "We have Mommy, me, Hannah, Anya, and Olivia." I point to my thumb when I say her name. "Olivia, you are like my thumb." I fold up my thumb into my hand. "You see, without my thumb, I really can't hold a fork to feed myself or hold a glass to drink. I can't turn a doorknob to open a door. I won't be able to brush my teeth. I won't be able to hold a phone. I don't think I could get dressed, either.

"Olivia, each finger and my thumb are so important to me; my life won't be the same if I no longer have them. The same with our family. Olivia, you are like my thumb. I need my thumb and my fingers, just like I need each member of my family. Without any of them, my life just doesn't work. Olivia, I need you." Olivia looks serious and thinks over things for a moment. "Olivia, can we go home?" She nods, and we turn around to head back home.

I reach for her hand. As we walk home, holding hands, I squeezed hers gently, thumb and all.

2009

Kelly

The day Mike and I dread finally arrives in the spring. Olivia has been coming home complaining about school and being pulled out of class to work privately with other teachers. She does not enjoy the attention it brings to her or the questions from her classmates. We have noticed her social network is changing. It's getting harder to keep up with lunchroom banter with friends, and she is often left out of get-togethers.

Mike and I consulted with various doctors over the years about when the right time to tell her about the accident. Some felt we should not tell her because it could become a crutch for her. Others felt it better to tell her rather than risk her finding out on her own and feeling we haven't been truthful.

We sit down with her to tell her what happened on November 27, 2001. I'm not sure what her reaction will be, so I prepare myself for anything. She quietly listens to Mike speak. Tears well up in my eyes.

I feel responsible and worry she will blame me. He tells her she was in the hospital for a few weeks and received services to assist in her healing. We tell her how her brain was shaken, and she must work harder than her peers to learn new information. We do not give any specifics unless she asks. She is stoic, but there is emotion behind the stoicism. She asks if she can go to her room, and we respond yes but also tell her we love her and that any time she has a question, we are here for her. She nods and walks out.

My heart is broken. Will this information help her understand the whys and hows? We hope eventually it will. As parents, all we can do right now is support her and love her as we have been doing since she was born.

2010

Mike

Olivia is very naive and gullible. Too many times, I feel that her "friends" take advantage of her for a joke at her expense. It seems that Olivia is constantly playing catchup in processing information even if engaged with her peers in a conversation.

I'm not quite sure if Kelly feels the same, but I want to give our eleven-year-old a head start before she starts middle school. I picture her peers saying something that she doesn't understand, and her just laughing and nodding. Then the friends will realize she doesn't comprehend what they are saying and will make fun of her, so . . . I teach her swear words. One day, I explain to Olivia that although we don't say these words, she will be hearing these and oftentimes will not understand what others are saying. This will be new to Olivia— well, at least I think so, since she doesn't hear those words in our house!

Kelly thinks we should have recorded the conversation, me

saying the word, defining it, and in the case of certain swear words, going into more detail, which is a bit awkward for a father merging this conversation with a talk of the birds and the bees.

After our talk, I can tell that this is quite a bit for Olivia to take in. We end our discussion, which is pretty much just me talking, and I see by Olivia's serious expression that she needs time to let this sink in. I think this has been a good idea. However, not sure this will be a good trait to put on some type of Father-of-the-Year nomination.

2012

Mike

Middle school is not kind to Olivia. Bullying is pervasive as students realize that Olivia is sometimes slow to process information and it's easy to make her upset. At only fourteen, Olivia is called stupid, among other things. Olivia can be with a group of kids, and as is common with middle-school girls, they talk a mile a minute. Kids laugh, talk over each other, and converse like typical middle-school girls. Olivia might catch the joke, but it takes her a bit longer. By the time she processes the information, the kids have moved on to another topic.

Olivia comes from an interfaith family but is being raised in my faith, Judaism. I am not sure what has led to the anti-Semitic slurs that are hurled her way. I think it started with a bracelet she wears with a Star of David. She's told that it's ugly and that she should just get rid of it, wear a cross, etc.

It gets worse as kids say that Jews are stupid and ugly and try to convince Olivia that she should just go to church. Olivia is intimidated and scared that things could get violent. It doesn't help when two other girls at her lunch table make jokes about the Holocaust!

Teachers and the school administration are made aware of the comments. As parents, Kelly and I are frustrated and concerned. We send emails, make calls, and meet on more than one occasion with the staff and administration. Apparently, our communications don't resonate as matters don't improve.

Since no progress is made and I am getting increasingly upset, I send a letter to the county superintendent. No response.

I follow up with the school, offering my assistance and support to increase sensitivity training by including information and contacts for local clergy of different denominations, social service agencies, websites offering training and resources, articles about bullying, and more. Let's just say that my phone remains silent.

Kelly

Middle school is a challenging time for any adolescent, but for one with a disability, it is even more so. Olivia is familiar with the school since her older sister went here, but the new daily schedule, locker, large noisy hallways, and finding classrooms is a challenge for her. Her teachers, case manager, and counselor tell me she is handling the transition into the sixth grade well.

At home we experience a lot of issues. She is angry. She storms off, pounding up the stairs and slamming her bedroom door daily. The cause may be a little irritation or not. We try speaking to her calmly once things settle, but the situation does not improve. One evening she punches her bedroom door so hard that she leaves an indentation. One thing I never worried about was her harming herself. I am not as confident now. The stress is affecting all of us. Every time she raises her voice, Anya puts her hands over her ears and starts crying. It's exactly how I feel.

One evening after an extremely loud outburst, I suggest we contact her neurologist, Dr. Parker. We have not seen him since Olivia was six years old. At that time, he thought she was progressing very well and referred to her as "the Miracle Child." At our first appointment, Dr. Parker reviewed her records and commented he had seen several children with traumatic brain injuries, and most had less severe injuries than Olivia. Many never learned to walk and talk again, and he feels her progress is a miracle.

I took Olivia to his office when she was four because we suspected seizures, but the testing was inconclusive. We continued follow-ups with him for a few years but then stopped because she was progressing and there was nothing further he could add to her care.

Mike accompanies us to the appointment. The office is decorated for children given it is affiliated with the Children's Hospital. Olivia has her vitals taken in an area with pictures of princesses, pirates, and monster trucks. She appears too old to be here, and yet she is not. Dr. Parker enters the examination room and chats a bit with the three of us. He looks over her file and asks which hand she writes with. When she replies her right hand, he chuckles and says he indicated in his notes she would be left handed because she exhibited right-hand weakness in the earlier years.

He conducts his examination, and we give him a few updates. He looks directly at Olivia and asks her, "When you get angry or frustrated, does it feel like your brain is on fire or you are getting so mad you cannot control anything?" She responds, "Yes, that is how it feels." He informs us her lack of control is a mechanism of her brain. Her injury makes her less capable of controlling these emotions, especially during the adolescent years. He makes some recommendations, and we leave. I feel so relieved. There is a mechanical reason she is so angry. If we can now help her to manage it better, then she will be all right.

2013

Kelly

Seventh grade is becoming exceedingly difficult for Olivia. She is often behind on assignments, and her organizational skills are severely limited. She is also having difficulties with some of her classmates, which must be affecting her ability to focus on school.

Approximately every two years, Olivia has neurological testing to determine her current cognitive and emotional abilities. These are intense days; we no longer travel to Baltimore but instead go to the Children's National Hospital in Washington, DC. It is a day of getting up incredibly early, driving to the hospital during rush-hour traffic, testing in the morning, a break for lunch, and more in the afternoon and leaving sometime after 3 p.m. The report is usually completed in three weeks, and we return to get the results.

These appointments allow Mike and me to get a clearer picture of where Olivia is as far as her brain injury healing and development. We also receive top-notch recommendations. We do not always follow up on all the suggestions but do consider or investigate most of them. Our follow-up this spring of her seventh-grade year is hard. The doctor requests to speak to both Mike and me and then meets separately with Olivia. The doctor realizes Olivia can only comprehend a small portion, and the information she shares with us is a bit more complicated.

The office is small and tucked back into a feeding disorders clinic. Colorful pictures of food items decorate the walls. Mike and I enter the office, and the doctor tells us what a lovely daughter Olivia is and how cooperative she was during the many hours of testing. She explains Olivia really did her best, but once the fatigue set in, the testing was over. As she goes over the results, my head is swelling. It's always such a massive amount of information to take in and retain. I usually go home with the report so I can read it over in my own time and make notes.

Two things really strike me as she gives us the results. Olivia is struggling with depression and anxiety. The doctor recommends it may be time to explore medication to help manage the symptoms. This is concerning. She believes some of the eating issues we report are related to both diagnoses as well. A list of recommendations is included with the report, and she gives us her business card and encourages us to contact her with any questions.

Mike and I walk out a bit stunned. I'm not sure where to begin, but we don't have time to discuss the options since Olivia is finished speaking with the doctor. We head to the car for the long ride home.

Kelly

I have been looking for ways to get more involved with brain injury issues. My relationship with the Brain Injury Association of Virginia has continued since my initial meeting with Anne McDonnell, the executive director, in 2002. I reach out to their office whenever I need assistance locating services or finding the correct avenues to advocate for Olivia's education. Reading their newsletter one day, I notice an article about applications to serve on the board of directors. I call Anne, and we discuss the time commitment, roles of board members, and her vision for the organization. I take some time to weigh the pros and cons. It will require a drive to Richmond every quarter for a Saturday-morning meeting. Mike and I discuss logistics, and I decide to apply. I hope this will be a new avenue for me to explore to feed the need of giving back.

I ultimately join the board of directors in January 2013. I am terrified. The week before the first meeting, I receive a five-inch binder full of financial reports, five-year strategic plans, fundraising initiatives, and bylaws. I sit down once everyone is in bed and start reviewing these materials.

Sitting on my family room sofa in the quiet evening, tears stream down my face. My heart is pounding, and the anxiety takes over. I do not understand all this information I'm reading. How can I sit on a board of directors? The following day I share these thoughts with some other moms while our kids play in my basement. I don't know them very well, but the feelings come pouring out like a waterfall. They validate my concerns but encourage me to go and think I will be surprised at my ability to handle it all. They remind me I have dealt with so much since that fateful day in November 2001 and are confident I will persevere.

I keep those thoughts in my head while driving to Richmond the next morning. I get up at 5:30 a.m. to give myself extra time. I enjoy my solo ride, listening to music, and realize I am building my confidence. I have not driven more than two hours by myself since our accident; it's not as bad as I thought it would be. I will be exhausted tomorrow, but hopefully, it will get easier over time.

I arrive early and get a cup of coffee before entering the cavernous meeting room. The room is lit with fluorescent lighting, and there are no windows to allow sunlight in. I sit through part of the meeting a bit overwhelmed, but then a sense of relief comes over me. I made it here, sitting in this room of attorneys, medical and business professionals, association staff, and a few other survivors. I realize I can do this.

Our search for a therapist continues as Olivia enters eighth grade. I ask doctors for recommendations, contact Brain Injury Services for suggestions, and search on my own. The one therapist we find seems to be a good fit, but then she isn't. Mike suggests someone we know. I immediately agree she will be a great fit if she is able to fit Olivia in her schedule.

We find a time that works. The only caveat is that it's during the school day. I pick her up, drive thirty minutes to the appointment, wait fifty minutes while they meet, and drive another thirty minutes back to school. If she and Olivia are a good fit, it will be worth the almost two hours.

Olivia continues struggling socially in school, and when it's time for her transitional IEP meeting in the spring, I ask her if she is willing to change high schools next year. The middle school sends all the students to one high school, the one Hannah is attending. The student body consists of the same students she has been with these past three years. Mike and I worry this group will continue to bully her. Maybe it's time for a change. There is another high school she can attend if we get special permission and agree to provide transportation. She knows some kids who will attend since they went to her elementary school.

Surprisingly, Olivia is agreeable to this change. At her IEP meeting, we decide she will attend a different school. I have mixed feelings. It would be nice for Hannah and Olivia to spend a year together in high school before Hannah's graduation, but I doubt they would see each other. It's a lot to consider, but overall, we all agree it's the best fit for Olivia, and that is what matters.

PART FIVE
THE HIGH SCHOOL YEARS

2013

Kelly

Once the decision that Olivia will attend a different high school is complete, another wave of anxiety rolls in. Is this the right decision for Olivia? Is this the right decision for our family—which really means for me? It will be my responsibility to drive her to and from school. She will not have access to bus transportation since it is our choice, not the school's. How will this new responsibility affect me and our family?

There are many other changes happening as well. Our oldest daughter is entering her senior year of high school, and a feeling of melancholy surrounds this time. Only one more year living in our house, and then she'll be off to college, coming home only a few times a year.

She continues to thrive and shine in all she does, and I know deep down this must affect Olivia. We make a point to encourage our children and ask, "Did you try your best?" We do not use the phrases

"If only you believed" or "If you want it hard enough, it will happen" or "You need to do better and get all As." We balance our praise. There is a lot to be proud of in all our children. They are individuals. Their triumphs and failures are individual.

The summer focus is getting Olivia ready for a new schedule and adapting to a brand-new school. Most schools in our county are built to resemble one another to make navigation easy. This school is the oldest and not laid out the same. As I have done every year, I set up a meeting with all her teachers and case manager the week before school starts. The case manager meets me in the lobby beforehand and escorts me to the room. We sit in a circle in what appears to be a small classroom. The teachers look uncomfortable sitting in the chairs with desks attached. They introduce themselves, and it's apparent some do not want to be here. They're slumped in their seats and looking a bit annoyed. I notice the case manager is a bit abrupt in her comments but attribute it to her overwhelm at the beginning of a new school year.

After the case manager introduces me, I give a brief overview of Olivia's history. One teacher appears upset he is required to attend this meeting. He questions some of the accommodations and remarks his curriculum is structured and there is not much extra time to alter deadlines. I immediately take note he is going to be a challenge.

The first day of school arrives, and I pick Olivia up after school, eagerly waiting to hear how her day went. So many questions have been on my mind—what she thinks of her teachers, classmates, etc. I make sure to arrive early since I don't know how busy the parking area will be and I don't want her to get anxious looking for the car. The outside of the school is beautiful. It has a white façade with tall Roman columns. There is a large green lawn in the front with old trees and a path leading to the parking areas.

I see her walk out the front doors with a bright smile on her face. *Phew, things must be all right.* She gets into the car, puts on her seat belt without looking at me, and immediately bursts into tears. The tears quickly escalate into sobs. My heart races, and I feel my breath getting shallow. I try to focus on driving while talking to her about her day. She tells me she tried to find her classrooms but was knocked into while walking because the halls are too crowded to navigate, and she does not want to go there anymore. I keep asking myself if this is a big mistake.

We return home to Mike, Anya, and Hannah, who are excited to see her. Mike is also eager to hear about her day as she storms upstairs, and I shake my head, signaling she isn't in any mood to talk yet. Whenever Olivia is upset or fatigued, she retreats to her room to rest, listen to music, or calm down.

Later that evening after dinner, we talk calmly about her experience. She seems better emotionally but still defeated. The routine gets better each day, and the halls seem less intimidating as she gets used to the unfamiliar environment. She continues seeing her therapist once a week, and I juggle these appointments around the rest of the family's schedule. Olivia is also pleased to resume therapeutic riding since taking the summer off and has music therapy now as well.

Kelly

By mid-September, we are in a groove with school. Olivia is getting used to the new schedule, as are Anya and me. I drive Olivia to school each morning and pick her up at dismissal. Anya is always with us since her kindergarten is a half-day program. There are some days I wake Anya so we can drive Olivia to school, which always tugs at my heart. I am the mom who does not like to wake a sleeping child if I don't have to.

Olivia enjoys therapeutic riding this session and really enjoys her instructor. This is her sixth year of riding, and she has progressed quite a lot from those early first lessons. She has participated in shows the program conducts over the summer, and her confidence has really grown. She is paired with another girl a few years younger. The girls both enjoy each other, and her mom and I chat during the riding time.

The indoor ring we are assigned is a newer one, and it has seating to accommodate the shows and events. Olivia forms a bond with each horse she rides and speaks so lovingly to them as if they are friends. She has always loved animals, so this isn't a surprise. She isn't as enamored with the current horse she's riding, though; he is much bigger than any of the others she has ridden and seems to have a mind of his own.

Since her lesson is in the early evening, I leave Anya at home with either Hannah or Mike. The evenings are getting darker earlier, and fall is in the air. Riding is hard in the summer since the dress requirement is long pants, boots, and a helmet. When it is over ninety degrees, this can make for an uncomfortable hour.

During our drive, I look at the sky and try to determine if it's going to rain or not. We arrive, and Olivia runs out of the car with her riding helmet in hand and enters the facility. Most evenings the horses are already saddled up and ready to ride. I walk to the opposite side of the ring where I can sit and observe. The girls start their lesson, and I turn my back to place my keys on the bench when I hear a loud noise. The roof and sides of the building are metal, and everything echoes, so I am not too startled. The other mom turns to me and says, "Olivia just fell."

I turn and see her lying on the ground in a fetal position. My heart stops. *Oh my god, how could this have happened?* I run over, and one of the instructors lets me in the ring, which normally isn't allowed. Her horse is being led away. I bend over and ask if she is all right, and all she manages to mumble is no. She keeps repeating her leg and stomach hurt. The instructor is truly kind and speaks to her in a calm voice, which is what Olivia needs. I try to help her stand a few times before she can steady herself. I decide we need to go to the emergency room as a precaution. Realizing my keys are still on the bench, I accompany her outside of the ring, and the other mom comes and hands me my keys. She puts her hand gently on my arm and says, "I am so sorry. I hope she is okay."

The instructors follow us to the car. We get in, and I drive as she moans. I try comforting her, but she is incapable of speaking. As I drive down the long gravel road leading through the gate of the facility, I am mindful of the speed limit set at fifteen miles per hour but focus on getting to the emergency room. She tells me she doesn't want to go to the hospital, but I explain it is only a precaution to make sure she's all right. It takes us about fifteen minutes, and I help her out of the car. Dusk gives the scene an eerie quality. We enter the building, the same one we had been wheeled into that fateful evening in 2001.

I always feel a pit in my stomach when we come into the emergency room. I do not remember that night, but the pit indicates that I have been here before and it wasn't fun. We check in with the triage nurse, and Olivia can barely speak. I complete the paperwork, being sure I give her complete history, including her prior traumatic brain injury. We sit in the waiting area, and I text Mike, updating him. He offers to come, but I tell him it isn't necessary. We watch as a young boy is carried in by his father. Since he's wearing a soccer uniform, I conclude he hurt his leg or foot playing soccer. He is sobbing in obvious pain. The room is bright with a lot of light, which I know is hurting Olivia's eyes and will ultimately lead to a migraine. I ask her if she wants something to drink or eat, and she declines. I always know when Olivia isn't feeling well because it's one of the rare times she refuses food.

A nurse calls us into the door behind the triage, where we sit in cold, hard chairs while the nurse looks over our forms and asks a lot of questions. She explains the pain scale to Olivia with a ten being a smiley face and a one being a mad face and asks her what level of pain she feels. Olivia is unable to answer. This question is too arbitrary for her, and I've never understood why children are given this scale. If they've never experienced pain, how are they expected to rate it? I answer the question based on her history. I am surprised and annoyed we aren't ushered into an examination room as soon as her traumatic brain injury is noted. In the past, when we have taken her to the emergency room, as soon as the previous injury was noted, she was seen quickly. A minor benefit to having a brain injury.

After waiting a while longer, we head to the examination room. The hallways are wide, and there is an open feel to this area. Each room has a glass door allowing a little more privacy than a curtain. Olivia is instructed to lie down on the stretcher, and the nurse takes her vitals while another comes in to confirm the insurance information and contact information. I try to talk with her while also listening to the conversation between the nurse and Olivia. I ask if the lights in the room can be dimmed since they are hurting her eyes but am told it's not possible. The migraine sets in. I can always tell when she's suffering because her eyes dim, and she develops a confused look. The nurse asks repeatedly if she lost consciousness, and Olivia keeps replying she doesn't remember. I fill in what I can, explaining it happened so quickly and I do not think she lost consciousness.

We are left to await the doctor's arrival. Whenever a person is anxiously awaiting answers, it always seems to take forever. It doesn't help that we're sitting in a bright but cold room, and the anxiety is bursting out of both of us.

At last, he arrives. He asks her several questions, turning to me when she is unable to answer appropriately. She keeps complaining about her stomach and remains in a fetal position. He asks her to straighten her legs so he can examine her, and she complies grudgingly. I mention her history, and he doesn't seem concerned. He asks whether she was wearing a riding helmet, which surprises me that he even has to ask! Does he think I'm a complete idiot? Does he think the therapeutic riding program would allow anyone to ride without a helmet?

He informs us since she didn't lose consciousness, he doesn't think a CT scan is necessary, but he orders X-rays for her abdominal pain. After another long wait, an attendant comes to take her to radiology. I ask if I can accompany them. I'm not sure how Olivia is emotionally at this point, and I don't want her to go alone. When we return to the room, Mike is there. He explains Hannah arrived home and she is watching Anya. Since the accident, he feels guilty. He wants to make sure he is present, which I appreciate, but I also know I can handle things on my own.

Another long wait, and finally the doctor returns with the X-ray results. He asks Olivia a lot of questions, and she immediately looks to me. I tell her these are things only she can answer. The doctor concludes she needs to eat more fiber, doesn't think there is a concussion, and there aren't any broken or fractured bones, so we are discharged. A red flag goes up in my mind. I instinctively know there's more going on than simply the need to eat more fiber.

The next few days are difficult for her.

Mike

Kelly and I get more concerned about Olivia's condition, so I take her to the emergency room. The doctor on duty orders a CT scan almost immediately and diagnoses her with a concussion. The doctor also notes her eye tracking is off as well, so she tells us that Olivia needs to remain in a dark room with no electronics and needs to get a lot of rest. She instructs us to contact the concussion clinic associated with the hospital on Monday morning for an appointment prior to her return to school.

Olivia rests the remainder of the weekend and is upset when we tell her she cannot go to school on Monday morning. She has acclimated to the groove of school and worries about the work she's missing. I call the concussion clinic Monday morning, and once I inform the receptionist about her previous TBI, I am instructed to contact her neurologist immediately. I think, *That's odd; the clinic noted her history when the hospital did not.*

I immediately call the neurologist and am surprised to get an appointment the next day. There is usually a long wait prior to securing an appointment. We were just there two weeks ago for her annual appointment, and the doctor informed us he is leaving to take another position in Boston.

As he enters the examination room, he comments he was surprised to see her name on his patient list. We explain why we are here. I am taken aback when he asks if she was wearing a helmet at the time of the fall. I think, *What is it with this question?* but realize it's probably protocol.

He performs a full neurologic work up and looks over her scan and indicates she is fine to return to school. He instructs her to rest when needed but feels she will be okay returning to her normal schedule. He does caution she may want to cease horseback riding. I thank him, and as we ride down the elevator, I think, *This was an interesting appointment—not sure I agree with him that she is fine.*

2014

Kelly

Two families in our neighborhood for years have tried to get Olivia to try A Place to Be, an organization focusing on music therapy. Olivia resisted for years, but we finally talk her into trying it out. The key factor is she knows the therapist through another program, therefore making the transition a bit easier. Ashley is the right mix of young, outgoing, and talented. Mike and I are not sure we understand what music therapy encompasses or how it will help but figure we have tried so many things already, and the organization is highly recommended by people we know.

As the school year progresses into 2014, Olivia's mood starts going down. She becomes much more agitated and quicker to anger. Her grades are affected, and she complains more about her case manager. Olivia feels she doesn't speak nicely and is quick to become annoyed if Olivia doesn't understand directions.

It is a very rough adjustment, but the eye-opening clue that things are off is the night of her Holiday Chorus Concert. We arrive home late following a long evening filled with too many performances, and she tells us she has a paper due for science and has not started it. We learn the assignment was given in September and tell her it is unreasonable to expect it to be written by the next morning.

After much arguing back and forth, I remind her she has extended time on all homework and needs to use this accommodation. Her winter break starts in two days, and she can use that time to complete the project. She argues a bit before agreeing, putting her notebook and pen down and going to bed. Unfortunately, sleep is not forthcoming for me. I cannot get over the fact that she thought a complex project could be completed in such a short amount of time. Even the most advanced student would not be able to pull it off; how did she think she would?

Mike and I decide to investigate an evaluation with a different doctor her therapist recommended. The therapist has spoken very highly of Dr. Lisa Meier for a long time, and we decide it's time. I call and give her some information pertaining to Olivia, and we schedule a parent consultation. Her evaluations are very thorough, and she asks me to gather all her medical records from birth to present. The records I cannot locate are ordered through the individual doctor offices. She asks provoking questions. I am confident she will pick apart Olivia's case and determine what's going on with our girl. As the appointment progresses past two hours, I look over at Mike, and he is glassy eyed.

Dr. Meier completes an afternoon of testing with Olivia, explaining she is not repeating any test previously done during her neuropsychological testing. Luckily, we've schedule Olivia's testing on the President's Day holiday so she doesn't have to miss any more school.

Things at home are deteriorating quickly. Schools have been closed several days because of bad weather, and when the routine changes suddenly, Olivia has a challenging time transitioning. She sleeps late, unaware of how much work she must complete and how to get it done. When school resumes, teachers are forced to quicken the pace of instruction to make up for the lost class time, which only slows her processing speed down even more. Olivia feels the anxiety ramp up, and instead of talking about it with her case manager, mental health therapist, or us, she internalizes all these feelings. Her grades plummet, and she is spiraling.

A few days after school resumes, I receive a phone call from her case manager. She begins the conversation saying, "Mrs. Lang, what are you trying to do? Olivia mentioned you are having testing done."

I pause, thinking, *Why did Olivia mention this information, and second, why does this concern the case manager? Is she worried the testing will prove her inabilities as a case manager? Is she concerned testing will require more of her or the school?* I am dumbfounded. My heart rate increases, and anger starts building. I take a deep breath and respond, "We do this every few years to assess Olivia's progress as it relates to her brain injury. Her doctors made this recommendation a few years ago. In addition, her grades are falling, and she is struggling. We want to figure out how else we can assist her to be successful." The case manager tells me it isn't necessary. She continues, "All students are having a tough time due to all the missed days of instruction, and things will settle once she gets caught up."

How many times will a school employee tell me about the other students? I am exhausted by the comparison. I tell her, "I am not worried about the other students, and quite frankly, they aren't my concern. Olivia is the only student I am referring to, and I am going to do whatever is possible to help her." The conversation does not end well as I hear anger in her voice. I am furious as I hang up the phone. The nerve of her. She doesn't have any right to question our motives.

Kelly

A few weeks later, the anger and hostility emanating from Olivia increases dramatically. The breaking point occurs while driving her to school one morning. She argues with me and becomes so enraged she throws a can of seltzer water from her lunch at me. It punctures, sending liquid all over me and the car. Anya is crying as it startles her. I pull over so as not to cause an accident. I turn to Olivia in the back seat and very sternly say to her, "Do not ever do that again." We ride the rest of the way in silence, and when we arrive, she gets out of the car angrily without bothering to close the door. I immediately take out my phone and call Dr. Meier, leaving her a message asking when her report will be complete. I explain things are getting worse and we need help.

In late March, Mike and I drive to Dr. Meier's office to get the results of Olivia's testing. Dr. Meier quickly escorts us to her office and welcomes us to sit on the couch opposite her. She has a very calm demeanor, which draws you in. She takes a deep breath and says, "First, I want to start off by saying you have been through so much over these years trying to manage Olivia's injury." Such a simple statement, and yet it holds so much compassion and empathy. The tears start rolling down my cheeks. No one has ever acknowledged this to Mike and me. Validation is so powerful.

The report is very complimentary of Olivia's innate traits of compassion, desire to please, and loving nature. The doctor is skilled in starting with the positives. However, she does point out a lot of unsettling issues. Olivia's cognitive functioning has declined considerably. Her math skills are so poor Dr. Meier is stunned she is on track to pass Algebra I. The recommendations are several pages long. The most startling discovery is a chart she includes in the report showing Olivia's intelligence quotient. The doctor has calculated her scores through the years of prior testing and illustrates the serious decline. She is now on the level of cognitively impaired.

Dr. Meier sees the devastation on our faces. She is gentle and reassuring, but I am unable to grasp any more information. She suggests we take the report, go home, and digest it.

As Mike drives home, I cry inconsolably. This is the most devastating report. Other reports consisted of both positive and negative outcomes, but this one makes such an impact on me. I am not sure Olivia is going to be all right. Up to this point, I thought she would get a job one day and live independently. This report is indicating a vastly different scenario.

I take a few days to decompress and then begin looking over the report. Dr. Meier makes several suggestions regarding Olivia's education plan. The state allows students with individual education plans (IEPs) to stay in high school longer than four years. We can prolong her graduation, giving her three extra years to complete her education and graduate at the age of twenty-one rather than eighteen. If she takes this route, her schedule will lighten considerably, possibly cutting her course load in half. We are not sure if the school will allow this scenario, but it is worth looking into if Olivia agrees.

It doesn't come as a surprise when she refuses this idea. She wants to graduate with her "friends." She will be embarrassed or shamed by this scenario, and we accept her decision. After all, what choice do we have at this point?

Dr. Meier also recommends additional math coursework since her basic math skills are so poor. I schedule a meeting with the IEP team. This is the first time this type of meeting is happening at this school. When I arrive, the case manager, two special education teachers, the dean of special education, and two representatives from the county school administration are sitting at a long table in the school library. The last comes as a surprise. In the twelve years we have navigated this process, we have only met with county school administration staff once. The school administration team usually conducts the meetings.

The team fights me hard on the additional instruction I request, even though the need is thoroughly documented in the report I share. We eventually agree on additional testing to determine her basic math skills. I walk out of the building exhausted but also triumphant. The school does not want to do additional work but in the end agrees to investigate her math skills.

Kelly

The annual IEP meeting is scheduled in the spring. I ask Mike to attend. After the difficulty I experienced before, I feel his presence is beneficial. Once again, as we enter the room, I am surprised there is a representative from the county administrative team. One of the diagnosticians reads her report on the additional math testing and explains her basic math skills are intact and denies our request for additional instruction.

The meeting continues, and the dean of special education and case manager take control. Dr. Meier's report is projected on an overhead screen. The dean proceeds to read the documents word for word. I think to myself, *We are going to be here all day.* As he reads, he glances at his watch and announces the meeting is adjourned, and since we did not complete the plan in the allotted time, another meeting will convene at another day and time. Mike and I are furious. This has never happened before.

Every year prior to this, the team keeps working until the IEP it is written. We have never met multiple times to complete the task. The dean explains this is school policy. I counter this was not communicated to us. As the team gets up to leave, Mike explains there is an important event we need to discuss since our daughter's safety is at risk. They stop and look at him. He informs them about a conversation we had with Olivia the previous evening.

I noticed marks on Olivia's arm and inquired what happened. After much stalling, she explained a girl approached her in the hallway and pushed her into the bay of lockers alongside the wall and then used the metal binding of her spiral notebook and scratched Olivia's arm. I learned this was not the first time this has occurred.

The dean informs us we need to speak with the principal regarding this matter, and the principal is called into the room. Most of the staff leave, and Mike retells the story. The principal responds, "Isn't your daughter attending this school because she is not at her home school? I think maybe she should go back there." I cannot explain the fury rising in me. We proceed to the front office and inform them we are picking Olivia up for early dismissal and she will not return until these incidents are investigated and her safety is assured.

The bullying incidents are investigated by the school, and the perpetrator is required to meet with the principal, but that is all the information that is divulged. We know the school's policy is that parents of the victim are not privy to the punishment of the perpetrator. Mike and I are not confident the bully receives any discipline.

We hire a special education advocate to assist with the follow-up IEP meeting. An advocate reviews the student's records and current plan and attends the meeting to assist the parents and advocate on behalf of the student. The advocate points out a few things in Dr. Meier's report we should pursue. As required, we inform the school that an education advocate will attend the meeting. As we enter the room, the atmosphere is quite different. The attendees are much more agreeable. They have worked with the advocate in the past and appear willing to work with us now.

The meeting flows much better this time around, and we obtain math tutoring for Olivia through the school to get her skills up to speed. As we walk out the door, Mike and I thank the advocate, and she suggests we investigate a reading program Dr. Meier referenced in her report. She explains in the past the school system has paid for the program and arranged services at the school rather than the center, which is forty minutes from our house. I arrange an evaluation for Olivia once I arrive home.

The center works on reading skills for all ages. The program helps children with phonics, retention, and comprehension. Olivia needs assistance with comprehension. The evaluation takes a few hours, and she is exhausted at the conclusion. I meet with the director, and she gives me a lot of information on the programs they offer. The key to their success appears to be consistency and repetitiveness. The program requires a commitment of daily lessons lasting one hour for a minimum of six months.

I look at her and comment, "Thank you, but there isn't any way I can make this work. We live forty minutes away, and I cannot take her out of school for the hour plus travel time, which will amount to almost three hours; it is not feasible." She understands and suggests I contact the director of special education. The center has worked with the school system in the past and has a relationship providing services for students. She suggests that when I contact the director, I ask her to approve the cost of the program and space in Olivia's current school. I am not very optimistic, but we don't have anything to lose. We have a long relationship with her.

Surprisingly, I secure an appointment with her quickly. The administration building is brand new and massive compared to the little school building I first entered in 2001. The director looks the same as when I first met her when Olivia was in preschool. A few years ago, I attended a town hall for parents of children receiving special education services. I was trying to obtain more reading assistance for Olivia, and the school principal told me she wasn't eligible because she received special education services. I attended the town hall hoping to get clarification, which I did. The following day, the principal called to let me know Olivia would start the program. I knew why her opinion changed.

The director and I speak for a bit before I ask for the reading services to be paid by the school system. She easily agrees and informs me I will have to coordinate with the school to fit the time into her schedule. I walk out of her office feeling victorious. I imagine her school will be very upset, but honestly, I do not care. The sunny, warm day helps boost my mood, but I honestly think if it were snowing and cold, I would feel as wonderful.

Another recommendation in Dr. Meier's report is an evaluation by a pediatric neuro-ophthalmologist. I'd never heard of this specialty when she mentioned it and learned it is a doctor trained in both neurology and ophthalmology. She was surprised we were never referred to one; apparently one of Olivia's brain bleeds was on her occipital lobe, and yet her vision was never evaluated by a doctor who was trained in both ophthalmology and neurology.

The day after school ends in mid-June, Olivia and I get up extremely early to make the long drive to Children's Hospital in Washington, DC. Olivia is a bit confused as to why we are meeting with yet another doctor. The office is in the basement, and it is very dark and dreary. I am surprised this portion of the building has not been spruced up a bit since it is a pediatric hospital. Upstairs there are colorful wall hangings and a lot of windows letting the sun in. We check in, and the receptionist instructs us to wait in the hallway where there are chairs lined up against the wall. It feels as if the office has been tucked into a dark corner, and they were left to set it up themselves.

A few minutes later, a technician escorts us into an examination room, confirms why we are here, and conducts a brief examination.

He speaks directly to Olivia, and when she is unable to answer, he turns to me. He explains, based on the technician's exam, he does not detect any vision issues but will do a more extensive exam in an adjacent room. I sit in the waiting area and once again am struck by the bleakness surrounding me.

The testing is rather quick. I enter another room where Olivia is sitting in the examination chair, looking around the room. She does not make eye contact with me. The doctor immediately explains she doesn't have any right peripheral vision. I try to comprehend this information. It is not what I expect to hear. How could she be walking around without part of her vision field, and this is the first time I'm learning such critical information? He sees the bewilderment and surprise written on my face. He acknowledges this information must be quite a shock. I still cannot understand how no one detected this on previous exams.

He proceeds to show me how Olivia sees the world. I am dumbfounded.

He asks a few further questions: Did she have a tough time learning to read? Were her pictures drawn without a right side? Did she walk into things on her right side? The answer to all of these is yes. I explain she was tested at Kennedy Krieger and the Wilmer Eye Institute, a world-renowned clinic at Johns Hopkins Hospital; how was this missed? He explains Olivia doesn't realize anything is different. At three years old, she did not remember how she viewed the world prior to the accident. Therefore, afterward, she assumed her lack of vision was normal. He further explains she learned to compensate for the lack of vision by turning her head very slightly. He mentions other doctors would not have noticed because the turn is so slight; he didn't notice it initially. I ask what we can do to rehabilitate her vision or fix it, and he says it cannot be reversed, nor could it have been reversed when she was initially injured. He concurs she should not pursue driving at this time.

Olivia looks dazed and does not ask any questions. She usually prefers to zone out during medical appointments and relies on Mike and me to relay the information to her. She is exhausted. We leave the appointment in a stupor. I have a hard time processing and understanding how this piece was missed for so long. So many questions have been answered during this visit. As I drive us home, Olivia asks me to explain what the doctor was saying. She is confused but not upset. Many of her questions surprise me since she usually does not comment about the appointments other than to complain about how long it takes or how tired she is.

We arrive home, and she immediately goes to her room where she usually retreats. I inform Mike of the appointment, but we don't have much time to dwell on it since we are preparing for Hannah's high school graduation party. At dinner, Olivia announces, "The doctor was right." She illustrates holding objects straight in front of her right eye and slowly moving them toward the right, and they disappear out of her line of sight. Tears well in my eyes as she explains. She didn't want to believe what the doctor told us, so she sat in her room most of the afternoon, testing herself, and my heart breaks again. An almost sixteen-year-old should not have to sit in her room and check her vision over and over. The gravity of what has been stolen from her hangs in the air. It is one thing if you are born without something, but to have it taken from you is quite another.

Mike

Olivia is enjoying A Place to Be's summer musical camp in June. It's a six-hour day, and she is tired, but I detect a brighter girl. She tells us about the others she's met who, like her, are dealing with various challenges. There are participants with autism, ADHD, obsessive compulsive disorder, anxiety, depression, low self-esteem, and brain injuries. She is getting to know others who share similar experiences and want to place their true selves out in the world. It is so refreshing to see a genuine smile on her face. The camp ends with a weekend of performances for the families as well as the local community. She has a nonspeaking role as a butterfly and wears the brightest smile on her face the entire time. It is such a thrill to see her so happy.

Kelly

We are delighted when the principal retires at the end of the school year. I hear great things about the incoming principal and set up an appointment for Olivia and me to meet her in July. She is very welcoming and listens to Olivia explain the issues she experienced in the past school year. The principal apologizes and remarks the situation was not handled appropriately and she will make sure things are different this school year. She is genuine, and I feel much better, and Olivia does as well.

In August, I schedule a meeting with Olivia's case manager and her teachers before the start of school. This is the first time Olivia willingly attends one of these meetings. I am impressed how she handles herself and explains her needs. The group at the table is overwhelming for me, so I can only imagine how she feels. Right away, I detect which teachers will be her allies and which will be difficult.

A Place to Be has asked her to participate in their show *Behind the Label*. We attended an earlier version of this show a few years ago and were impressed by how it teaches empathy and kindness. Mike and I are proud and excited for her. Rehearsals are held two times per week. It is a lot for her, but it also energizes her. She is meeting more peers and enjoying the camaraderie. She doesn't share much about her role, saying she wants to surprise us on opening night. One of the directors asks for pictures of Olivia when she was in the hospital, and I send her what I have, but it isn't much. One afternoon, Anya and I take Olivia to rehearsal and sit quietly in the audience while the cast rehearses. The director wants the cast to feel they are performing in front of an audience. I come armed with snacks and a lot of books and coloring activities to keep Anya entertained.

I half listen to the other performers while coloring with Anya. Some are hard to hear, especially when they aren't comfortable talking into the microphone. They are on a stage, and the staff tries to get them to project and pretend they are performing for an audience. Olivia approaches the microphone and performs her piece, "I Couldn't Get the Words Out," and follows up with a short monologue. She talks about going to her sister's *Nutcracker* rehearsal and getting into an accident and the resulting hospital stays and her traumatic brain injury. It is hard to hear.

As soon as her piece is complete, Anya turns to me and says, "Was I in the accident?" Surprised she was listening, I reply, "No, she was speaking about Hannah's *Nutcracker* rehearsal. The accident occurred before you were born." I wonder what other things she has overheard over the years and never questioned. Not that we speak about tragedies or difficult issues, but she is only in first grade at this point. She then asks, "Does Olivia have a brain injury?"

WOW! I explain a little bit to her about the accident and Olivia's work to heal but only as much as I think she can process. Mike and I have always wondered when these conversations would start. Such a scary subject matter for a six-year-old. I wait for the questions regarding herself, but they never come.

Mike

The debut performance is on a weekend in October coinciding with Hannah's family weekend at college. Luckily, we live close enough to accomplish both. The show is at a private-school theater. The school is generous, donating the facilities whenever possible for these productions and summer camps. The theater is packed, and Kelly and I cannot sit next to each other. Kelly sits in a chair with Anya on her lap. We are wet from our day walking around in the rain, and the air-conditioning is turned up to accommodate all the body heat and bright lights focused on the performers.

The stories of the performers are full of sadness, and yet there is so much hope and inspiration built into the program. They reflect on times they were dealt a devastating diagnosis and yet learned to adapt or persevere. The stories revolve around autism, visual impairments, learning disabilities, attention deficit disorder, cancer, anxiety, depression, cerebral palsy, and many more. One after another, they enter the stage holding clouds with their diagnoses written across. The ending number brings them back holding clouds with words of affirmation. It is beautiful and heartbreaking at the same time.

Olivia is thrilled. She is walking on cloud nine. The group tours to middle and high schools in the area. Kelly notifies her teachers and the principal she will miss class on all the performance days and explains what she is doing. The principal is the first to respond, and she compliments Olivia on courageously teaching empathy. Therefore, none of her teachers complain about her missing class. Kelly attends all the performances as the group teaches the message of empathy. Each performance, Kelly cries. When Olivia arrives on stage, singing along with her castmates, she is so happy and beautiful. She skips along, holding her cloud with pride. It's as if she is with her group.

I brace myself when it is her turn to sing as pictures of her appear on the screen behind her. Seeing the pictures of her in the hospital with me, Kelly, and Hannah break me each time. The tears well in our eyes, and I am unable to stop them. All the parents and guests of the cast sit together in the front rows, and one person always reaches out in support, illustrating empathy and acceptance. After all, we are all in this together. Surrounded by others who have spent years advocating for their children, I realize they are part of our "group." Our stories and challenges are different and yet similar. We and especially Olivia finally feel a sense of belonging.

In Manassas, Virginia, there is a wonderful venue called the Hylton Performing Arts Center. Hylton's Merchant Hall contains more than 1,100 seats in an elegantly styled opera house with a hundred–foot stage and orchestra pit. A Place to Be's performance of *Behind the Label* is performing two shows for all middle school children in Prince William County, Virginia. Olivia is nervous, but who wouldn't be? Especially since she is performing a solo in a packed auditorium filled with students and teachers and staff. Kelly and I aren't sure who is more nervous, the parents or the cast members. The parents and guests sit high in the balcony, allowing the students closer seating to the stage.

Several of the performers come to the stage before Olivia, singing, dancing, or reciting poems about their disabilities. Finally, the moment comes. Olivia takes the microphone on stage and gives a short monologue of her traumatic brain injury story, then leads into a short song about her experience. On the expansive stage, there is only our daughter, who confidently exposes the suffering—physical, mental, and emotional—that came with her injury. The applause following her performance brings tears to our eyes.

At the end of each performance, a short question-and-answer session is held so that the students can ask anything they want of the cast. You never know what the kids will say; you have to pray they are kind and supportive. Some of the students take the microphone and, in front of a thousand of their peers, say how they relate to one or more of the performances. Several give wonderful messages of empathy and what seems to me genuine understanding.

One girl stands up and says loud and clear into the microphone, "Olivia, I thought your story was beautiful, and you know what? You are a beautiful person." As the other parents of the performers around us offer words of support, I can only smile and nod; anything more will cause us to burst into a cascade of tears. When the session is over, the kids file out in the lobby of the building, waiting for school buses to take them back to school. Kelly and I stand in the back; we want Olivia to have her space with the other performers as they talk with each other and thank the kids for coming to the show. I notice the girl who complimented Olivia walking with an adult. I'm not sure if it is a teacher or a chaperone, but she leads the adult to Olivia. Although I am too far to hear the conversation among the three, Olivia is beaming. The girl gives Olivia a big hug after they talk.

It is a moment that we will never forget. It feels as if we are part of the warm embrace, and I supposed we are, one of empathy.

2016

Kelly

We learn in May that *Behind the Label* will be the keynote at a conference at the National Institute of Health in Bethesda, MD. One of the planners of the National Center for Medical Rehabilitation Research read an article in *The Washington Post* about the work A Place to Be was doing and specifically how the *Behind the Label* show is teaching local students about living and coping with disabilities. She was so moved by the story and felt the group would be an excellent start to the conference and reached out.

Olivia and I drive to Bethesda the day before the conference to attend a stage rehearsal along with most of the other cast members. We are staying in a hotel, and anyone whose parent is unable to attend is paired with others for the overnight stay. It takes a bit for everyone to get their bearings on the larger stage, but once the rehearsal is underway, it runs smoothly. Once dismissed, we drive to the hotel, check in, and meet others for dinner. It is a wonderful opportunity for all of us to relax and socialize before running off to other obligations.

Our shuttle ride leaves the hotel early, so we are up, dressed, and ready to go. The cast members are teenagers and young adults, and it is apparent mornings are not their best times of day. Once we arrive, the energy returns, and the excitement and nerves are felt by all. The cast rehearses and works out any technical difficulties before the conference attendees arrive. The audience consists of physical, occupational, speech, and vocational therapists as well as researchers and other professionals.

The show is beautiful, and the audience gives the cast a standing ovation. The energy these performers receive from this never ceases to amaze me. Cast and family members leave feeling excitement and hope. Olivia and I return to the hotel along with the others. We say our goodbyes, and I observe her energy fading. She is always so excited for these events, but once they are over, the fatigue hits hard. Her eyes aren't as bright, and I sense a migraine coming. We drive home on this beautiful spring day. The sun is shining, but the air is still a bit crisp, and there is so much hope circling around us. I remind myself not to engage in much conversation because she doesn't like to talk once we are on our way home, but I'm still feeling wonderful after such an experience.

Earlier in the spring, Mike and I met with an attorney to discuss getting power of attorney for Olivia. We have always worried she will get taken advantage of or manipulated by someone into handing over her money or making rash decisions before first discussing with us. I have spoken to other parents who have children with special needs and know that once she turns eighteen, it will be much harder to get these documents approved. At her last neuropsychological testing, the doctor informed me we would have a hard time obtaining guardianship since most states were drawing a hard line and not allowing parents to take over. Rather, she suggested the power of attorney so Olivia would not be able to sign any legal documents.

At our initial meeting, we give the attorney a brief history and explain our goals. We also need to set up a special needs trust for her to hold the money she will begin receiving at age eighteen from the accident settlement. As the attorney listens and asks further questions, she recommends we pursue guardianship. She explains power of attorney can be revoked by Olivia; if she and the guardian disagree, she can destroy the document without court approval. She gives us a few examples, and Mike and I nod in agreement. She also explains not all states have a strict guideline, and she feels Olivia will qualify under the current Virginia statute. We provide all the documentation, including medical reports, and once she reads them, she assures us we will not have any problem obtaining guardianship.

We explain the potential guardianship to Olivia, and she meets with another attorney, guardian ad litem, who interviews her to determine if she should be covered by a guardianship. Olivia chooses not to attend the court hearing, which is a bit of a relief. We aren't sure how she would handle it, and as she presents so well, a judge may question the need. She has an invisible injury that cannot be detected unless a person speaks to her for an extended period and gets to know her better.

The morning of the hearing is a typical hot and humid July day in Northern Virginia. Mike and I drive to the courthouse in Leesburg, a beautiful building in the center of town. As he drives, I feel a pit in my stomach. I am surprised by how this process is affecting me physically. We arrive very early and check in to security, handing over our cell phones and walking through metal detectors. The last time we were in this building was for the hearing to settle our civil cases. Another horrible day.

We learn the court is a busy place. A long line of cases is listed on the board, and we wait our turn. Both attorneys accompany us and explain how the proceeding will run. When our names are called, we enter and walk up to the judge sitting behind a high desk. It is just like you see in the movies or on Court TV, except we are able to approach without sitting at one of the tables.

The judge asks why we are here, and the attorneys explain our request for both guardianship and a special needs trust to protect her assets. She asks Mike and me a few questions, including why Olivia chose not to attend. Within ten minutes, she approves our request, and we are ushered out of the room to file paperwork and get the certified documents we need. Once the paperwork is complete, Mike and I thank the attorneys and retrieve our phones and walk outside. We are initially blinded by the bright the sun. I begin crying.

We head to a local coffee shop and talk. It is pretty quiet since we are between the breakfast and lunch times; it's nice to have a bit of time to decompress. I tell him I didn't expect this to hurt so much. This is so unfair. No parent ever thinks they will have to take their child's independence away before they turn eighteen. Why do we have to continue this painful reminder of all she lost?

Olivia's last year of high school is met with both excitement and uncertainty. In the spring, we discuss her desire to take an Advanced Placement science class. Her advisor suggests a suitable alternative. The schools recently began offering dual enrollment classes. He explains she will earn the equivalent of six college credits and satisfy her high school English requirement. Olivia agrees to this compromise, but we are still apprehensive. Some members of the IEP team think it will be a good fit for her, but others, especially her case manager, are not proponents.

Once again, we meet with her teachers prior to the school year. I feel much better about the class after meeting the teacher and hearing how it is structured. She is wonderful and seems to make a connection with Olivia during our brief meeting. We mention Olivia participates in the *Behind the Label* project with A Place to Be, and her teacher says she has seen the production, and this is why she recognizes Olivia.

Rehearsal for *Behind the Label* once again coincides with

the beginning of school. We are back in the thick of things. The rehearsals and anticipation of a new season brightens Olivia a great deal. She enjoys both the social opportunity this affords her and being on stage. We are lucky to have one other person with whom to carpool to and from rehearsals. Each season, the production changes a bit. Some performers move on to other things and new ones are brought in. Some of the songs and music change, and there is always a different energy.

Mike and I remark in October how performing has brought out Olivia's self-confidence. She usually shies away from any attention, but getting up in front of an audience and telling her story has invigorated her. I remark to the cofounders how thankful we are they have brought her back to life. It is such a joy to behold.

When I look at the calendar dates filled with rehearsals and performances, it always looks so overwhelming. I wonder, *When am I going to get anything done?* I enjoy the shows and attend all of them. Each one is different, depending on the mood of the cast and the reactions of the audience. I also really enjoy the camaraderie I feel with the other parents. Special needs parents do not have a lot of opportunities to interact with other parents going through similar experiences. This isolation seems much more pronounced as the kids get older. I do not know if it's because some parents check out at this point or they move on to other things, but it becomes a lonelier place.

Kelly

I start to notice a shift in Olivia. When the cast does their final bows as a group, she positions herself toward the back, not wanting to stand out. It appears she is hiding. I also feel that she is "off." It's hard to describe in words, but it seems she is very distracted, withdrawn, and irritable. I mention my thoughts to Olivia's therapist, who is trying to get her to open a bit more about her feelings. She comments a lot of seniors in high school are feeling this way given all the pressures they are under to get college applications complete and make plans for after graduation. She notes Olivia may be feeling down since she cannot contribute to these conversations but is most likely feeling the same angst as everyone else.

I share my thoughts with the director of the show, and she offers to speak with Olivia. I do not want Olivia to know I set this up because I want her to be authentic and honest. I'm not looking for her to put on her "happy" face, which always leads to, "Oh, she is fine. Probably just being a typical moody girl." I drive to the meeting and make myself scarce. I don't think it will last long, so I am surprised when I look at my watch and realize almost an hour has passed. They return to the building and tell me they had a nice talk. Olivia and I leave, and she doesn't say anything about their discussion, which is not too surprising since she rarely does. She usually needs a bit of time to process all the information.

The next show is at a private school in a neighboring county. As the cast is rehearsing, the director asks to speak with me. She mentions she wants to follow up regarding her conversation with Olivia. Olivia told her she was feeling "lost" and disconnected with friends at school. She spoke about her desires to pursue an acting career but being frustrated by some of the comments others made, such as "Acting is only for less than one percent of the population" or "You can do acting as a hobby but don't expect to make any money," etc. She offers to work with Olivia.

Then all my concerns and fears come to fruition. Mike and I are having coffee in our living room in the midafternoon. He has declared this time "Montana," indicating to our children we are having time to ourselves, visualizing we are far away. Olivia and Anya have an argument, and Mike and I are trying to understand the conflict when Olivia storms upstairs to her room and slams the door.

A little while later, we ask Olivia to come down and explain what happened, figuring she's had time to cool off. Mike and I are sitting on the couch, and she stands across from us with her back to the opposite wall. She is still upset, and her eyes are bloodshot from crying. I notice she keeps rubbing her arm. She is wearing a sweater, so I wonder if the material is irritating her skin. I observe this behavior for a few minutes while she explains what happened, and I ask her to show me her forearm. My fears are then brought to light when I see that she has cut herself in the area above her wrist. I calmly ask her what happened to her arm, and she cries some more and tells us she was upset and feeling frustrated, so she took something in her room and cut herself out of frustration and anger.

Mike and I speak to her gently and tell her she needs to text her therapist. I immediately contact A Place to Be and let them know. I am sick to my stomach. I never thought she would hurt herself. Over the years, I've heard so many parents say those words following horrific events. Honestly, part of me feels vindicated that I was right. I did read all her signs correctly. Why didn't anyone believe me when I said she was having a difficult time? I know my daughter better than anyone else, and I cannot help wondering why no one took my concerns seriously. Every time someone dismisses my concerns and assumes I am being an overprotective parent, it makes me feel foolish and belittled. They may not intend to elicit this feeling, but they do.

We immediately increase her therapy to get over this bump. She seems to rebound. Many parents and professionals explain that when teens participate in these behaviors, it is not because they want to hurt themselves; rather, they use it as a way to deal with an overwhelm of emotions. I hope this is the case!

Kelly

On a Wednesday afternoon, one week prior to Thanksgiving, I'm home, rushing to vacuum before picking Anya up from Girl Scouts and then driving carpool to religious school. Wednesdays are always busy between 3 and 6 p.m. with ensuring everyone gets where they need to be without meltdowns and tears. Luckily, I do not have to drive to Olivia's school today; the mom I sometimes carpool with is picking up today, so I have a little more time to finish these chores.

As I shut off the vacuum, the phone rings. I detect something is wrong as soon as I hear Olivia's voice. She sounds shaky and is sobbing. I ask her what's wrong. I speak calmly, hoping this will help her keep calm, but I know it's not working. She explains they were in an accident on the way home, but everyone is okay. She asks me to come get her but cannot tell me where they are. Her description sounds like a minor fender bender. She starts speaking again but goes into hysterics and passes the phone to the mom, Emily.

Emily tries to describe where they are, but it's hard for me to hear since I also detect Olivia sobbing in the background. I ask if Olivia is okay, and she says yes but that she's very shaken up. I explain I must pick Anya up first and then can come get everyone else. She agrees but then indicates she will call me back as the police arrived.

I am not very worried about their physical safety. I assume Olivia is upset because her post-traumatic stress has kicked into gear. As I drive, I think, *At least everyone is all right.* I drive to the elementary school and plan the best way to get everyone where they need to be. I will pick up Anya, get our carpool mate, drive them to religious school, and then go to the accident site and pick everyone else up. As I exit my car to walk inside the school, I notice another parent waiting at the entrance. The front doors are always locked, and someone in the office front lobby must unlock the doors to allow us in. This is always so frustrating since I pick Anya up early and we are rushing, which makes the wait even worse.

We chat, but I am impatient. I walk to the window of the classroom the girls are in and my phone rings. It's Emily informing me the ambulance is taking Olivia to the local emergency room. I am confused. I respond, "Why is there an ambulance? I thought it was a minor fender bender." She doesn't answer my question and tells me to hold on. As I wait for her reply, I tap on the window to get the girls' attention. Of course, a few of the girls see me through the blinds but only wave. As I walk back to the front door, I hear Emily get back on the line and say, "Everyone is going to the emergency room." My mind is spinning. WHAT? Finally, the front doors are unlocked, and I rush into the building to get Anya.

Anya and I quickly get her stuff and hurry to the car, and she senses my concern. She asks if Olivia is okay, and I tell her I think so. Once we are in the car, before pulling out of the parking lot, I quickly text the mom of the girl I am supposed to drive to religious school and tell her what's happening. As I drive, I am very calm and answer Anya's questions as best as I can.

We arrive at the ER before the ambulances. The receptionist instructs us to wait in the lobby. While we sit, I call A Place to Be and notify them she will not be at her music therapy session today and give them the little information I have. As expected, they are supportive and ask me to update them when possible. A few minutes later, I see a few ambulances pull into the emergency room bay. My heart is pounding. I am unsure what to expect since the story keeps changing. I wonder, *How can it have only been less than sixty minutes ago that I learned about all this?* It has felt much longer. While we wait, I try to prepare Anya for what may happen once Olivia arrives. It's hard to explain to an eight-year-old when you aren't sure what the situation is.

The receptionist escorts us to the triage area, which looks like a typical patient floor in a hospital. There is a large nurses' station in the center and several stalls on the left-hand side. Anya and I follow the hallway and walk past a few rooms on the left side. Each room is identical and sterile looking. We notice Emily and her daughters in two separate rooms. As we get closer, I hear Olivia crying and moaning. By the time we reach her, she is hysterical. I am surprised to see her on a stretcher with a C-spine collar around her neck and strapped to a backboard. I flash back to that fateful night on November 27, 2001, when I was wheeled to the back hallway of the emergency room to say goodbye to her. I know she is likely having a subconscious memory from that time. Of course, I am not going to approach that topic with her now or any time soon.

I am deeply shaken to see her like this. I never envisioned this was the scene I would walk into. Again, all the information I have suggests a minor fender bender. I immediately walk to her side and tell her Anya and I are here, hold her hand, and keep reassuring her everything will be alright. Anya joins me on her bedside and strokes Olivia's arm and speaks softly to her, trying to soothe her. If it weren't such a horrific scene, I would take pictures. The love is apparent.

The emergency medical technician in the room introduces himself and asks if this is a normal reaction for her. I explain her medical history and tell him she is probably having a subconscious reaction. He nods and writes something in his notes. He explains she told him about her previous TBI and that is why they insisted she come to the ER. I am still trying to understand what happened, where she was in the car, if she hit her head, is in pain, etc. I approach her bedside and ask her a few questions, but all she can say is her head and side hurt. Luckily, I don't see any blood. Emily is standing in the doorway the entire time, and I am not sure if it is out of concern or if she wants to talk to me. The nurses enter and ask a lot of questions and confirm insurance before proceeding to take a closer look. I overhear a police officer talking to Emily outside the room near the nurses' station and am quite surprised to hear she is being charged with reckless driving. Again, fender bender and reckless driving do not fit. The driver who caused our accident in 2001 was also charged with reckless driving. Granted, fifteen years have passed, and laws change, but a fender bender this is not.

The officer asks to speak with me outside of Olivia's room, so I explain to her and Anya I will be in the hallway for a few minutes. He introduces himself and asks a few questions. He shows me a diagram on the police report and repeats Emily is being charged with reckless driving. I don't have much to say at this point.

As I return to the room, the nurses are trying to move her so they can determine if the backboard and C-spine collar can be extricated to make Olivia more comfortable. They try getting her to scoot off the board. This is quite an ordeal. She is so terrified they are going to drop her, which in turn makes it more difficult. We finally get her off the board. The C-spine collar cannot be removed until X-rays and a scan are complete to ensure nothing is broken, etc. While we sit, I notice Emily's husband walk through to pick up her daughters and then her ex-husband as well. He pokes his head in and mouths, "Sorry" to me. I nod and thank him. I need to text Mike and update him. As I left the house earlier, I left a voice message for him. I know how upset he will be, especially since he's in Arizona for his company's large conference.

He asks if I want him to come home early, but the conference ends in one day, and his return flight is two days from now. I respond that no, we are okay. He is upset because he wants to be here to support us, but I don't want him to rush home when we are handling it. He texts a few minutes later, informing me he changed his flight and will be home tomorrow morning.

A technician finally comes to take Olivia to radiology, and Anya and I wait in the room. Again, Anya manages to entertain herself quite well. We look through the bag of stuff I usually keep in the car for her and find some coloring books. I am reminded of how much time is spent sitting around and waiting in hospitals. Emily comes to the room and informs us her husband took her girls home, but she doesn't want to leave until she knows Olivia is okay. She asks if I will drive her home as well. I think, *Seriously, I don't have enough to worry about and you want me to drive you home.* I now must sit and talk and "take care of her." She keeps apologizing.

Olivia arrives back at the room, and I am happy to see she is no longer wearing the C-spine collar. She appears a bit more comfortable. Emily keeps apologizing to her, and Olivia says, "It's okay." What else can she say?

The doctor enters the room and informs me her X-ray is clear. He checks her vitals, asks her to stand and if she is in pain. My heart breaks for her; she looks miserable and tormented. He explains she will be sore the following few days and instructs her to take Advil or Motrin. He informs us her computerized tomography (CAT) scan is clear and continues, "So, no evidence of concussion." I feel my blood pressure rise. Here we are in 2016, and medical professionals have been taught a concussion does not necessarily appear on scans; they are diagnosed through symptoms. I cannot stop thinking what an idiot he is. I decide not to address it with him, knowing it will be futile. I want to get both girls home as soon as possible.

Once we get home, I encourage Olivia to eat or drink since she is in a lot of pain. She takes some Advil and keeps telling me she has schoolwork due the following day. I tell her not to worry about it. I will notify her teachers and the school she will not be going the following day anyway. She doesn't protest and goes upstairs to lie down.

Again, I am amazed at how adaptable and caring Anya has been. It is during these challenging times that I see how much she loves her sister. She showed her so much love in the emergency room and during our ride home. I am proud of her and tell her so.

Olivia is a mess the day after the accident. She has difficulty adjusting to lights and prefers to sit in a dark room. She is extremely fatigued, confused, doesn't have an appetite, and is very sore. I reassure her the soreness is expected as the doctor explained. I also inform her some of the teachers responded to my email and send their best and encourage her to take her time getting back to school until she is fully healed. They also reassure us any missed assignments will be accepted without penalty. This is a huge relief for both of us.

It has been a few days, and she still isn't much better. I phone the neurologist's office and make an appointment for an evaluation for a possible concussion. We need answers, and the quicker the better.

Mike

My association holds its annual meeting each November. This year, the event is held at the Biltmore in Phoenix. Presidents, CEOs, and other key decision-makers make this conference the most widely attended and important event of the year in our industry. It's a long week beginning on Sunday for the staff.

On Wednesday, sitting outside and enjoying the beautiful November Phoenix weather, meeting with the membership committee, I receive a voicemail from Kelly about Olivia.

I excuse myself from the meeting and call her. Kelly seems to downplay the incident. As she tells me about the Olivia being in the hospital, I think, *This can't be happening . . .*

Kelly says there is nothing that I can do and I do not need to come home early. I wish that she could drop her guard down a bit and say, "Please come home" or "I need you," but Kelly tries to take on things herself. Anyway, I book myself on the next available flight home.

Kelly

Olivia and I drive to the outpatient Children's Hospital for an appointment with the concussion clinic affiliated with her neurologist a few weeks later. She is a bit anxious and keeps asking me what the doctors will do. I explain I am not sure but assume some testing, possibly like neuropsychiatric testing. Of course, this is not her favorite, and I cannot blame her since it is long and tedious.

It feels as if we have just sat down when an assistant calls her name and escorts us back to the doctor's office. When she notices there is not an examination table in the office, she appears to relax a bit. The doctor informs us she read over Olivia's medical history and spoke to the neurologist before our arrival. She plans to conduct a few tests to establish what is going on and compare the results to the previous testing on file. I return to the waiting room and let Olivia know she can find me there if she needs anything.

It doesn't feel like a long time before I am ushered back to the office. Olivia appears exhausted and glassy eyed. Over the years, I have learned to prepare myself for unwelcome news. So much has happened, it is better to have a plan in place than to be caught off guard. As I suspected, the doctor explains Olivia has a concussion. The testing shows a significant decrease in scores compared to her last round of testing a year ago.

Olivia seems surprised by the outcome. The doctor turns to me and indicates she doesn't think I'm surprised, which is true. She tells us she is writing recommendations for the school to follow as well as things we need to do at home to assist Olivia's healing. Some of these are the routine concussion protocols and general health recommendations such as getting enough rest, eating a well-balanced diet, and drinking a lot of water. All of these are important reminders to Olivia on an average day. Then the doctor informs her she does not want her to take any tests or quizzes until our follow-up appointment in four weeks. I see the look of terror on Olivia's face and know immediately I will need to work with her to come up with another plan. If she waits to take any tests, she will be more behind. I am confident many of the teachers will try to finish sections prior to Christmas break, and if she waits until January, her memory will not be as clear.

The doctor also recommends Olivia attend school for only half of the day. She wants her to take several rest breaks during the day as well. The doctor and I negotiate with Olivia as to when these will be appropriate given her schedule. One of the rest times we agree upon is during chorus since it isn't a core class and there are a lot of high-sensory items in the classroom, such as noise, lights, commotion, spacing, etc. Olivia reluctantly agrees to this one.

One other thing the doctor suggests is exercise. I am pleased with this one. The concussion protocol has changed a bit since her last concussion. Previously patients were instructed to rest in a dark room with no stimulation, no electronics, and hardly any movement. The new theory is moderate exercise is essential for the recovering brain. Olivia asks a lot of questions about the exercise piece, and the doctor does an excellent job explaining it.

On the way home, Olivia repeatedly asks if I am surprised about the concussion diagnosis, and I keep telling her I suspected this. I explain that I didn't think the doctor in the ER diagnosed her correctly and many in the medical community theorize once an individual has a head injury, she is prone to more. Unfortunately, no one is sure why this is. It could be because our bodies remember trauma and when trauma returns, the body goes directly into that state. I have asked quite a few doctors this question over the years, and no one has been able to provide a definitive answer.

Olivia's surprise about her diagnosis is very telling for Mike and me. It confirms, once again, how out of touch she is with her own body. Whenever doctors ask her questions about how she feels or if a medication is helping, she cannot answer. Her reply is always that she doesn't know or doesn't feel any differently. This is frustrating for us and I'm sure for her doctors as well.

Mike and I know how anxious Olivia gets when she has schoolwork hanging over her, so we make the decision to allow her to finish up as much as she can prior to the holiday break. This will allow her time to rest and recover during the extended time off from school. Her headaches increase during this time, but she handles it much better than expected. It may help that, for the most part, she is enjoying her classes and her teachers. Her case manager has also been supportive of her. This is the best gift.

2017

Kelly

Senior year of high school is filled with so much emotion. Luckily, we have been through this before. Mike and I do not recall this much stress when we were this age, but maybe we forgot. One question is asked numerous times: "Olivia, what are your plans next year?" I let her answer but cringe. She gives the usual noncommittal answer: "I don't know. I applied to Mary Washington University but haven't heard back yet." This is a great response for her since it is the usual response a senior gives midway through the year unless she commits early.

Of course, my entire body tightens each time this question is asked since Mike and I know going away to a four-year school is not the best direction for her. She applied to a small university we toured in the spring. The school met most of her "wants"; it is small, less than two hours away, and is SAT optional with the right GPA. She was overwhelmed during the tour and shut down. At the time we were not confident this was an excellent choice on her part but were advised to let her apply and see what happens. She also applied to a community college and received an acceptance to their Pathways Program, which assists students who plan on transferring to a larger university after earning an associate degree. We are unsure if this is the right path for her but agree this is a stepping-stone.

In January, I receive phone messages from the admissions department of the university indicating Olivia's application cannot be processed due to incomplete information. I remind her quite a few times to return the calls, but she doesn't. Finally, one day I decide to call on her behalf. There are a few advantages to having guardianship—I can get information that normally is not released to a parent of an eighteen-year-old.

When I speak to the admission office, my heart drops.

Her application is incomplete because ACT or SAT scores were not received. I explain she is applying under the "test optional" category that allows applicants to submit only the application with required essays, high school transcript, and recommendations without the college entrance exams. The staff member explains since she does not have a 3.5 grade point average, they will not review her application without scores. Her current grade point average is 3.46. I explain she has a disability which makes it difficult for her to take these tests but am told I will have to speak with the admissions counselor assigned to her high school.

My heart breaks, even though we warned her, as did her high school guidance counselor, that though her GPA is close, she may not get admitted. I am sick to my stomach. How am I going to explain this to her? Her dreams were stolen fifteen years ago, and ever since, she has had work harder than anyone else just to stay afloat. Life is so unfair sometimes.

I speak to the admission counselor assigned to her high school later that day. I realize he speaks to hundreds of parents each year, but I reiterate the conversation I had with his staff regarding Olivia's disability. He tells me there isn't anything he can do. He is unable to waive the requirement, even though her GPA is so close to a 3.5. I am disheartened as we were told by so many experts that exceptions are made—just ask.

I tell Mike, and he is relieved. He reminds me we were extremely uncomfortable with the thought of Olivia going away to school since we are unsure she could handle it physically, emotionally, and/ or academically. I know this intellectually, but emotionally I am distraught. To make things even worse, Mike is out of town, and I need to break the news to her.

Anya is at a neighbor's house, celebrating a birthday, so it allows me some time with Olivia. We finish eating dinner, and I tell her about my conversation with the admissions department. The look on her face is heart wrenching. She bursts into tears and runs upstairs. I clean up before going to speak with her and find her lying on her bed, sobbing. She tells me she really wants to go to school there. The campus layout is perfect for her as well as the small size. I agree and tell her I believe it is unfair they are unwilling to accept her application. She keeps sobbing and repeats it is the only school she likes over and over.

I let her cry for a bit before reminding her of our visit. She was overwhelmed after the admissions session was completed. When the tour guide took us into the dormitory, she refused to look at the rooms; instead, she pushed me to enter. She did not interact with anyone and seemed very disinterested the remainder of the tour. I also remind her of the conversation we had at lunch following the tour.

As we sat in a local restaurant decorated with college banners, we spoke about the noisy dormitory living and her need for quiet, especially when a migraine occurs, and her need to eat properly and how difficult that can be on a college campus. She tells me she remembers, but she wants to be the one to make the decision. Right there is exactly what I feel! She is so much wiser than I sometimes give her credit for.

I think back to the ride home after that one and only college visit. It was very emotional for me. I sat in the passenger seat as Mike drove. My head rested on the car window as tears rolled down my face. I knew she wouldn't be able to handle the rigors of a college campus even though this particular one would be perfect for anyone like her. So many things were taken away from her during the accident, and I feel as if it never ends. The gift that keeps on giving.

Mike

I'm not sure who is most worried and excited for the Brain Injury Awareness Day held in March on Capitol Hill, sponsored by Congressman Bill Pascrell Jr. (D-NJ) and Congressman Thomas J. Rooney (R-FL). Each year a panel comprised of survivors, government agencies, and a military representative convenes in the afternoon and is the highlight for those in attendance. The theme for 2017 is pediatric brain injuries, and Olivia is asked to speak about her experience.

Kelly is a current board member of the Brain Injury Association of Virginia and is a member of the Brain Injury Association of America Brain Injury Advisory Council and has been increasing her advocacy efforts over the last several years. It's only natural she would be asked if Olivia would be willing to participate in this event.

Olivia is the first pediatric panelist to speak at this event. Over the past weeks, we worked a great deal with Olivia, getting her speech written and having her practice. It was difficult at times. Kelly and I sat in our living room as she read the speech aloud and we made suggestions. Now as she walks to the front, we look at each other and try to support ourselves and her. It is a silent show of solidarity and strength many couples share.

Olivia speaks for almost fifteen minutes about her injury, challenges, and notable events in her life. The packed room is silent as she speaks. At the conclusion, she receives thunderous applause and a standing ovation. I finally exhale; anxiety strangled me during those minutes of uncertainty, wondering if Olivia would be able to present herself in front of the crowd. She handles it beautifully, and my heart swells with pride—maybe all the more because she later says that her knees were knocking before she was asked to speak.

Kelly

The morning arrives, and the three of us leave the house early. It is a ninety-minute ride to Capitol Hill during rush-hour traffic. As we drive, I reminisce about how far Olivia has come since the original accident. No one could have imagined her speaking at an event such as this eighteen years ago.

Upon arrival, the beauty of the buildings on Capitol Hill strike me, as they do every time. It is such a serene area in a bustling city center. The buildings are white stone with beautiful columns and broad stairs leading up to the entrances. As we walk in, we are ushered into a line to walk through security. We enter the main hallway, and the sounds echo off the marble floors and high ceiling, making it seem larger than it is. I see fear on Olivia's face mixed with confusion. We walk to the main exhibit hall where tables are set up for vendors with information on brain injury, recovery, and programs. We stop by the Brain Injury Association of America's table, and I introduce Mike and Olivia to the staff and introduce Olivia to Anne McDonnell. Anne has become a friend and fellow advocate. She recommended Olivia for this panel. She warmly embraces Olivia, which I hope alleviates some of the butterflies.

Mike offers to take Olivia to lunch and get her to the appropriate room early so she has time to relax before the panel discussion. It's best for her to be one of the first in the room to minimize some of the nerves. Meanwhile, I attend congressional meetings Anne has set up along with another board member. We arrive at the room thirty minutes early and find Mike and Olivia sitting in the hallway.

There is a delay in setting up the room. Once we are allowed inside, the organizers bring her in first and make sure Mike and I have a front-row seat. There are usually one hundred or more people in attendance, and seats are at a minimum. The moderator introduces the panel and decides Olivia should be given the option to go first. As she stands at the podium, Mike and I squeeze each other's hands. My stomach is swimming with butterflies, and I cannot imagine what she is feeling. I look around the room and see some faces I know and more I do not. The room is at capacity, and they are all here to listen to my daughter tell her story.

As soon as she begins to talk, the microphone dies. Why during her speech? Mike and I both glance at each other in another secret sign of support and encourage her to keep going. After the microphone is fixed, Olivia gives a very impressive and impactful speech. As she speaks about her recovery, the successes, and the struggles she has endured, my eyes water, but I hold off the downpour. She concludes, and the tears come streaming down. Tears filled with guilt, pride, sadness, and joy. She receives a standing ovation from every person in attendance. Once the panel concludes, everyone files out and immediately surrounds her with congratulations and awe. She gets overwhelmed with all the people approaching her and congratulating her on a job well done. Mike and I glow. We are so proud of her and all she has endured.

High School Graduation, June 12, 2017
Kelly

After sleeping fitfully all night, my alarm sounds, and I jump out of bed like a rocket going to the moon. I attempt to collect my thoughts as I recall that this is the day we all have been working toward for the past fifteen years. I hurriedly shower and dress, moving on autopilot. It's still dark outside, but I know from the previous day's forecast it is going to be a hot and humid day here in Virginia, even for June.

I wake Olivia gently since I know she is very anxious about the morning and festivities. I suggest she eat something since I know it will be quite a while before she has an opportunity again. I enter worry mode, trying to preempt a migraine. The past fifteen years have been spent trying to control whatever I can since so much has happened that was out of my control. She's ready to leave but is still fussing with her cap and gown and worrying nonstop about getting it dirty since it is white, after all.

Once we arrive and park, Olivia is ready to bolt for the gymnasium where all the graduating seniors are waiting for their big moment. The past few months we have kept asking her how she feels about graduating high school, and each time she says the same thing: "It hasn't hit me yet. It probably won't hit me until I start classes in August." I never believe her when she uses this response. She learned to internalize her feelings a long time ago, and even though she has thousands of hours of therapies under her belt, she still uses the same response.

Once I find good seats, I sit and look over the scenery. Olivia is not our first daughter to graduate high school, but she is the first to graduate from this high school, the oldest high school in the county where we live. The ceremony is on the front lawn of the school, weather permitting, and it is truly a magnificent backdrop to this day. The school is unique in its architecture and large front lawn with a sprinkling of trees. At 7 a.m., it is still shaded and at times chilly, though I know that will change very soon. Other families and friends begin arriving and soon fill many of the seats around us. Mike arrives with Anya, armed with cold drinks and coloring activities to keep her amused during our wait and the ceremony. Hannah drives separately since she is going to her internship immediately following.

As more people surround us, I feel the familiar anxiety stir up in me. I cannot believe we finally are at this pivotal juncture. I don't know if anyone else in the crowd has ever wondered if their child would graduate high school. We live in an area that prides itself on accomplishments, especially those of their children. Most, if not all, assume their children will finish high school and immediately go to a four-year traditional college setting. Of course, I can safely assume most did not sit in the Pediatric Intensive Care Unit fifteen years ago, wondering if their child would ever wake up and, if she did, what obstacles she would face. I try not to focus on that, but it is difficult not to when you have gone through as much as our family has.

Once the ceremony starts and the pomp and circumstance begins, chills shoot up my arms. The music gets me every time! I find Olivia in the crowd and start snapping photos since this will keep me focused—for a brief time anyway. She never sees us; she wears a serious expression. I am reminded of her as a little girl, usually a bit more serious than her older sister, who she looked to as her guide through life. Of course, Hannah isn't with her now, and she can only rely on herself, which is a scary thing for Olivia.

Finally, after what seems to be a hundred speeches, the presentation of the diplomas begins. We are lucky to have a last name that begins with L as we fall right in the middle of the ceremony. I always feel bad for the kids who are closer to Z, since the audience is usually a bit rambunctious and bored by the time their names are read. I see her approaching the front of the line, and of course, my nerves are completely shot by this point. Finally, I hear her name, and I am overcome with emotion. Mike turns and hugs me, and I can't believe that we made it to this momentous day. I always joke he and I deserve the diploma as much as she does. I have never worked as hard at anything as we did to ensure Olivia received every accommodation she deserved. We fought like our lives depended on it. In hindsight, I believe we fight for her fiercely because no matter how hard we try, we can never undo the events of November 27, 2001. This is the only way we know to make it up to her.

Mike

The day we have worked so hard for has finally arrived. When I say "we," I am referring to our entire family, medical team, friends, teachers, etc. Not the usual group to thank when thinking about a high school graduation. Having already been through one with our oldest daughter, I know the difference.

Olivia's graduation is her accomplishment. She worked hard for her grades, and she took full responsibility for the choices she made during her four years in high school. There were countless days and nights of tears, outbursts, frustration, and other emotions in that time.

On the other hand, as her parents, it is our triumph also. Kelly is truly a champion of Olivia's education. She spoke with Olivia's counselors, teachers, administrators, and, well, pretty much everyone she could. Although I participated in some of those conversations and meetings, Kelly was the driving force behind making sure this day would happen.

Now we are sitting outdoors in front of the oldest high school in the county with the four white Tuscan columns serving as the entryway into the school on a beautiful, late-spring day. I keep Anya busy with coloring books as we wait for the ceremony to begin. I am not the most patient person as the ceremony drags on and on. But I do appreciate the other families and their graduates, too. Who knows how they made it to this momentous day?

I clap, and Anya follows my lead as each name is called. After about fifteen names, Anya stops clapping. After about one hundred names, I do the same and fumble with the camera.

My heart starts to pound around the *H* names.

Finally, " . . . Olivia Lang!"

I hug Kelly and say, "We did it!"

EPILOGUE

Kelly

The event of November 27, 2001, left us feeling isolated and fearful for survival as well as financial stability, but we persevered and came out stronger on the other side. We slowly began to see the light. The brightness of the light changes during different periods, but it never truly disappears. We remind ourselves to look back upon all the highs and lows and rejoice in how far we have come. Every one of our family members have felt the pain and joy, even Anya, who had not yet been born. Her life has been altered during this ongoing event. I believe it has shaped her in ways we have not yet witnessed. How could it not?

In 2018, Olivia and I paid a visit to the Leesburg Rescue Squad to deliver a handwritten thank-you note and treats for the first responders. Mike and I started this tradition many years ago, and once Olivia understood the significance, she took on the primary role. It is important for her to visit on the date of the accident,

November 27, as a reminder and give thanks. It was a very cold and windy day this particular year, and she and I walked to the front of the building as a siren sounded. We entered the kitchen area and were greeted by two career employees. She handed them her note, and we chatted a few minutes before I took some photos by the trucks outside the garage area. I exchanged contact information with one of the men before Olivia and I went on our way. Imagine my surprise the following day when I received this note:

> Good morning and hope you all had a great holiday. I was made aware of a visit you and your daughter made to Loudoun Rescue in Leesburg. I had seen the note last year after stopping by on a station visit and was curious as to the location of your accident. My partner and I ran a very similar call when assigned to Loudoun Rescue during that time frame which was at E. Market and Cardinal Park. I'm so happy that she is doing well and wish you all the best.
>
> Sean C Scott, Battalion Chief Battalion 602 "B" Shift
> Loudoun County Department of Fire and Rescue

As I read the email, my heart leaped. I couldn't believe it. We had tried to find the first responders who saved her life for seventeen years, and here he was, I hoped. I replied and gave him some information before he immediately responded that yes, he and his partner had been assigned to our car and took care of Olivia at the scene and during the ride to the hospital. We arranged a time to talk, and he told me all he recalled from the accident scene. I was amazed how much detail he remembered. He replied, "I don't normally remember so much about a call, but this one really struck me and stayed with me all these years. I have always wondered what happened to her."

As much as I wanted to hear those details, it was heart wrenching. He explained the scene. He approached the car amazed at the damage and saw the "baby" through the shattered window. He told me his first thought was *Oh, look at that, the baby slept through the entire accident.* Only as he laid his hand on her and repeated the words, "Baby, wake up" did he realize she was not sleeping. She wasn't breathing. He was unable to lift the entire car seat, so he cut the straps and ran with her in his arms to the waiting ambulance and rushed her to the hospital. "No one thought she had any chance of survival" were the words that resonated. He recalled the scene in the hospital hallway where I was wheeled on a stretcher to say goodbye before she was transferred to the hospital with a trauma center. He said it was emotional and noted there wasn't a dry eye in that hallway filled with first responders, doctors, nurses, and my friend, Kristin. They never expected her to survive the ride.

Mike and I wanted to meet him and his partner so we could thank them in some way for saving our daughter's life. I was surprised when Olivia overheard us and indicated she also wanted to be present. The opportunity arrived on a very cold yet sunny day. I had butterflies in my stomach and was not sure why. Mike had the idea of notifying local media. The reporter and photographer arrived shortly afterward. It was surreal, meeting these men who perform heroic feats to save others. They were the ones who had provided the first step of care for our daughter, ultimately saving her life.

During this day, Olivia asked to see pictures of our car. I suggested she wait until we arrived home before looking them over, but she insisted. I warned her the pictures were devastating, but she persisted. Again, her persistence is strong when she wants something. I opened the manila file folder and showed her the photos printed on copier paper. She asked if the seat with the missing window and car seat still inside was where she was sitting, and I replied softly yes. She burst into tears, and for the first time in years, she allowed me to hold her. She is resistant to many forms of physical affection, so this was a powerful moment in our relationship. I stood there holding her and let her sob quietly. She has never asked to see those photos again.

Through this experience, we advocated for Olivia every day. This led all of us, but especially me, to a new community. I became involved with the hospital, speaking to groups about our experience, joining a speaker's bureau, going to brain injury conferences, serving on the board of the Brain Injury Association of Virginia, and much more. These experiences have brought me to a new career in advocacy.

We still do not know what the future holds for Olivia but remain hopeful that her resilience will bring her to a place of love and security. Parents never receive a crystal ball forecasting the future. Yes, our road has been paved with more obstacles than most, but we also have experienced such profound moments of joy. It is the joy I carry along in my heart.

Mike

As I write this, I am now the father of two adult daughters, Hannah and Olivia, and a teenage daughter, Anya. Why has this book been written? Is it to unload some heavy burden from our heart? Perhaps.

After Kelly and I had Olivia, we went back and forth about having another child, especially after she had another miscarriage. Later, Kelly became pregnant, and we made the mistake of telling people right before her first trimester. That joy was short-lived when a few days after our announcement, Kelly miscarried.

When Kelly became pregnant again in 2007, I didn't know how we would manage if something went wrong. When our baby was born, we still had not decided on a name. Ultimately, we gave her the name Anya after her maternal grandmother Ann, who had passed away. Her middle name is Faith, named after my grandmother Fanny, but, well, that name was never in consideration! The name Faith means so much more to us. Faith represents the feeling that our family has in each other and in God. As stated earlier, we don't know why certain events in life happen, but we know that God watches over us.

Anya is such a joy, and her sisters dote on her constantly. I have felt a sense of happiness I've never experienced before. As I looked within myself one day in early 2010 when Anya hadn't quite turned two yet, it occurred to me: Olivia—and our family—had missed a lot of her childhood during those early years. Part of me withered away and died that day in November 2001. The very existence of Anya allowed me to resurrect those areas of death and to experience once again the beauty of life and the innocence and sanctity of a baby girl. Part of me was reborn.

Perhaps my "rebirth" is complicated by the fact that misfortune seems to plague me when I travel. I still have a sense of guilt that I was not home when the car incident happened. That guilt was exasperated later when a fire broke out in our house and when my father-in-law passed away—both occurring when I was out of town, attending work-related events.

My social life has also changed. I've turned down certain offers and events because I feel that I need to be home. Hobbies? None, really. I used to enjoy catching football on Sundays, watching my Steelers and other teams throughout the day. Now even when my team is televised, I find that choosing between watching TV or playing with Anya, well, there really isn't a decision after all. I tried at one point to do both at the same time. That didn't work out. The TV was turned off.

I know it isn't healthy to feel bitterness toward the person who altered our lives forever. To remain angry, especially after all these years, certainly doesn't benefit me or my family. However, I can't get beyond it. Every day, I am reminded of the car incident. I stopped calling it an accident years ago. I don't believe that it was intentional, but having hit several vehicles, driving through a red light, and rear-ending a minivan with a mother and two small children, resulting in a three-year-old in a coma, there must have been some negligence on the driver's part, right? But there was never an apology or recognition of how he changed our lives. Surely he must feel remorse. If not, what type of person can that be?

HOPEFUL FOR THE TOMORROWS THAT FOLLOW

Mike and Kelly Lang

So why the book? And why after all these years? We suppose a written discourse on these pivotal events in our family was cathartic. Just to unload was therapeutic. We are hopeful, though, that this book will be helpful to others who are challenged by tragic events. Most importantly, our goal is to instill one thought with you: cherish life!

Relish the grand opportunities that you have been given. Tell your loved ones how much they mean to you. Tell them they fill your life with meaning and hope. Tell them they give you the reason for your very existence. Tell your spouse or significant other how the world matters when they are in it. Tell your parents and other loved ones how fortunate you are to experience the beauty of life because of them.

How fortunate we are as parents to have the amazing privilege to hold a baby and watch her sleep peacefully in a warm, loving home; the chance to witness the first steps and hear the first words; to witness the times when your child reaches for your hand, the bedtime stories, and the times your child says, "I love you."

If you are a parent of a child, tell them every night when they go to bed that you love them. How gratifying and heartwarming it is to see the smile broaden on their face and the brightness in their eyes. It is amazing that even at times when you and your spouse have been arguing or perhaps when your child is upset that they were not invited to a friend's party, there is a certain glow and warmth elicited by those truly magical words. Say you love them today and embrace them literally and collectively. Tomorrow may be too late, and you will regret that missed opportunity for the rest of your life. As you kiss your little ones good night, breathe in the sanctity of their life and be thankful and hopeful for the tomorrows that follow.

ACKNOWLEDGMENTS

There are so many people who have assisted us in this journey. First of all, thank you to Hannah and Anya for your unconditional love, sacrifices, and support you have given us. Thank you, Olivia, for trusting us to share your story. We can never thank our dear friend Kristin Campbell enough for all she has done for Olivia and our family. She not only rode in the ambulance with Olivia, but she also watched our girls and provided levity when we most needed it. She continues to support us twenty years later. Similarly, special thanks to Charles Fleet, as longtime friends like him are rare.

Our family, especially Sam and Estelle, for coming to our home and taking care of Hannah in our moment of fear. Jeff and Leslie for always being there and supporting Olivia whenever she needs it.

The many doctors, therapists, and teachers who assisted us along the way, especially Michele Zuckerman, Mary Lynn Hicks, Gayle Massey, and Tammy Bullock. Thank you, Kathy Hallissey and Dr. Lisa Meier, as you were invaluable to us through Olivia's middle and high school years. Your compassion and insight are unmeasurable.

Thank you, Lisa Fong, for always striving to be Olivia's advocate.

Please support your emergency responders. Our thanks are never enough to express our gratitude to the men and women of the Loudoun County Volunteer Rescue Squad, Company 13 (http://www.loudounrescue.org). You saved our daughter's life and kept our family whole.

Also, thank you to A Place to Be (Middleburg, VA, http://www.aplacetobeva.org). Although your slogan is "Where Music Meets Therapy," it is much more than that. You helped Olivia find her voice.

There are many others who have been so supportive to our family over the years. Please note that we thank and think of you pretty much every day.

A year after our journey began, Kelly had the pleasure of meeting Anne McDonnell at the first brain injury conference she attended. Somehow, she knew Anne was the person to turn to with questions. Anne has been there to guide our family through this journey, giving us answers to a litany of questions and bringing me and Kelly on the Board of the Brain Injury Association of Virginia. Anne's guidance and support is immeasurable.

The numerous brain injury survivors I have met throughout the past twenty years. I have formed wonderful relationships of support while we all navigate this club none of us asked to join.

RESOURCES

A Place to Be, http://www.aplacetobeva.org/

Alzheimer's Association, https://www.alz.org/

American Congress of Rehabilitation Medicine (ACRM), https://acrm.org/

Arts for All Loudoun, https://www.artsforallloudoun.org/

Beamer Learns about Traumatic Brain Injury: The Beamer Book Series, https://www.amazon.com/Beamer-Learns-About-Traumatic-Injury/dp/1457559072

Bob Woodruff Foundation, https://bobwoodrufffoundation.org/

The Brain Injury Association of America (BIAA), https://www.biausa.org/

Brain Injury Services, https://braininjurysvcs.org/

Brainline, https://www.brainline.org/

Centers for Disease Control (CDC), https://www.cdc.gov/

Family Caregiver Alliance (FCA), https://www.caregiver.org/

Guiding Eyes for the Blind, https://www.guidingeyes.org/

The Loudoun County Volunteer Rescue Squad, http://www.loudounrescue.org/

The Miracle Child (authors' website), https://www.themiraclechild.org/

The National Association of State Head Injury Administrators (NASHIA)

National Institute on Disability, Independent Living, and Rehabilitation Research (NIDILRR), https://acl.gov/about-acl/about-national-institute-disability-independent-living-and-rehabilitation-research

National Resource Center for TBI, https://www.washington.edu/doit/national-resource-center-traumatic-brain-injury-nrctbi

Ohio State University College of Medicine, Ohio Valley Center for Brain Injury Prevention and Rehabilitation, https://wexnermedical.osu.edu/physical-therapy-rehabilitation/ohio-valley-center-for-brain-injury-prevention-rehabilitation

TBI Model Systems, https://msktc.org/tbi/model-system-centers

Wrightslaw, https://www.wrightslaw.com/